THE TWENTY-FIRST CENTURY CONFRONTS ITS GODS

# The Twenty-First Century Confronts Its Gods

## Globalization, Technology, and War

EDITED BY
David J. Hawkin

STATE UNIVERSITY OF NEW YORK PRESS

Published by
State University of New York Press, Albany

© 2004 State University of New York

For information, address State University of New York Press,
90 State Street, Suite 700, Albany, NY 12207

Production by Kelli Williams
Marketing by Susan Petrie

Library of Congress Cataloging in Publication Data

The twenty-first century confronts its gods : globalization, technology, and war /
   edited by David J. Hawkin.
      p. cm.
   Includes bibliographical references and index.
   ISBN 0-7914-6181-5 — ISBN 0-7914-6182-3 (pbk.)
     1. Globalization—Religious aspects. 2. Technology—religious aspects.
   3. War—Religious aspects. I. Title: 21st century confronts its gods.

BL65.G55T86 2004
201'.7—dc22

                                                              2003190069

              10 9 8 7 6 5 4 3 2 1

*For Harold Coward*

# Contents

PART ONE

# New Gods for Old?

# Introduction

Not too long ago it was conventional wisdom to regard religion as a thing of the past. During the 1940s, for example, the influential scientist C. H. Waddington wrote that religion was irrelevant to modern life and that only science "unadulterated by any contrary ideal" was able to provide the milieu for the "harmonious conditions" of the rational life.[1] He was espousing a view that was to become prevalent for many years: religion had nothing more to say; the only way forward was through science and technology. Few people, however, would make this argument today. Not only has it become very evident that science and technology cannot by themselves deliver the "harmonious" and "rational" life, it has also become apparent that religion is far from irrelevant. Three events in particular have illustrated how significant religion is, not just in the lives of individuals, but also in the lives of nations.

First, there was the revolution in Iran in 1979. Quite unexpectedly, the West was brought face-to-face with an unfamiliar phenomenon in modern times: a religious revolution that completely changed the political and social fabric of a nation. The religion behind this revolution was Islam. It became clear that if we are to understand the modern world, we need more than economic and military analyses. We need also to understand what animates religions such as Islam.

The second event took place in 1989. In that year the Soviet Union began to fall apart. The communist block, so long seen as a danger and a threat to the Western way of life, disintegrated to the point of impotence. But as the danger from communism faded, new threats emerged. Democracy and liberalism did not replace communism, as had been hoped. What resurfaced were old rivalries. Bitter conflicts erupted in Central Asia and in the Balkans, fueled by ethnic and religious alliances. Once again, it became apparent that religion was still very much a force to be reckoned with in the modern world.

3

The third event was the terrorist attacks on the United States on September 11, 2001. Much has been written about these attacks, but a clear picture of their significance will probably not become apparent for some time. What does seem clear, however, is that once again religion was a factor in shaping global events.

Even if it is acknowledged, however, that religion plays a significant role in non-Western societies, and must therefore be taken into account when discussing world events, there are still those who would claim that religion has little significance for the lives of those of us in the Western world. In Islamic states, such as Pakistan and Iran, religion is clearly identified with public and political life, and there is no Western distinction between Church and State. But, it is argued, in the West it is different. The West has gone through the Enlightenment and is thoroughly secularized. There is a clear distinction between Church and State. It follows that the gods of the Western world have been vanquished and relegated to the private sphere.

This argument is a strong one if one thinks of religion in a narrow and traditional sense. But if we peer below the surface of our Western assumptions, we find that the twenty-first century still has its gods, and these gods are playing a very significant role in lives of ordinary citizens and in the making of the future.

In *The Eighteenth Century Confronts the Gods*, Frank Manuel argued that the intelligentsia of the eighteenth century rejected religion, only to erect in its place other gods such as Progress and Reason. He says: "If the eighteenth-century myth of origins ultimately destroyed the ancient gods, pagan and Christian, *les progrès* became the new deities of the age."[2] Similarly, the twenty-first century also has its gods, erected after the process of secularization had supposedly vanquished religion. Walter Wink, for example, in *The Powers That Be: Theology for a New Millennium,*[3] identifies a number of "Powers"—the market, the military, technology, and nationalism—that have become integrated and have given rise to what he calls "idolatrous values" and "the Domination System." These "Powers" are invested with their own belief systems and orthodoxies. Thus, the "gods" of the twenty-first century are not only the traditional gods of Judaism, Christianity, Islam, Hinduism, and other world faiths, but also those powers to which our Western hegemonic culture seems increasingly to grant ultimacy.

The present volume argues that we must confront these gods of the twenty-first century. Early Buddhism teaches us that we must "see things as they really are" (*yathabhutam*). Never was it more essential that we follow this Buddhist precept and see things as they really are, and not as they appear to be. If we are to understand the twenty-first century, we must see how and why Western secular culture has placed its faith in such things as globalization and why it sees the power of the Market as able to bring happiness to citizens through consumerism.

## What Will the Twenty-First Century Be Like?

It is now over a decade ago that Francis Fukuyama advanced his thesis that we were witnessing the "end of history," that is, the end point of humankind's ideological evolution. "Democratic capitalism" constituted the "final form of human government" and its global reach "the triumph of the Western idea." There was, he argued, a "Universal History" of humankind "in the direction of liberal democracy."[4] Thus, he declares triumphantly:

> The enormous productive and dynamic economic world created by advancing technology and the rational organization of labor has a tremendous homogenizing power. It is capable of linking different societies around the world to one another physically through the creation of global markets, and of creating parallel economic aspirations and practices in a host of diverse societies. The attractive power of this world creates a very strong predisposition for all human societies to participate in it, while success in this participation requires the adoption of the principles of economic liberalism. This is the ultimate victory of the VCR [video cassette recorder].[5]

When Fukuyama first advanced his thesis there seemed good reason to take him seriously. The Cold War was no more and the United States reigned supreme as the world's only superpower. It seemed to follow that the American democratic ideals of individualism and unfettered economic activity in a global free market, powered by technological drive and innovation, would now also reign supreme. But as communism faded from the picture, new menaces appeared. As John Gray observes:

> A defining feature of the period after the Second World War has been a metamorphosis in the nature of war. Organized violence has slipped from the control of states and passed into that of other institutions. Political organizations such as the Palestine Liberation Organization and the African National Congress, tribal, ethnic and clan militias in Rwanda, Chechnya and Bosnia, drug

cartels and mafias in Colombia, Russia and Ireland—such diverse institutions have deprived sovereign states of their effective monopoly of violence. To a considerable degree war has become an activity waged by irregular armies which acknowledge no sovereign power.[6]

The liberal democratic ideal has not been universally embraced, and there has been unexpected and unforeseen resistance to the "new world order" of the *Pax Americana*.

The situation we face in the twenty-first century is quite paradoxical. On the one hand there is unprecedented economic integration and cultural homogenization, and on the other unrelenting cultural and religious factionalism. But are these two trends simply contradictory, or are they, on some deep level, linked? That is, are cultural and religious wars and rivalries actually a *result* of globalization and its homogenizing power? Certainly some explanation is warranted for the fact that, contrary to expectations, the *Pax Americana* has not made the world a safer place in which to live. In fact, as September 11, 2001, showed, America itself is very vulnerable to attack. One of the best-known explanations of why the world seems to be growing more anti-Western and more fractious than ever is given by Samuel Huntington. Huntington's ideas first appeared in *Foreign Affairs* in an article entitled, "The Clash of Civilizations?" Later he expanded his views into a book, *The Clash of Civilizations and the Remaking of World Order.*[7]

Huntington argued that wars in the future will no longer be wars of ideologies, but primarily "wars of civilizations." By "civilizations" Huntington means the "cultural groupings" that extend beyond regions and states. In these "cultural groupings" religion is a basic component of belief and a motivating force of action. Religions, therefore, must be seen as having a fundamental role in world politics. Says Huntington: "In the modern world religion is a central, perhaps *the* central, force that motivates and mobilizes people. . . . What ultimately counts for people is not political ideology or economic interest. Faith and family, blood and belief, are what people identify with and what they will fight and die for."[8]

There are many problems with Huntington's thesis, and these will be discussed by David R. Loy in chapter 5. But Huntington's central insight is completely sound: religion is central to understanding the twenty-first century.

Increasingly, the modern world seems a fragile place. It is threatened not only by weapons of mass destruction, but also by ecological devastation and social and economic disintegration. Our destiny is not, however, tied simply to political, economic, and social factors. There are other, deeper forces at work, and it is one of the strengths of Huntington's writings that they make this very point. In order to truly comprehend our destiny we must confront these forces and try to understand them. The chapters in this volume are an attempt to contribute to such understanding.

## The Modern World and Secular Religion

One of the shortcomings of Huntington's writings is that he fails to really grasp and analyze the *Zeitgeist* of the Western world. By labeling the West a "Christian civilization," he gives the impression that it is Christianity that animates the West. But the Western world is animated by a very different spirit and a very different religion from Christianity. The spirit that animates the West is religious, but it is also secular—that is, it is *a secular or quasireligious* spirit. To speak of a "secular religious spirit" and of "secular religion" seems a contradiction in terms and requires some explanation.

It is difficult to define what religion is. It seems easy enough at first: most would say that religion entails belief in a god or gods, involves ritual and worship, and has a system of beliefs. C. A. Campbell accordingly defined religion as "A state of mind, comprising belief in the reality of a supernatural being or beings, endued with transcendent power and worth, together with the complex emotive attitudes of worship intrinsically appropriate thereto."[9] Yet this definition does not include, for example, Theravada Buddhism, which does not have a transcendental being in its belief system. Nor does this definition reflect the fact that in popular usage the term "religion" is used very broadly (as in, for example, references to New Age "religion"). Paul Tillich recognized this when, in *Dynamics of Faith*,[10] he defined religion as being grasped by an "ultimate concern." What Tillich meant was that for most people all other concerns are preliminary to a main concern that supplies the answer to the question, "What is the meaning of my life?" What makes this primary concern religious is that it is the primary motivating concern of one's life: it makes an absolute demand on one's allegiance and promises ultimate fulfillment. Using this definition, we may distinguish three types of religion. First, *theistic religions*, in which the object of ultimate concern is a transcendental being (as in Judaism, Christianity, and Islam). Second, *nontheistic religions*, in which the object of concern is some higher principle or abstract power (as in Theravada Buddhism and some types of Hinduism). Third, *secular* or *quasireligions*, where the object of ultimate concern is such that it resembles theistic or nontheistic religions. What the person holds as ultimate concern gives that person's belief a character (often unintentional) similar to that found in more traditional religions.

Seen in this light, the ideology that underlies globalization—the fervent belief in an unfettered omnipotent Market that will eventually bring goods and the good life to everyone—may be seen as quasireligious. Certainly, there is a firm belief in the salvific power of consumerism found in such writers as Fukuyama, who not only speaks of the "victory of the VCR," but also explicitly sees this as the goal of all humans. So he says, "The revolutionaries in Romania and China imagine that they would be happy when one day they get to the Promised Land of consumerism. One day they too will all have dishwashers and VCRs and private automobiles."[11] Fukuyama does rhetorically ask whether this is "what the human story has been about these past few millennia," but clearly cannot see humans giving up the joys promised by consumerism and global capitalism to be dragged back "into history with all its wars, injustice, and revolution."[12]

After the events of September 11, 2001, officials in the U.S. government urged Americans to go shopping. This advice was meant to try to stimulate the flagging economy, but it also served to remind people what the Western world was about. The Western "way of life" was clearly identified with the values of consumerism. In this commodified and consumer-driven world, "the Market" has come to function like religion. It has its statements of faith, its catechisms, and its rhetoric of salvation. As Harvey Cox pointed out in his popular account in *The Atlantic Monthly* (March 1999), the Market—with its honorific capital *M*—bears all the characteristics of Deity: omnipotence, omniscience, and omnipresence. For Cox, we are now living in an entirely new dispensation. Its prophets and seers are the "econologians" of liberal economics. Other scholars agree. David Loy's exploration of this religion of the market explains, among other things, that modern economics is an example of a religion trying to act like a science.[13] William Greider has written of the "utopian vision of the marketplace" offering its followers "an enthralling religion, a self-satisfied belief system." Indeed, people are seen to "worship" principles of the free market economy as though they constituted a "spiritual code" capable of solving all human problems "so long as no one interferes with its authority." Secular society, with its this-worldly preoccupations of individuality and personal success is a paradoxical culture: "Many who think of themselves as rational and urbane have put their faith in this idea of the self-regulating market as piously as others put their trust in God."[14]

## New Gods for Old?

The chapters in Part 1 of this volume seek to penetrate behind the assumptions that inform our Western technological society and that are rapidly and inexorably imposing themselves globally. They seek to bring various perspectives and methods of analysis to bear on our modern culture, with the goal of helping us to "see things as they really are."

In chapter 1 David Hawkin discusses the origins of Western techno-logical society and argues that it signals a decisive break with the past. The beginnings of this break may be traced back to the thought of William of Ockham, who sought to defend the truth of the Christian revelation while at the same time acknowledge the knowledge to be gained through empiri-cism and the logical method. His defense was brilliant in its simplicity. He completely separated the knowledge gained through the Christian revela-tion from that gained through the senses. Sensory experience may give us knowledge of the world, but it does not give us knowledge of God. The classical view, rooted in Platonic thought, perceived the world as rational. This rational world was the way it was because it reflected a divine order. Ockham's thought is thus very significant because he is essentially repudi-ating this classical tradition. Hawkin argues, similarly to Hans Blumenberg, that a precondition of the coming of the modern age was this belief that the eternal order was not reflected in nature. This change in the attitude to nature was coupled with an equally significant change in the attitude to contemplation. In the classical view of things the highest form of philo-sophic activity was to contemplate and behold the Good. But because in Ockham's thought nature does not reflect a divine order and therefore one cannot perceive God in nature, the intrinsic value of the natural world is undermined and with it the value of contemplation. Contemplation was valuable because its object, the natural world, was valuable.

Thus, when nature comes to be seen as a mere object, contemplation ceases to be of vital importance. The full significance of these developments, argues Hawkin, is contained in the thought of Francis Bacon. Bacon's writ-ings exude the spirit of modernity. Bacon attacks the contemplative life and elevates above it the life of action. He sees nature as a mere artifact that humans should manipulate and control. He thus paves the way for the men-tality of the technological society in which efficiency, pragmatism, and util-ity are the chief virtues. Hawkin concludes that there is an irony at the heart of the technological worldview. We have abandoned the notion that life has transcendent goals, but in bringing heaven down to earth we have divinized human life itself. It is thus that science and technology have received "an imperious ordinance to gratify a proliferation of human 'needs.'"[15] We have banished the contemplative quest for the Good, only to replace it with a feverish quest for goods. We have created new gods to replace the old. Our supposedly secular technological society is, in fact, driven by a fundamen-tally religious spirit.

The technological society has brought many benefits, especially to the privileged in the West. It has not only given us an impressive array of goods, but on a more basic level it has increased life expectancy and eliminated food shortages. Recent biotechnological developments conjure up a future in which we live even longer and in which genetically modified food will make scarcity unheard of. Yet there are many people who are concerned that such developments pose significant risks to our health and welfare. In chapter 2 Conrad Brunk examines this concept of risk assessment in the technological society. He argues that discussions of such issues are couched in the language of risk assessment, in which the merits or otherwise of a particular technology are presented in terms of a cost/benefit calculation. Such analyses fail to take adequate account of more fundamental values rooted in a philosophic or religious understanding of the world. Brunk further points out that globalization has exacerbated the problem, especially in liberal pluralistic societies. In an effort to find common ground for public discourse about ethical matters, public policy mandarins have settled on values that are themselves dictated by the very characteristics of the technological society. So the key concern becomes to maximize good and avoid harm. This concern is allied to the liberal belief in individual autonomy and equality. But such a moral framework is too restrictive to be applied to discussions about such issues as genetic engineering. Brunk argues that those using "risk assessment" techniques fail to understand that a significant number of people see nature as either sacred or as a creation of God and do not approve of changing its fundamental character. To put it in terms of the discussion in chapter 1, they do not, in fact, subscribe to the Baconian worldview and do not regard nature as an artifact to be manipulated in any way we see fit. Brunk concludes that we need to understand better what values actually shape public attitude towards technology. We need to better understand the moral values of different communities and incorporate them into public discourse about ethical issues.

Rosemary Ommer, in chapter 3, offers some reflections that illuminate our "new gods for old" theme, which was adumbrated in chapter 1. The trust we have placed in the god of the Market is misplaced, for it cannot deliver what it should: prosperity and human well-being. Ommer explains how the global market has come into being. It developed from the first global system of trade established by Britain in the mid-1800s. As multinational corporations evolved and became larger, they became truly *trans*national, breaking down national and cultural barriers in the name of "free" trade. The results have been disastrous, especially for small communities in the developing world. Ommer discusses at length the case of Canada, which is a developed country, yet some of its regions, such as the province of Newfoundland and Labrador, have been exploited in ways similar to what has taken place in the underdeveloped world. The environment seems to be particularly vulnerable when the market is allowed free rein, as is evidenced in the disappearance of the cod from the the Grand Banks, off the coast of Newfoundland. The Grand Banks once had more cod than any other fishing grounds in the world, but now there are not enough cod left to support a modest "food fishery." Ommer concludes that we need to see more clearly the true nature of the global market and act accordingly.

The theme of "new gods for old" is taken up again by Jay Newman in chapter 4. Newman focuses on modern media technologies—especially television and the Internet—and examines their relevance to religious culture. Appropriately, Newman takes his cue from Harold Coward, to whom the present volume is dedicated. Indeed, the title of Newman's essay, "Media Technology and the Future of Religions," is taken from the title of a chapter in Coward's book, *Sacred Word, Sacred Text*. Newman focuses in particular on Coward's assertion of the "primacy of the oral." Newman acknowledges the force of Coward's claim, but says that the value of the written word must be recognized, as must the value of new media technologies. He points out that the printing press, so vital in the dissemination of the written word, was perhaps an invention of greater importance in its time than the creation of new media technologies is today. This leads him to consider the charges of "idolatry" that are often made against new media technologies such as television. Television is of particular interest because of the way it features "televangelists." Newman argues, however, that the "idol" here is not television but the written word, which features so prominently in the presentation of the television evangelist. What television has done in this instance is to focus attention on a more classical version of idolatry—that of bibliolatry, where the written word is taken literally. As Paul Tillich reminds us, "Faith, if it takes its symbols literally, becomes idolatrous!"[16] Newman is reminding us that idolatry is not something that has only just emerged in the modern world. It is a phenomenon we see throughout history, from the idols condemned by the prophets of the Hebrew Bible to the bibliolatry evident in television evangelism today. He concludes that we should not be afraid of modern media technologies, as they are "likely to foster more than retard civilization."

In the final chapter in Part 1 David R. Loy discusses Huntington's "Clash of Civilizations" thesis. Huntington's essay is really about how to determine the security needs of the United States in a post–Cold War world. Huntington argues that we are entering a new era in which rivalries between ideologies and nation states are over. The conflicts in the world today are caused by clashes between civilizations. Contrary to conventional wisdom, Huntington argues that increasing intercivilization contact increases tensions in the world, because at a basic level civilizations are incompatible.

Loy argues that the "fault lines" in the modern world are caused more by a clash of values that arise as a result of globalization. Globalization confronts us with a very particular set of values. The modern Western culture that drives globalization exudes values that are, in fact, religious.

Modern Western culture, Loy maintains, is a secular religion. Its values clash with religions such as Buddhism and Islam. The very qualities engendered by globalization—greed, ill will, and delusion—a Buddhist would say should be transformed into generosity, compassion, and wisdom. Similarly, central to Islam is a concern for social justice, something not evident in globalization. Through globalization, says Loy, the West is imposing its values on the rest of the world. Much of the conflict in the world is not caused by civilizational differences, but rather is a result of resistence to this process. Globalization brings with it a set of values—a religion—that conflicts with those held by adherents of the major traditional religions of the world.

## Religion and War

Loy takes issue with Huntington when he says, "The next world war, if there is one, will be a war between civilizations."[17] Loy argues that the fault lines in the modern world cannot be attributed simply to a clash of civilizations. Their causes are complex, but we must not underestimate the power of technology and the forces of globalization to create global disharmony and conflict. Huntington's assertion that the fault lines of the modern world are civilizational fails to take adequate account of the stresses that cut across civilizational boundaries and that are caused by globalization. As Cynthia D. Moe Lobeda argues in *Healing a Broken World: Globalization and God*, the prevailing model of globalization widens the gap between the wealthy and the rest of humanity, assaults the earth's life-support systems, and jeopardizes cultural diversity.[18] Much of the violent reaction to the West that we have seen recently is fueled by rage against the injustices and barrenness of the materialistic, corporately governed, liberal state.[19] The forces of globalization, which are powered by American corporate capitalism and the unwavering belief in the individual, are extremely powerful and uncompromising.[20] We should not be surprised, therefore, if these forces cause global disharmony and conflict. To repeat once again what Huntington himself says, what is globalization to the West is imperialism to the rest.

Huntington further argues that religion is a major constituent of identity within civilizations. The implication of this is that as civilizations clash, the religion that drives each one is a major source of the conflict. We do not see religion in this way. To be sure, people will sometimes justify violence in the name of religion and will countenance extremely violent acts. But extremists are not just found within religious circles, and not only religious people perpetrate atrocities. In the past century leaders of secular governments (Stalin and Pol Pot come to mind) have killed more people in the name of the state (176 million worldwide) than anyone has in the name of religion. Yet it is conventional wisdom to blame religion for wars, from the one in Northern Ireland to the one in Bosnia. Moreover, there is much media talk these days of "Islamic Extremists," "Hindu extremists," "Zionist extremists," and so on. They are never simply "extremists." This assumption is similar to the one made by Huntington, that there is some kind of intrinsic link between religion and conflict. So the question becomes insistent and in need of an answer: Are the gods of traditional religions such as Christianity, Islam, Judaism, Hinduism, and Buddhism gods of war?

## A Test Case: Christianity

Let us first discuss this question of war and religion by focusing on the religion most familiar to Westerners: Christianity. There is no denying that institutional Christianity has been responsible for wars: one thinks, for example, of the Crusades. There is also no denying that Christians in good conscience have supported wars.[21] But Christians of equally good conscience have also been pacificists.[22] So the Christian tradition as such is unlikely to give a clear answer to the question of whether there is an intrinsic link between war and Christianity. We are therefore driven back to the very origins of Christianity and to Jesus himself. What attitude did Jesus take toward war? This seems a simple question, and yet it turns out to be far from simple. For an argument can be made that Jesus was a pacificist, but it can also be contended that he was a revolutionary who, in fact, countenanced violence.

During Christmas 1969, West Berlin clergy received a letter from the so-called Palestinian Front. The letter contained the following paragraph:

> The revolutionary liberation front, Al Fatah, has been organizing the Palestinian people for many years and is preparing in theory and practice for an armed revolt. *As Christ fought against the Roman occupation power, so also Al Fatah fights against the Zionists and their supporters*, the German and American capitalists.[23]

In this paragraph Al Fatah is attempting to justify its violence by appealing to the example of Jesus, alleging that he fought against the Romans.

The idea that Jesus was a revolutionary who believed in violent means to achieve his ends is not original to Al Fatah. It was first proposed in a systematic form in 1778 by Hermann Samuel Reimarus, who claimed that Jesus was a revolutionary who failed, and that after his death his disciples put out a spiritualized interpretation of his life to cover up his failure.[24]

Since Reimarus, there have been many reformulations of this thesis, especially by Jewish scholars, the most notable being Robert Eisler,[25] Joel
Carmichael,[26] and Hyam Maccoby.[27] If such scholars were right, and Jesus
were a violent revolutionary, it would surely have an impact on Christian
ethics, especially with regard to war. For Christians, Jesus is the Christ, the
Son of God, and it is difficult to see how, if he did counsel the use of violence, Christians could resist the argument that they should follow suit. So
the question of whether or not Jesus embraced the "Zealot option," as it is
sometimes called, is not simply an obscure academic question: it has practical implications.

The Zealots[28] of Jesus' time held the conviction that God's rule must
be made manifest in concrete political ways and that the acknowledgment
of God's rule conflicts with submission to Rome. The Romans must therefore be driven out by force. Jesus, it is claimed, shared these views. There
are two major arguments to support this contention. The first concerns
what Jesus did and said. The focal point of Jesus' message was the Kingdom
of God. In Jewish thought the Kingdom of God was not some otherworldly
reality: it was to be established in the here and now. Had Jesus taught an
otherworldly kingdom he would hardly have been arrested and crucified.
Crucifixion was a serious punishment reserved for serious crimes, especially
treason. It is no coincidence that Jesus was crucified with two other gueril-
las or "revolutionary bandits" (Lk 23:32). Moreover, some scholars maintain that when Jesus "cleanses" the temple and drives out the merchants
and money changers with a whip (Jn 2:15), he was, in fact, inciting a riot.
Temple trade was vital to the Jewish authorities who collaborated with the
Romans. Any attack on the Temple, it is claimed, would be seen as an
attack on the whole political system of the day.

The second argument focuses on Jesus' disciples. They were a motley
crew, but among them was a "Simon the Zealot" (Lk 6:15). It could be
argued that Judas was also a Zealot, as his name "Iscariot" could possibly
come from "sicarius," meaning an assassin. Moreover, Jesus nicknames
James and John "boanerges," which means "Sons of Thunder," a possible
allusion to Zealot affiliation (Mk 3:17 cf. Lk 9:51ff.). So there might well
have been a significant Zealot presence among the disciples. Furthermore,
they are armed: Luke tells us they had two swords apiece (Lk 22:38), and
in the Garden of Gethsemane Peter cuts off the ear of one of those who
comes to arrest Jesus (Jn 18:10). So some scholars ask the question: Would
Jesus be the leader of a band with such obvious Zealot sympathies unless
he himself was a sympathizer?

None of this evidence is as conclusive as it appears, however. Jesus *was*
indeed crucified as a messianic pretender and a danger to the Roman state.

But the Gospel writers claim that these were false charges: Jesus was not a threat to the Romans. His enemies claimed he was a threat in order to get rid of him. The cleansing of the Temple seems more like an act of righteousness indignation than a violent act meant to provoke a revolt. And Jesus may have had one or more disciples who were sympathetic to the Zealot cause, but he had at least one other disciple, Matthew the tax-collector, who definitely was not. As for the fact that they carried weapons, all prudent travelers of the day carried weapons for protection. The Jewish historian Josephus tells us that even the nonaggressive Essenes carried weapons on long journeys. Moreover, the disciples were not arrested along with Jesus, which seems to indicate that the Romans did not see them as Zealots and did not consider them a threat. It thus goes beyond the evidence we have to link Jesus to the Zealot cause through his disciples.

The evidence we have examined so far does not suggest that Jesus embraced the Zealot option. There is, however, one particular incident that is crucial to the debate and to which we have not yet referred, and that concerns the question about paying taxes to the Romans. This question is meant to at least embarrass Jesus and, it was hoped, to discredit him. Paying taxes to the Romans was a sign of subservience to the idolatry of Rome, and for a true Jewish nationalist it was unacceptable. If Jesus advises people to pay taxes, he loses popular support. If he advises against paying taxes, he is publicly counseling treason against Rome, a very dangerous thing to do.

The traditional Christian interpretation of this passage emphasizes how adroit the reply of Jesus was. He asked to be shown a specific coin, a denarius. This was a silver coin minted outside of Palestine. The time was the reign of Tiberius. His denarius bore a bust of the emperor crowned with laurel as the sign of his future divinity and bore the inscription "Augustus son of the divine Augustus." On the reverse side of the coin was an image of the emperor's mother seated on the divine throne. The emperor was thus celebrated as the head of the pagan religion and as the divine son of divine parents. The coins were a very effective way of emphasizing the cult of the deified ruler. As such, they were offensive to Jewish nationalists.[29] Jesus accordingly asked to be shown a denarius and inquired whose head and inscription it bore. His questioners answered simply, "The Emperor's." His reply might be paraphrased, "If then you trifle with your scruples and carry the tainted coins, give back to Caesar what he has given to you, but remember your prime allegiance is to God." It seems like a very clever answer, yet Jesus was crucified shortly afterward for sedition. Clearly his answer was too ambiguous: Jesus was crucified by the Romans as a Zealot. He had, according to one of the three charges brought against him at his trial, "forbidden taxes to the Romans" (Lk 23:2). Yet for large numbers of the crowd he clearly was not a Zealot, as they shouted for the release of Barabbas, not Jesus (Lk 23:18). And the story is perhaps more complex than it first appears. Jesus says, "Bring me a denarius and let me *look* at it." This statement implies two things: that he does not possess a denarius, and second that he does not wish to handle the denarius, only look at it. In this he is like the Zealots, for they would neither possess the denarius, nor would they touch it. To touch a denarius with its graven image would be to become religiously impure. And when Jesus says, "Give to God the things that are God's," for the Jewish nationalists among his audience this would mean one thing: give the land of Israel back to God. It did not belong to the Romans and they must be driven out. This interpretation suggests Jesus was embracing the Zealot option and that the Romans understood his answer correctly, and that is why they killed him.

The story about taxes is thus open to interpretation and leaves a question mark over the attitude of Jesus to the Romans. Paul, in Rom 13, urges Christians to obey the imperial power and seems to regard such secular rule as part of the price we pay for living in a fallen world. Most Christians have taken their cue from Paul and assumed that this reflects what Jesus thought. But it is not really clear that Jesus thought as Paul did. What does seem clear is that Jesus was crucified by the Romans and that *he offered no resistance*. This implies that, no matter what his attitude to the Romans was, he did not countenance violence for religious ends.[30] But we cannot go much further than that.[31] So, for example, the question of whether one may go to war in self-defense is open to debate.[32] Christianity does not have a simple, unequivocal position on the question of whether war may be justified. And so it is with the other religions of the world.

### Religion and Violence

Marc Gopin explains very well the challenge religions face when confronting the twenty-first century. He says:

> The character of religion, how opposed or supportive it is of science, of the human mind, of human rights, of civil society, will depend completely on the hermeneutic of engagement of its adherents. That, in turn, will depend on the degree to which its adherents can honestly see a creative interaction of ancient traditions and modern constructs. Both elements of the equation, ancient traditions and modern constructs of civil society and scientific

investigation, will have to be respected in this artful process of weaving the future.[33]

This process of "weaving the future" and successfully negotiating with the modern world is a challenge for all religions. Postmodern theorists, most notably Jean-Francois Lyotard,[34] speak of the collapse of "metanarratives," those all-encompassing stories that undergird cultures and religions and give them their values and goals. In the modern world, where cultures and religions all interact with each other through the process of globalization, these metanarratives are seen to be relative. They cannot all be true. The new metanarrative is therefore one of cultural diversity.[35]

Some religions find this easier to accept than others. Hinduism and Buddhism do not find such a plurality of metanarratives all that disturbing. The Western faiths of Judaism, Christianity, and Islam, however, because they are missionary faiths, view such accommodation as more difficult. Of the three monotheistic faiths Islam is often singled out as the one that has the most difficulty adjusting to the modern world, and which therefore poses the greatest threat to "the new world order." Huntington says:

> The underlying problem for the West is not Islamic fundamentalism. It is Islam, a different civilization whose people are convinced of the superiority of their culture and are obsessed with the inferiority of their power. The problem for Islam is not the CIA or the U.S. Department of Defense. It is the West, a different civilization whose people are convinced of the universality of their culture and believe that their superior, if declining, power imposes on them the obligation to extend that culture throughout the world. These are the basic ingredients that fuel conflict between Islam and the West.[36]

Huntington is not alone in this view. Philip Jenkins, in his provocative book *The Next Christendom: The Coming of Global Christianity,* when speaking of the future, says:

> At the turn of the third millennium, religious loyalties are at the root of many of the world's ongoing civil wars and political violence, and in most cases, the critical division is the age-old battle between Christianity and Islam. However much this would have surprised political analysts a generation or two ago, the critical political frontiers around the world are not decided by attitudes toward class or dialectical materialism, but by rival concepts of God.[37]

When one approaches the question with a broader perspective, however, new insights emerge. One may well argue that from a Western, post-Enlightenment perspective bitter disputes over rival conceptions of God stem from an outdated concept of exclusive religious truth. The claims to truth in the "grand," all-encompassing metanarratives found in the religions of the world are relativized in our pluralistic modern world. But such a critique also applies to the metanarrative which undergirds globalization. Fukuyama's conception of a Universal History moving towards a homogenized world culture is just as much a metanarrative as those found in the religions of the world. The Western story of scientific-technological progress is also a metanarrative which should be seen as subject to the same critique as that which applies to other religions.

Diversity relativizes all narratives. The chapters in Part 1 of this volume show how we will gain greater insight into our modern predicament when we see that there are other ways to view the role of technology in our lives and its concomitant development, the Western project of globalization.[38] The primary task, however, when thinking of war and religion is to understand the dynamic of each religion and to see what drives it, so that we may understand why religions do sometimes clash with each other. As Hans Küng has argued, there will be no peace among the nations unless there is peace among the religions; there will be no peace among the religions unless there is dialogue between them; and there will be no dialogue between them unless there is investigation into their foundations.[39] The chapters in Part 2 accordingly seek to discuss various interpretative cruxes in each of the major religions to see what light can be thrown on the question of religion and war.

The first chapter in Part 2 offers some theological reflections on terrorism. Timothy Gorringe first discusses how we might define terrorism. He argues that conventional understandings of terrorism are inadequate because terrorism comes in many guises and supports many different causes. Most terrorists do not think of themselves as such: they see themselves rather as freedom fighters or resisters of oppression. Gorringe therefore discusses what validity there is to this claim. Can terrorism, for example, ever be considered a form of just war? Gorringe argues that we should judge wars waged by legitimate states and wars waged by terrorists by the same "just war" criteria. There are some wars waged by states that are not morally defensible, and there are some—for example, the war against Nazi Germany—that may be justified as a necessary evil. Similarly, some forms of terrorism may be justified as evil but necessary, and others may be deemed as simply unjustifiable.

Gorringe then moves on to a discussion of religiously motivated terror and discusses the vexed question of whether there is a causal link between religion and violence. He concludes that "religiously motivated terrorism clothes fanaticism in the stolen robes of faith." It is a false god. Yet there is a link between religion and violence, especially in the myth of redemptive violence that permeates Western culture, but that is especially prominent in America. This myth is really a theological perversion of the symbol of the crucifixion, in its interpretation of violent death as a response to sin. Gorringe condemns such a misappropriation of the message of Christianity and argues for a "nonviolent militancy." All violence, he says, whether of the state or of a terrorist cell, ultimately will destroy us. Violence is pathological and will vanquish the very foundations of any culture that does not see it as such.

Islam is singled out by Huntington as being a special threat to peace in the "new world order." Islam, he says, has "bloody borders."[40] The events of September 11, 2001, have especially focused attention on "Islamic extremists." But what exactly is the relationship between Islam and violent extremists? Rippin examines the question in an indirect way in chapter 7. His starting point is the question of Muslim identity, and he points out that Muhammad combined the roles of religious leader and political–military leader. Muhammad's authority to decide on both religious and sociopolitical matters was thus clear. But when he died, the question of where such authority resided became a disputed one. It was this question which led to the schism in Islam between the Sunnis and the Shiites (beginning in 661 C.E.). The question has continued down to the present: How does one determine who is a genuine Muslim? Or, to put it more graphically, who are the "insiders" and who are the "outsiders"? One of the most famous statements on this issue was by Muhammad Ibn Abd al-Wahab in the eighteenth century in a tract *The Things which Nullify Islam*. This tract has been revised in the modern period by a Saudi cleric Shaikh Abdul Aziz ibn Abdullah ibn Baz (1912–1999).

Rippin examines this revision and shows how it reflects some of the concerns of modern Islam. Rippin sees the "ghost of Salman Rushdie" lurking in the background. For many Muslims Rushdie represents the threat of modernity. This is seen in many of the particular "dangers" that are referred to. There is a concern with a perceived lack of respect for Islam. Israel and its relationship with the Islamic world is also an issue. And the Western notion that religion is a private and entirely spiritual affair is also seen as unacceptable. Westerners may be surprised that Ibn Baz sees such "dangers" as so threatening. But looking at Ibn Baz is illuminating for this very reason: his writings help us to understand better why so many Muslims feel that Western modernity is such a menace, and why sometimes the response is a violent one.

In *The Next Christendom* Jenkins sees Islam coming more and more into conflict with Judaism. The political situation in the Middle East doubtless exacerbates such conflicts, but Jenkins' work, like that of Huntington, raises the question of whether there is something in the religion itself that promotes violence. The state of Israel has been relentless in its violent response to the violence perpetrated against it. But does this reflect the philosophy inherent in the Jewish religion, or is it more a philosophy of *Realpolitik*? Eliezer Segal argues that the Jewish tradition emphasizes free and rational discussion, not passion and subjectivity, and it puts definite limits on the use of violence for religious purposes.

Segal focuses on the famous case of Phineas, who in Num 25:7–8 kills a man and a woman who were engaging in the cult of Baalpeor—that is, he kills for religious reasons. In *Sifre on Numbers* it is related that Phineas' action was accompanied by a series of uniquely miraculous events. The implication was that his action was to be thought of as unique and not to be seen as a precedent for emulation. Rabbinic discussions generally suggest that Phineas' violent act should not be condoned. Jewish exegetes in the medieval period and in early modern times saw Phineas' attack as justified by a special combination of circumstances that were "virtually irreproducible." Segal concludes from this that there is a shift away from the Bible and Second Temple documents that extolled Phineas' actions. In the midrashic and talmudic sources Phineas' actions are relegated to the past and were not a model for the present. Segal says this indicates a philosophical mind-set that emphasized free and rational discussion and deprecated actions guided solely by emotions and unreasoned conviction. The rabbis, in fact, tried to carefully circumscribe the boundaries of justified violence.

Huntington suggests that the major constituent of civilization, or of the consciousness of civilization, is religion. Neufeldt's article is illuminating here. He examines the language of *Hindutva: Who is a Hindu?* by V. D. Savarkar in 1923, and its influence on the Bharatiya Janata Party (BJP). Sarvarkar was discussing what it means to be a Hindu. He understands "Hinduness" as going beyond mere religious affiliation. A Hindu is one who shares a history and a consciousness going back to the Rig Veda. Sarvarkar contended that to be a Hindu one has to be "of the soil" of India, recognize India as the Father- and Motherland, and further recognize it as a Holyland. To be a Hindu was, moreover, to recognize Hindu *dharma*. Thus, for Sarvarkar Muslim Indians and Christian Indians had abandoned their true heritage and could not partake in their true destiny. For Sarvarkar the true identity of India as a country was inextricably bound to the Hindu religion, and it was not possible to be loyal to the Indian state on the one hand and have loyalty to a non-indigenous religion on the other. Sarvarkar's thought influenced Constituent Assembly Debates, Reports of Missionary Activities, and Freedom of Religion Bills in the post–World War II era. In the vision espoused by the *Hindutva* India was to be a Hindu state. There was no room in the state for dual cultural or religious loyalties.

This was quite foreign to the thinking of Mohandas Gandhi. Gandhi spoke of an India whose inhabitants were "citizens" and that took seriously the needs and rights of its minorities. There could be a pan-Indian civilization that recognized diverse identities. Gandhi thought that civilizations could communicate across the sharpest divide. The philosophy of the Hindutva, on the other hand, sets up barriers that can lead to violence.

Neufeldt's study illustrates the same point that was made in our brief examination of Christianity and violence: religious traditions do not have a monolithic position on this matter. Hinduism has produced the nonviolent and inclusive philosophy of Gandhi as well as the strident cultural and religious exclusivism of Sarvarkar. One tradition generally perceived to have a coherent and uniform view on violence, however, is Buddhism. The conventional wisdom is that Buddhism is a pacificist religion. The religion conjures up images of gentle monks walking, with head bowed, anxiously trying to avoid harming any living creature. Robert Florida's essay in chapter 10 shows that this is a simplistic picture. He looks at Buddhist attitudes to violence in Thailand and Tibet. The choice of these examples is not meant to present contemporary Buddhists in a bad light, but rather to highlight what for many may seem a sharp departure from Buddhist teaching and practice.

Florida begins by reminding us that although Buddhists extol peace, the Buddha himself never actually condemned anyone for being a soldier. Moreover, the famous Buddhist emperor Ashoka (who reigned approximately 269–232 B.C.E.) tempered the violence of traditional rule, but he did not renounce violence altogether and he maintained a standing army that he was quite willing to use. Florida then moves on to a specific examination of the situation in Thailand and a discussion of the Buddhist monk Bhikku Kitthiwuttho, who, in the 1970s, countenanced violence. In Tibet there is a history of Buddhist monks being associated with violence as for many years the *dobdos* or warrior monks were found in the three largest monasteries (often referred to as the "Three Seats"). Florida concludes that although individually Buddhists are encouraged to cleanse their own hearts of violent acts, in general the Buddhist traditions have not advocated pacificism as something the state should follow.

In chapter 11 Michael Hadley returns to the "new gods of old" theme. Hadley agrees with Walter Wink that "redemptive violence" is the most dominant religion in our society today. In the media and popular culture violence is portrayed as able to solve the basic evils of the world, bringing justice, destroying evil, and promoting good. Violence is seen as redemptive. The language that promotes this belief is fundamentally religious. It has, moreover, become the American civil religion. Hadley goes on to show that the speeches after September 11, 2001, are couched in the rhetoric of "sacred duty," which requires the United States to bring "evildoers to justice." President George W. Bush is, in fact, drawing on a fervent patriotism that sees the United States as having a "manifest destiny." Hadley relates this language to Huntington's thesis on the "clash of civilizations": civilization (the United States) on the one hand, and the "enemies of freedom" on the other. The fault lines dividing "us" from "them" are those drawn in a world where "freedom is under attack." Bush's famous dictum, "You are either with us or against us," invokes the saying of Jesus and thus gives a religious identity to those "fighting the forces of terrorism." Hadley concludes that the post-9/11 language that is used in the "war on terror" and the symbols this language evokes are about salvation, ultimacy, and power. Current military and political discourse has appropriated the power of "might and dominion," which was once the preserve of God alone.

The chapters in this volume seek to present new insights into the nature of globalization, technology, and war. Each emphasizes the value of seeing issues and problems from a different perspective. It is fitting, therefore, that the volume is dedicated to Harold Coward. Harold founded the Centre for Studies in Religion and Society at the University of Victoria in Canada in 1992 and was its director until he retired in 2002. Under his leadership the Centre attracted scholars from all over the world. One of the keys to its success was Harold's insistence on the primary role of interdisciplinary research teams bringing knowledge of science, social science, humanities, and the world's religions to bear on major problems facing the world today. These major team projects have highlighted critical aspects of modern life, for example: religious conscience, the state, and the law; cross-cultural approaches to health care ethics; the crisis in the fisheries; environmental degradation; overpopulation and consumption; the spiritual roots of restorative justice; and the greenhouse effect. The present volume is in that tradition.

Harold is not only an accomplished organizer and team leader, but he is also an outstanding scholar and prolific author in his own right. This volume is a token of the esteem in which he is held by his colleagues and friends and a public way of acknowledging his scholarly and intellectual achievements.[41]

## Notes

1. C. H. Waddington, *The Scientific Attitude* (London: Hutchinson Educational, 1941; 2nd ed. 1968), p. 144: "Science by itself is able to provide mankind with a way of life which is, firstly self-consistent and harmonious, and, secondly, free for the exercise of that objective reason on which our civilization depends."

2. Frank E. Manuel, *The Eighteenth Century Confronts the Gods* (Cambridge, Mass.: Harvard, 1959), p. 11.

3. Walter Wink, *The Powers That Be: Theology for a New Millennium* (New York: Doubleday, 1998).

4. Francis Fukuyama, "The End of History," *The National Interest* 16 (1989): 4, 8.

5. Francis Fukuyama, *The End of History and the Last Man* (New York: The Free Press, 1992), p. 48.

6. John Gray, *Endgames: Questions in Late Modern Political Thought* (Cambridge: Polity Press, 1977), pp. 178f.

7. Samuel P. Huntington, "The Clash of Civilizations?" *Foreign Affairs* 72, no. 3 (1993): 22–49; *The Clash of Civilizations and the Remaking of World Order* (New York: Simon and Schuster, 1996).

8. Samuel P. Huntington, "If Not Civilizations, What? Paradigms of the Post-Cold War World," *Foreign Affairs* 72, no. 5 (1993): 191–192.

9. C. A. Campbell, *On Selfhood and Godhood* (London: Allen and Unwin, 1957), p. 248.

10. Paul Tillich, *Dynamics of Faith* (New York: Harper and Row, 1957).

11. Fukuyama, *The End of History*, p. 312.

12. Fukuyama, *The End of History*, p. 312.

13. David R. Loy, "The Religion of the Market," *Journal of the American Academy of Religion* 65, no. 2: 275–289.

14. William Greider, *One World, Ready or Not* (New York: Simon & Schuster, 1997), p. 473.

15. Warren Winiarski, "Niccolò Machiavelli," in *History of Political Philosophy*, ed. Leo Strauss and Joseph Cropsey (Chicago: Rand McNally, 1963), p. 273.

16. Tillich, *Dynamics of Faith*, p. 52.

17. Huntington, "The Clash of Civilizations?" p. 39.

18. Cynthia D. Moe Lobeda, *Healing a Broken World: Globalization and God* (Minneapolis: Fortress Press, 2002), pp. 19ff.

19. Cf. Dieter Senghaas, "A Clash of Civilizations—An Idée Fixe?" *Journal of Peace Research* 35, no. 1 (1998): 130: "Cultural, and as a rule, religious factors, are rarely of great relevance at the very beginning of a conflict escalation. Socio-economic problems with no prospect of a solution are more important."

20. Kishore Mahbubani, "The Dangers of Decadence: What the Rest Can Teach the West," *Foreign Affairs* 72, no. 4 (1993): 14, puts it pointedly: "The United States has undertaken a massive social experiment, tearing down social institution after social institution that restrained the individual. The results have been disastrous. Since 1960 the U.S. population has increased 41 percent while violent crime has risen 560%, single mother births by 419%, divorce rates by 300% and the

percentage of children in single parent homes by 300%. This is massive social decay. Many a society shudders at the prospects of this happening on its shores. But instead of traveling overseas with humility, Americans confidently preach the virtues of unfettered individual freedom, blithely ignoring the visible social consequences."

21. For example, just before World War II Leslie Weatherhead abandoned his pacificism. See Leslie D. Weatherhead, *Thinking Aloud in War Time: An Attempt to See the Present Position in the Light of the Christian Faith* (London: Hodder and Stoughton, 1939).

22. See C. E. Raven, *War and the Christian* (London: SCM, 1938).

23. Quoted in Martin Hengel, *Was Jesus a Revolutionist?* (Philadelphia: Fortress, 1971), p. 36.

24. Hermann Samuel Reimarus, *Reimarus: Fragments*, ed. Charles H. Talbert, trans. Ralph S. Fraser (Philadelphia: Fortress, 1970).

25. Robert Eisler, *The Messiah Jesus and John the Baptist* (New York: Dial, 1931).

26. Joel Carmichael, *The Death of Jesus* (New York: Macmillan, 1962).

27. Hyam Maccoby, *Revolution in Judaea* (New York: Taplinger, 1981).

28. The word "Zealot" is a general term that refers to those in Palestine who resisted the Romans by force of arms during, and after, the time of Jesus. But, in fact, the resistance to the Romans should be differentiated. See Dennis C. Duling and Norman Perrin, *The New Testament: Proclamation and Parenesis, Myth and History*, 3rd ed. (New York: Harcourt Brace College Publishers, 1994), pp. 55–58.

29. During the Jewish revolt against the Romans of 132–135 C.E. under Bar Cochbah, the Jews hammered the Roman coins flat and stamped them afresh with Hebrew characters.

30. Hengel, *Was Jesus a Revolutionist?*, pp. 26–29, argues that at the very heart of Jesus' message lies a conscious rejection of violence.

31. The evidence of the New Testament *as a whole* is ambiguous. See Michel Desjardins, *Peace, Violence, and the New Testament* (Sheffield: Sheffield Acdemic Press, 1999).

32. Roland H. Bainton, *Christian Attitudes Toward War and Peace: A Historical Survey and Critical Re-evaluation* (Nashville: Abingdon, 1960), esp. pp. 85–151.

33. Marc Gopin, *Between Eden and Armageddon: The Future of World Religions, Violence and Peacemaking* (Oxford: Oxford University Press, 2000), p. 223. It is interesting to note that there are now some Marxist writers who are also arguing that we must engage the forces of global capitalism and not simply reject them. See, for example, Michael Hardt and Antonio Negri, *Empire* (Cambridge: Harvard University Press, 2000). Hardt and Negri argue that we must "accept the

challenge and learn to think globally and act globally," and contrary to many socialists, they are optimistic that if the present globalizing processes are "pushed past their present limitations" (p. 206) a just and equitable world society can be established.

34. Jean-Francois Lyotard, *The Postmodern Condition: A Report on Knowledge* (Manchester: Manchester University Press, 1984).

35. You can, of course, reject the implications of cultural and religious diversity and maintain that only *your* metanarrative is true. This is precisely what fundamentalists do.

36. Huntington, *Clash of Civilizations*, p. 217.

37. Philip Jenkins, *The Next Christendom: The Coming of Global Christianity* (Oxford: Oxford University Press, 2002), p. 163.

38. There is a growing literature that offers a critique of globalization. Most of this literature, however, does not take the tack that globalization is a religious phenomenon. See, however, William Greider, *One World Ready or Not: The Manic Logic of Global Capitalism* (New York: Touchstone, 1997). See also: Richard Barnet and John Cavanagh, *Global Dreams: Imperial Corporations and the New World Order* (New York: Simon and Schuster, 1994); Jeremy Brecher and Tim Costello, *Global Village or Global Pillage: Economic Reconstruction from the Bottom Up* (Boston: South End Press, 1994); and David Korten, *When Corporations Rule the World* (San Francisco: Kumarian and Barrett-Koehler, 1995).

39. See Hans Küng, *Global Responsibility: In Search of a New World Ethic* (New York: Crossroad, 1991).

40. Huntington, *Clash of Civilizations*, pp. 254–259.

41. More detail about Harold Coward may be found in the Canadian *Who's Who*.

Note: All of the chapters in this book were written before the U.S. and Allied invasion of Iraq in 2003—Ed.

# CHAPTER ONE

# The Origins of Modernity
# and the Technological Society

### DAVID J. HAWKIN

"The past is a foreign country; they do things differently there." So begins L. P. Hartley's novel *The Go-Between*.[1] In this epigrammatic statement Hartley summarizes the thoughts and feelings of many in the modern world, for contemporary society is very different from that which has gone before. As Jacques Ellul has said, "We are conditioned by something new: technological civilization."[2] Technology has altered everything: cars have changed transportation; computers have changed communication; dishwashers and vacuum cleaners have changed work; televisions and video games have changed leisure; powerful medical drugs have changed health care. The evidence of dramatic change through technology is there for all to see. A world full of such labor-saving devices, leisure activities, and life-saving drugs and machines, if described to our grandparents, would probably have sounded utopian to them. Yet there are many who consider the modern world very distopian. Robert Pippin, for example, avers that "Modernity promised a culture of unintimidated, curious, rational, self-reliant individuals, and instead it produced . . . a herd society, a race of anxious, timid, conforming sheep, and a culture of utter banality."[3] Many would be less grandiloquous but make a similar point by pointing specifically to increasing global conflict, an escalating ecological crisis, and an AIDS epidemic in the Third World of catastrophic proportions as examples of how, despite the many advantages the modern world has given us, we are unable to solve some of our most basic human problems.

Why is this? There are those who argue that we need to look at the origins of modernity and the technological society if we are to fully understand the dilemma in which we find ourselves.[4] When we do so, we see clearly that there has been a discontinuity in the Western tradition, and that the nature of this discontinuity explains much of the character of the modern world. We will accordingly turn to an examination of the origins of modernity to see how this came about.

In a well-known article, Lynn White claimed that the origins of the modern worldview, in which technological mastery is the dominant feature, can be traced back to the influence of medieval Christianity. Many of the unfortunate consequences of the modern worldview can thus be laid at the feet of Christianity, which bears a "huge burden of guilt," for example, for the ecological crisis.[5] White made two essential points in support of his argument. First, he claimed that Western Christianity came to emphasize more and more that salvation was to be found through right conduct. Gradually, therefore, the classical ideal in which contemplation was superior to action was abandoned, and action was elevated above contemplation. This was coupled, he further argued, with a fundamental change in the perception of nature. This change was generated by monks, who, through their investigations of the workings of nature, laid the groundwork for an explosion in knowledge of the natural world. The most prominent of these monks was Roger Bacon. The rise of a voluntarist Christianity, combined with a dramatic increase in knowledge about the way the world works, laid the foundation for the conquest of nature and ultimately led to its exploitation.

White is to be commended for his insight, for he has latched on to two of the most important developments of the medieval period. But he overextends his argument when he singles out Roger Bacon and claims that he helped to bring about an exploitative attitude to nature. Roger Bacon (ca. 1214–1292 C.E.) is one of the great medieval scholars, renowned for his works on nature.[6] But while Roger Bacon may have investigated the workings of nature, he never suggested that nature should be exploited. Nature showed us the mind of God: to understand how it worked was to more fully appreciate how God worked. And while nature was there for human use, Roger Bacon at no time suggested that it would be appropriate to manipulate nature in a spirit of mastery and domination.

The problem with White's argument is that, like the curate in the boardinghouse, he has chosen the wrong Bacon. Some three centuries later *Francis* Bacon (1561–1626 C.E.) did what Roger Bacon never did—urged humans to conquer nature "for the relief of man's estate."[7] Nature must not be "a courtesan for pleasure" but a "spouse, for generation, fruit and comfort."[8] Similarly, White has exaggerated the extent to which contemplation and action were divorced in the medieval period. It is again Francis Bacon who finally severs the two and who attacks in a most uncompromising way the life of contemplation, which he regarded as concerned with pointless abstractions or, as he put it, "a whirling round about."[9]

Francis Bacon is, in fact, a key figure in the development of modernity. Although much of what he said had been said before, the way in which Bacon articulated his philosophy was quite novel and explicit. Bacon makes very clear two things: nature is for human use, and we have a duty to use it. Bacon saw himself as a pioneer and took to task those of previous generations because they had not used knowledge of the natural world for practical purposes. In a well-known passage he says:

> Being convinced that the human intellect makes its own difficulties, not using the true helps which are at man's disposal soberly and judiciously; whence follows manifold ignorance of things, and by reason of that ignorance mischiefs innumerable; he thought all trial should be made, whether that commerce between the mind of man and the nature of things, which is more precious than anything on earth, or at least than anything that is of the earth, might by any means be restored to its perfect and original condition, or if that may not be, yet reduced to a better condition than that in which it now is.[10]

Here Bacon lays out his agenda clearly: the "commerce between the mind of man and the nature of things" must be facilitated so that the earth may be "restored to its original and perfect condition." Bacon is a utopian. He believes that humans can, by their own efforts, improve their "estate," their lot in this world. But what is needed to bring this about is to jettison the baggage that has kept us back so that we have so far made only "contemptible progress." Humans in the past had been too busy puzzling over pointless abstractions. They needed to understand that their true calling was to reestablish control over a perfectible nature. In his major writings, *The Advancement of Learning*, *Novum Organum*, and *The New Atlantis*, Bacon recounts how this is to be done.

A basic premise of Bacon's is that the manipulation of nature could only take place when humans realized the importance of experiments and the practical application of knowledge. Thus, he rejected "the opinion, or inveterate conceit, which is both vainglorious and prejudicial, namely, that the dignity of the human mind is lowered by long and frequent intercourse with experiments and particulars, which are the objects of sense, confined to matter; especially since such matters generally require labour and investigation."[11]

Thus, for Bacon knowledge is practical; but even more than that, human knowledge and human power are identical (*scientia et potentia humana in idem coincidunt*). In the preface to *The Great Instauration* he says that the "true and lawful goal of the sciences" is to endow human life with "new discoveries and powers." He describes his ideal state in *New Atlantis* as a place where the new science results in lots of practical achievements, from the discovery of new chemical compounds and the artificial change of climate to the breeding of new species of plants and animals. In *The Advancement of Learning* Bacon describes how to set up an institution for inventors. It sounds remarkably like the Massachusetts Institute of Technology. Bacon envisages the government providing inventors with allowances for their experiments and for traveling. He also believes that there should be scholarly journals and international associations. He is, in fact, very modern: he conceives of the control and domination of nature as organized and controlled by an elite and supposedly our best weapon in the quest to improve the human condition.

There is much in the thought of Francis Bacon to dwell upon and analyze if we are to fully understand what it means to live in the age of modernity, for his writings exude its very essence. But there are two points in particular that are worth focusing on: what Bacon says about nature and what he says about contemplation.

The basic assumption in Bacon's thinking is that nature is impersonal and inanimate and can—and indeed should—be dealt with in an objective manner. He says:

> For as all works do shew forth the power and skill of the workman, and not his image; so it is of the works of God; which do shew the omnipotency and wisdom of the maker, but not his image; and therefore therein the heathen opinion differeth from the sacred truth; for they supposed the world to be the image of God, and man to be an extract or compendious image of the world; but the Scriptures never vouchsafe to attribute to the world that honour, as to be the image of God, but only *the work of his hands*; neither do they speak of any other image of God, but man.[12]

Thus, for Bacon nature has to be understood and studied as an artifact, as the work of God's hands, not as something that has purpose and worth of its own. There is no impediment, therefore, to humans putting it to their use. The language that Bacon employs in describing how humans should use nature is very revealing. He speaks of "putting nature to the test," for example, which is a phrase associated with torture during the Inquisition, and talks of the need to "conquer," "woo," "unveil," and "disrobe" nature in order to "force" her to give up her secrets. This graphic language reflects a culture of control in which nature becomes a "virgin" awaiting domination and exploitation. Carolyn Merchant has argued that the uncritical acceptance of this Baconian language has had disastrous consequences for those of us in the modern world. The forceful taking of nature's "virgin" resources and the emphasis on domination and conquest, such evident traits in the modern world, find their origins in Bacon.[13]

Bacon draws on the Bible to support his view that nature is an artifact. Nature is a creation of God and is in no way divine or suffused with the divine. It is matter, "stuff," an inanimate resource awaiting human use. Bacon gives the impression that he has derived this view solely from the Bible, but its origins are more complex than that. Bacon could not have found fertile soil for his argument that we must change our attitude toward nature if there had not been other fundamental changes in worldview as well. In particular, a change in the attitude toward nature could not take place unless there was first a change in how one understood the contemplative life. Bacon knows this well, and that is why he attacks Aristotle and the contemplative life.

Bacon criticized Aristotle for preferring the contemplative life to the life of action. He said that the common good "decides the question touching the preferment of the contemplative or active life, and decides it against Aristotle."[14] As he made Aristotle the object of his attack, Bacon managed to obscure the fact that he is attacking his own Christian tradition, which also elevated contemplation over action. As George Ovitt's *The Restoration of Perfection*[15] has shown, the Middle Ages remained true to the classical Christian tradition found in such writers as Origen, Gregory of Nyssa, Cassian, and Augustine, all of whom thought that although the active life is more productive than the contemplative, the contemplative is better and greater than the active.[16] Bacon is thus doing something very significant when he attacks the contemplative life and stresses the value of the active life. He is repudiating a tradition in which the life of action received its meaning from the life of contemplation. "All knowledge," Bacon asseverated, is to be referred to use and action, to "the relief of man's estate."[17] He thus makes *the life of action intrinsically worthwhile for its own sake* and paves the way for a view of the world in which efficiency, pragmatism, and utility are the key virtues. In short, this was a vital step in laying the ground work for the view of the world that has led to our modern technological worldview.

Bacon's influence on later practitioners of modernity has been enormous. In his thought we have nothing less than a repudiation of a way of thinking about nature and contemplation that had endured for a thousand years in the Christian tradition. But Bacon could not have undermined this complex superstructure of Christian thought all by himself: the edifice was already crumbling and all it needed was a hammer blow to bring it all tumbling down. It will be instructive now to focus more intently on how ideas about nature and contemplation changed before and during Bacon's time. By doing so we will understand better the nature of Bacon's achievement and see more clearly our own position in the modern world.

## Nature

It is important to consider again how Bacon arrived at his conception of nature. He claimed that the idea of nature as an artifact, as the handiwork of God, was derived from the biblical doctrine of creation. God was transcendent; the world was his creation. Nature and God were thus quite separate. But more than that, so conceived nature was an object and thus devoid of will; it was in no sense a subject. Humans thus became distinguished from nature by having will, a will that they could impose on nature. In grounding his idea of nature exclusively in what the Bible says, Bacon was implying that the true understanding of nature had been eclipsed in the Christian tradition by the influence of Greek thought. Bacon's argument carried the day, and the modern world is a testament to this. Bacon was, however, so successful in propagating his views because they had some antecedents; the time had to be right. What had brought about this change in attitude toward nature?

Christianity is a syncretistic phenomenon. More particularly, it is a synthesis of neo-Platonic thought and Jewish biblical religion. These two streams of thought had radically different approaches to understanding reality. Neo-Platonic thought, derived from the works of Plato, focused on the contrast between the eternal and the temporal. The central question was how to reconcile eternal realities (the Forms or Ideas) with their spatiotemporal counterparts. Plato himself sometimes spoke as if these spatiotemporal realities *copied* eternal Forms, and at other times he seemed to suggest that spatiotemporal realities *participated* in the eternal and were expressions of it. But the fundamental point was that for Plato and his followers the good life for the human consisted in conforming to the way things really are. Thus, cosmology, the inquiry into the whole of reality, cannot be separated from questions of what is good for humans. The way humans should live is inextricably bound up with the cosmic order. This cosmic order is eternal. What we see as temporal events are but the "moving image of eternity."[18] The spatio-temporal world is, in some sense, an expression of the eternal, and as such, cannot at any time "not be." It cannot have a beginning and it cannot have an end. The world is eternal, necessary, and ordered. Moreover, humans are inextricably bound up in the cosmic order that they can discern through the use of reason. Reason is what links humans to the eternal realities.

At the heart of the Jewish biblical religion, on the other hand, lies the idea of the creation of the world. A transcendent God creates the world. The world had a beginning, that is, it is contingent, and it does not participate in any way in the being of God. So in the Greek view of things the world is necessary and reflects an eternal origin, whereas in the Jewish biblical view it is contingent and has a beginning. In Greek thought the eternity of the world was not merely an assertion of temporal fact, it was a metaphysical claim of great significance. In the *Timaeus*, Plato tells of how the Demiurge creates this world by modeling it on the eternal forms. This implies that there is an intelligibility and order in the world that is itself eternal. In the *Republic*, when Socrates asks, "What is justice?" he was not looking for the list of the acts of a just person. He was looking for a definition that captured the nature of justice and was applicable to justice alone. In other words, Socrates was seeking insight into the essence of things, not into the use of words. The answer Plato gives in *The Republic* is to ground justice in the eternal order. When incorporated into the Christian tradition this "essentialist" view proved normative for a thousand years of Western philosophy.

Thus, as a synthesis of neo-Platonic thought and Jewish biblical religion, early Christianity incorporated into itself two conflicting views of creation. It is a remarkable fact that the Christian tradition was able to hold these two views together in dialectical tension for over a thousand years. But the neo-Platonic view gradually became eclipsed by the Jewish biblical view, which eventually found its secularized expression in the work of Francis Bacon. The turning point came in the Middle Ages. There were many factors involved in the transition from the medieval to the modern. Among them are the rise of the cities that eroded the feudal order and the concurrent rise of national monarchies; the expansion of trade; the dissemination of information by means of the printing press; and the voyages of discovery that widened not only the physical but also the mental horizons of the West.[19] There are two movements of thought, however, that were particularly influential in bringing about an environment of thought in which the ideas of Bacon could flourish. The first important movement was that associated with the nominalists.

### The Nominalists

The nominalists of the thirteenth century argued in typical medieval scholastic style that the omnipotence of the transcendent God would be compromised if he were limited by the laws of eternal reason. They did not like the Greek idea that the eternal order itself was governed by reason. This could imply, by analogy, that God himself was governed by the laws of eternal reason, thus imposing limits on God: he could only act according to these laws. But in the Bible it is revealed that God created the world through his will. For the nominalists this made the will of God paramount. By an act of will God created the world. By an act of will he gave the commandments. The commandments are valid precisely because he willed them, not because they express some eternal Good. Such an argument removes the sanction for moral precepts from the cosmic and eternal order and locates it in the will of God alone.

It was William of Ockham (ca. 1300–1349) who gave a vital and dynamic force to nominalism. A man of powerful and rigorous intellect, he defended Christian revelation while at the same time adhering to empiricism and the logical method. He did so by separating them. The reality of God, given in revelation, was to be separated from the reality of the world, given in sensory experience. God was beyond the senses and could not be known through the senses. Ockham was aware of the thought of Thomas Aquinas (ca. 1225–1274) and disagreed with him in a fundamental way over the limits of reason. Ockham believed that Aquinas did not fully appreciate how limited reason was in its ability to know God. The mind possessed no "divine light" by which it could know God. Only concrete experience could serve as a basis for knowledge, and God was not to be found in such experience. In fact—and this was a vital point—our experience of this world, mediated to us through the senses, gave us only knowledge of concrete particulars, and inferring a separate and independent reality (such as in Platonic thought) from such particulars was mistaken. Ockham not only separates the world of sense experience from God, he also denies that through such experience one can come to know God. God can only be known through revelation. Ockham is repudiating the classical view, rooted in Platonic thought, that one can see in the world a rationality reflective of divine order. It is a very short step from this to the view in which the world has no intrinsic value of its own and is there merely for our use. The nominalist thus prepared the way for the Baconian argument that nature was a mere artifact created by God for our use. But although the nominalists were important in this development, it was the thinkers of the so-called scientific revolution who really created an environment of thought suitable for the Baconian view.

## The Scientific Revolution

In 1543 two books appeared that ushered in the scientific revolution: Copernicus' *De Revolutionibus Orbium Coelestium (On the Revolutions of the Celestial Orbs)* and Vesalius' *De Humanis Corporis Fabris (On the Fabric of the Human Body)*. The fact that these two books appeared in the same year is symbolic of the two sides of the scientific revolution: the macrocosmic and the microcosmic, the abstract and the concrete, the mathematical and the empirical. Yet it was the revolution in thinking brought about by Copernicus' book that had the most far-reaching consequences. Copernicus' book repudiated the Aristotelian worldview in which the earth was at the center of the universe and instead proposed a heliocentric model. The medieval view of the world was thus severely compromised and eventually replaced by a more mechanistic understanding. In this new way of thinking the world was not permeated by the divine; neither did it reflect a divine order. It was impersonal and mechanistic and operated according to laws best described in the language of mathematics, not in the language of theology. This new way of thinking is epitomized in the work of Galileo (1564–1642).

Galileo had become convinced that Copernicus was right as early as 1594. Copernicus had been somewhat circumspect in his conclusions. Galileo was, however, a very different personality. Unlike Copernicus, Galileo saw himself rather as a kind of embodiment of a new way of thinking. He proposed to deal only with efficient causes rather than final causes. Moreover, he saw the world as a mechanism, which could be described in the language of mathematics. As he put it, the Book of Nature was written in the language of mathematics, not in the language of theology. Thus, the mathematical laws operative in nature could be demonstrated empirically or experimentally.

The importance of what Galileo was saying lay not just in proving medieval cosmology wrong, but in the way he set about his proof. Galileo set up a whole new paradigm in place of the old theological one. One could unlock nature's secrets by the use of mathematics and experiments. It was no longer necessary to look at nature through theological spectacles.

Galileo was not, in fact, able to prove Copernicus right until he came into possession of a new invention—the magnifying glass. By lining up a series of lenses Galileo came up with a telescope. And when he turned this telescope to the heavens he found the proof he needed that Copernicus was right and the medieval system (based on the thought of Aristotle) was wrong. He discovered that there were mountains on the moon and spots on the sun. This suggested that the heavenly bodies were of the same substance as earthly bodies. Moreover, Jupiter had moons. If Jupiter possessed moons, then Aristotle's notion of crystalline spheres was wrong. Moreover, as these moons orbited Jupiter they lent more proof to Copernicus's theory, for if not all heavenly bodies had Earth as their center, then it made sense that Earth may not be the center at all.

Galileo published his findings in *Sidereus Nuntius* (*The Message from the Stars*) in 1610. In this book Galileo attacked Aristotelianism and, more significantly, claimed that the Bible could not be taken literally, as it was so obviously contradicted by the Copernican understanding of the world. Galileo went on to argue that God had "written" two books: a Book of Nature and a Book of Scripture. The Book of Nature was the empirical, experiential world in which we live. Through it God revealed himself as the Creator. The world was God's artifact and it behaved according to the laws he had designed. Humans could discover these laws and thus see how the world worked. The language of the Book of Nature was mathematics, and it was through mathematics that we could understand the workings of the world. The Book of Scripture, however, was God's revelation through symbol and metaphor. It was open to interpretation and subject to misunderstanding. Thus, it did not give the same account of the world as the Book of Nature because it spoke a different language. But—and this is the crucial point—where the Book of Nature contradicted the Book of Scripture, it was our understanding of the Book of Scripture that had to be revised. What Galileo was implying was extremely significant: he was separating the world of faith from the world of science. This was yet another nail driven into the classical view of the world as a unity, with its concomitant view that political and social realities were rooted in divine and sacred realities. Galileo was proposing a new paradigm to replace theological inquiry: the scientific method. The issues for Galileo's opponents, then, appeared weighty indeed. Bellarmino, a contemporary of Galileo, saw clearly what the real issue was: Galileo had separated the divine from nature. As he put it:

> Rise thou up a little higher, if thou canst, and as thou observest the great splendour of the sun, the beauty of the moon, the number and variety of other luminaries, the wonderful harmony of the heavens and the delightful movement of the stars, consider: what it will be to see God above the heavens, as it were a sun, "Dwelling in the light which no man can approach unto" [1 Tm 6:16]. . . . Thus it will come to pass that the beauty of the heavens will not appear so very great, and the things that are beneath the sky will seem altogether insignificant, indeed almost nothing, and to be considered despicable and worthy of contempt.[20]

The ultimate clash between Galileo and the Church came as a result of both Galileo's imprudence and his impudence. In 1632, in his book *Dialogo dei due Massimi Sistemi del Mondo* (*A Dialogue on the Two Chief World Systems* ), he presents his case in the form of a dialogue between three people: Salviati, Sagredo, and Simplicio. It was ostensibly a discussion of the merits of the Copernican system. Salviati (obviously speaking for Galileo himself) was the proponent of the Copernican view; Sagredo was the impartial one who, however, was easily convinced by Salviati of the merits of the Copernican system; and Simplicio (the "simple one") was the opponent of the Copernican view. Galileo's propensity for diatribe and invective got the better of him in this piece of work, for he gave Salviati an utterly convincing case and made Simplicio look, as his name implies, quite simpleminded. Galileo's mistake was to put into the mouth of Simplicio some of the arguments of the then pope, Urban VIII. Urban VIII was, in fact, a friend of Galileo, and they had spent considerable time discussing Copernicus's views, so Galileo knew the pope's views very well. For Galileo, to put the pope's arguments into the mouth of Simplicio and make him look a complete fool was, to say the least, quite impolitic. When Urban VIII was finally acquainted with the contents of the book he was infuriated. Galileo was summoned to Rome to answer charges that he had openly advocated a heliocentric view of the world, which had in 1616 been declared heresy by the Church. Galileo was found guilty and forbidden to teach or write and put under house arrest. He was urged "even with the threat of torture" to retract what he had written. Galileo was an old man by now, and he begged forgiveness on his knees and dutifully said that he was wrong and that the earth did not move.

Galileo was officially confined to his house and not allowed to teach or write. But students still came to him in secret, and he continued to write and had his manuscripts smuggled to the Netherlands, a Protestant country, where he had them published. Thus, he continued to be influential, and when he died in 1642 his ideas lived on. The Scientific Revolution was in full swing, and great thinkers such as Kepler and Newton came along to further the cause of the new way of looking at things.

The full implications of the scientific revolution were perhaps not immediately obvious. It was not just that in the scientific method expounded by Galileo we had a new paradigm for understanding the world. On a deeper level, it gradually became evident that if nature sanctions nothing, then it permits everything. Whatever humans do to it, they do not violate an immanent integrity. In a nature that is contingent, that is accidental, each thing can be other than what it is without being any the less natural. Nature can no longer be seen as participating in an eternal order and providing humans with a normative understanding of how things should be. Moreover, by reducing nature to an object it becomes an impersonal artifact, devoid of will. This leaves us with a worldview in which humans alone have will, and human will thus becomes paramount. It is human will that remakes and shapes the world. Human will no longer has an ontological grounding: it is thrown back on itself in its quest for meaning and value. Values and meaning are no longer grounded in a cosmic reality or in an eternal order, but are creations of the human will that has no reference point outside itself.

In his justly famous book, *The Legitimacy of the Modern Age*,[21] Hans Blumenberg concurs with the argument that a precondition of the coming of the modern age was the belief that an eternal order was not reflected in nature. He also argues that the essential feature of modernity is the belief in the legitimacy of human self-assertion, which expresses itself in the will to dominate and manipulate the natural world.[22] William of Ockham had made explicit the extreme implications of God's transcendence. This had created a crisis, turning God into a "hidden God" who could not be known through reason. A *Deus Absconditus* implied a "speechless" world that lacked the marks of the Divine Word (cf. Jn 1:1ff.). But this crisis also had a liberating effect. For if the intelligible order of the world can no longer be maintained, then the traditional view that there are limits beyond which human knowledge may not go is also destroyed. Thus, argues Blumenberg, curiosity was released from its constrictive boundaries, and human self-assertion was able to legitimately express itself.

Blumenberg contributes to our understanding of the modern world by explicitly linking the rise of human self-assertion with the corresponding demise of the idea that nature was a worthy object of contemplation. We have already seen how the change in the attitude to nature came about. Now we must turn to how that change was linked to a change in the status of *contemplatio* or contemplation.

### Contemplation

The Gospel according to St. Luke (10:38–42) recounts the story of Mary and Martha, two sisters who invited Jesus to their home. Mary sat at Jesus' feet and listened to what he was saying. Martha, however, was distracted by her work and complained to Jesus that Mary should be helping her. But Jesus chided Martha and said that Mary had "chosen the better part" (Lk 10:42).

This story was an important text in early Christianity and medieval times. It was cited by such figures as Origen, Gregory the Great, Cassian, and Augustine in support of the argument that the life of contemplation was superior to the life of action. Dom Cuthbert Butler says: "St Augustine has no hesitation in affirming the superiority of the contemplative life over the active. This judgement he, in common with the rest of theologians, bases in the story of Mary and Martha, which forms the theme of his discourses in various of the *Sermons*."[23] Gregory the Great, similarly to Augustine, argues that although the active life is more productive than the contemplative, the contemplative is better and greater. The attitude of antiquity in general is perhaps best summed up by Julianus Pomerius: "The active life is the journeying, the contemplative life is the summit."[24]

This emphasis on contemplation goes back to the pre-Socratic philosophers. In an often quoted analogy, Pythagoras spoke about those who attended the Games. Some were to make money by selling and trading. Some were there for the glory that comes from competition. And some were there just to watch. Pythagoras said that those who were merely spectators, who were just there to watch and not to make money or compete, were the ones to be emulated. Pythagoras went on to suggest that by analogy we could see the spectators as similar to those who pursued the contemplative life. Contemplation was the highest form of activity. Another pre-Socratic, Anaxagoras, was asked what he thought was the purpose of his life. He replied that he lived in order to contemplate the heavens and the stars, the sun, and moon. He was clearly talking about contemplating the cosmos.[25]

Plato continued the emphasis on contemplation when he said that the goal of the philosophic life was to behold the Good. It was Aristotle, however, who endorsed most strongly the views of Pythagoras and Anaxagoras. Aristotle said that one obtained fulfillment through contemplation. This was because "by nature all men desire to know."[26] This being the case, it follows that fulfilling this desire is one of the ends of humans. But for Aristotle, knowledge became intrinsically valuable when its object was intrinsically valuable. This condition is only fully satisfied in contemplation. Contemplation incorporates into itself not only knowledge but also admiration and wonder. In its highest form *contemplatio* is love (*eros*) of its object. As Gruner says: "In contemplation the object is loved because it is as it is and not otherwise, because it is seen to be noble and thus intrinsically worthy of love, because it is recognized that love is the only appropriate attitude that can be taken towards it, not out of duty or due to a divine command but simply because of the nature of the thing."[27]

Once Christianity came onto the scene, the Aristotelean conception became modified. Under the influence of neo-Platonism, Christianity redefined the object of contemplation as the transcendent God and its goal as redemption. The transcendent God who had created the world was alone worthy of worship. The world was still seen as of value, not in its own right, but as a creation of God. Nature's harmony and beauty were still praised, but only in order to praise its creator. The value of the world was, in short, derivative and secondary.

But the status of contemplation remained unchanged. So Aquinas could insist that *vita activa est dispositio ad contemplativam*, the active life prepares one for contemplation.[28] There is no question that Aquinas agrees with Aristotle that the contemplative life is higher than the active, and this position is almost universally held in the high Middle Ages. But Okham's thought threw into question the intrinsic value of the natural world. And if the world has no intrinsic value, then it is not a worthy object of contemplation. The nature and superiority of contemplation become undermined. By the time of Francis Bacon the time is ripe for the value of the contemplative life to be discredited. Bacon rejected the analogy of Pythagoras and asserted that "in this theatre of man's life it is reserved only for God and Angels to be lookers on."[29] Bacon, in fact, saw nothing but vanity and pride in those who extolled the life of contemplation. It was, in short, a selfish life and inferior to the life of action. In the process of inverting the importance of contemplation and action Bacon made the world, instead of being something to contemplate, raw material for humans to use.

We can perhaps see most clearly where Bacon's thought leads when we look at the thought of Thomas Hobbes (1588–1679) some fifty years after Bacon. Hobbes appropriated Bacon's notion that humans are not part of a larger harmonious whole. Hobbes pushed this further: humans are locked in a perpetual conflict with a hostile nature. In their original state humans are exposed to a life that is nasty, brutish, and short. Only human knowledge helps to ameliorate this condition. Significantly, Hobbes saw no end to this struggle to subdue nature. He says:

> So that in the first place, I put for a generall inclination of all mankind, a perpetuall and restlesse desire of Power after power, that ceaseth onely in Death. And the cause of this, is not alwayes that a man hopes for a more intensive delight, than he has already attained to; or that he cannot be content with a moderate power: *but because he cannot assure the power and means to live well, which he hath present, without the acquisition of more.*[30]

Thus, human power over nature must be continually reasserted. As Gruner says, "Here, we might say, are the beginnings of a theory of infinite scientific progress in terms of power."[31] The question of ends is entirely limited to the alleviation of the physical hardships caused by human existence. There is no thought beyond that.

The full significance of Bacon's discrediting of the contemplative life is not, however, fully clear until much later, with the attack on belief in transcendental norms. The greatest and most profound expression of the view that there is no transcendental ground of permanence is found in Nietzsche (1844–1900). It is in Nietzsche's writings that we see most clearly the implications of emphasizing the historicity of human existence.

If it is accepted that the natural sciences have demonstrated how unnecessary it is to assume purpose in unraveling the mysteries of nonhuman nature, how much more should it apply to human nature! Humans do not have purpose—the historic sense tells us so. Nietzsche was a great admirer of the Greek tragedies because he saw in them humans inspired by nobility—they understood life had no purpose but were resolutely defiant in the face of it. Socrates destroyed Greek tragedy by maintaining that life did have purpose and that this could be revealed through rationality. Nietzsche attacks Socrates. The historic sense destroys belief in any transcendent ground of purpose. We live within horizons that are our own creations; there is no transcendental sanction for them. The horizon of the transcendent has been wiped away.

As we have seen, the way knowledge is conceived is inextricably bound up with what its end is thought to be. Contemplation was believed to be a valuable end because its object was valuable—that is, the natural world. And this natural world, it was thought, was valuable because, in the famous words of Aristotle, "all things have by nature something divine [in them]."[32] The divine reveals itself in the natural sphere. Such a view made it virtually impossible to see in nature an artifact that may be remade and reshaped by humans into whatever they desire. But after the nominalists the view that nature reflected a divine order became harder to maintain, and Francis Bacon's attack on contemplation had a receptive audience. Bacon was a turning point: after him, nature came to be seen as an object that was subject to manipulation and control by human will.

## Conclusion

What has our inquiry into the origins of modernity told us about its characteristics? First, it is clear that modernity signals a break with traditional Western thinking. It is a matter of some dispute as to whether the break should be seen as a *radical* discontinuity, but it is clear that the break is significant.[33] Our analysis indicates that the most significant development leading to modernity was the rise of what Blumenberg calls human self-assertion. The notion that there is an eternal order that limits what humans can do has been jettisoned. The belief in the efficacy of human agency to determine not only the direction of events in time, but also to remake the natural world in any way we deem fit, has had paradoxical consequences, as Leon Kass observes: "Our conquest of nature has made us the slaves of blind chance. We triumph over nature's unpredictabilities only to subject ourselves to the still greater unpredictability of our capricious wills and fickle opinions. That we have a method is no proof against our madness.

Thus, engineering the engineer as well as the engine, we race our train we know not where."[34]

The break with the ancient and medieval mode of philosophical inquiry, in which the focus was on the formal patterns underlying space and time, and the turn to analysis of the sensory world through mathematics and experiments, gave rise to science and technology. Science focuses on this world, a world of space and time, not on some transcendental reality, and gives us knowledge of that world. Technology combines what we have come to know about this world with practical applications of that knowledge, and does so in a unique way. Through science and technology we have gained unprecedented power to manipulate and order the world in the way we want. But what we want is no longer found in a Good grounded in an eternal order, and so, as Warren Winiarski observes: "As transcendent goals for human life are abandoned . . . human life as such is divinized, made into something transcendent; and it is thus that the sciences and the technological arts receive an imperious ordinance to gratify a proliferation of human 'needs.'"[35]

There lies the major irony at the heart of modernity. God and the Good have been banished, only to be replaced by Man and his goods.[36] "New lamps for old!" cried the evil magician in *Aladdin and the Wonderful Lamp,* and the wonderful old lamp was eagerly traded in for a new one, without it being realized that it was no bargain. In a similar fashion we have substituted new gods for old, without perhaps fully understanding what we have given up and what we have in return. Frederick Jameson has referred to the Market as that "consoling replacement for the divinity."[37] But, like the Hindu god Shiva, it is a divinity with many faces, and not all of them are consoling. Globalization and technology may have brought many benefits, but they have also created many problems. In the chapters that follow we will explore some of the challenges that face us as a result of globalization and technology.

## Notes

1. L. P. Hartley, *The Go-Between* (New York: Stein and Day Publishers, 1967), p. 3.
2. Jacques Ellul, *The Technological Society*, trans. John Wilkinson (New York: Vintage, 1964), p. xxix.
3. Robert B. Pippin, *Modernism as a Philosophical Problem: On the Dissatisfactions of European High Culture* (Cambridge, Mass.: B. Blackwell, 1991), p. 22.
4. There are a large number of writers who have pursued this line of inquiry. Of special note, however, is George P. Grant, who was Harold

Coward's thesis supervisor. See his *Technology and Empire* (Toronto: House of Anansi, 1969) and *Time as History* (Toronto: CBC, 1969). On the importance of Grant's work, see Arthur Davis, *George Grant and the Subversion of Modernity: Art, Philosophy, Politics, Religion, and Education* (Toronto: University of Toronto Press, 1997) and William Christian, *George Grant: A Biography* (Toronto: University of Toronto Press, 1993).

5. Lynn White Jr., "The Historical Roots of our Ecologic Crisis," *Science* 155 (1967): 1203–1207.

6. See David Lindberg, *Roger Bacon's Philosophy of Nature* (Oxford: Clarendon Press, 1983).

7. Francis Bacon, *The Advancement of Learning*, in *Selected Writings of Francis Bacon*, ed. H. G. Dick (New York: Random House, 1955), bk I, p. 193.

8. Bacon, *Advancement of Learning*, p. 194.

9. Francis Bacon, in the *Prooemium* of *The Great Instauration*, in *The English Philosophers from Bacon to Mill*, ed. Edwin A. Burtt (New York: Modern Library, 1967), p. 6.

10. Bacon, *The Great Instauration*, p. 5.

11. Francis Bacon, *Novum Organum*, bk. I, aphorism 83.

12. Bacon, *Advancement of Learning*, bk. II, pp. 250f.

13. Carolyn Merchant, *The Death of Nature: Woman, Ecology, and the Scientific Revolution* (San Francisco: Harper and Row, 1980).

14. Bacon, *Advancement of Learning*, bk. II, p. 321.

15. George Ovitt Jr., *The Restoration of Perfection: Labour and Technology in Medieval Culture* (London: Rutgers University Press, 1987).

16. See Dom Cuthbert Butler, *Western Mysticism: The Teaching of Augustine, Gregory and Bernard on Contemplation and the Contemplative Life* (London: Constable, 1967), p. 160.

17. Bacon, *Advancement of Learning*, bk I, p. 193.

18. Plato, *Timaeus* 37d.

19. Richard Tarnas, *The Passion of the Western Mind: Understanding the Ideas That Have Shaped Our World View* (New York: Ballantine Books, 1991), pp. 225–228.

20. Quoted in Richard S. Westfall, *Essays on the Trial of Galileo* (Notre Dame: University of Notre Dame Press, 1989), p. 20.

21. Hans Blumenberg, *The Legitimacy of the Modern Age*, trans. Robert M. Wallace (Cambridge, Mass.: MIT Press, 1983).

22. Blumenberg says that "the essence of the modern age's understanding of itself" (*Legitimacy*, p. 196) is that humans assert themselves "both *against* and *by means of* nature" (*Legitimacy*, p. 318).

23. Butler, *Western Mysticism*, p. 160.

24. Julianus Pomerius, *The Contemplative Life*, Ancient Christian Writers, vol. 4 (Cambridge: Cambridge University Press, 1947), p. 31.
25. See Gruner, *Theory and Power*, pp. 12f.
26. Aristotle, *Metaphysics* 980a, line 22.
27. Gruner, *Theory and Power*, p. 16.
28. Thomas Aquinas, *Commentary on the Third Book of the Sentences of Peter Lombard*, chap. 35, pt.1, sec. 3, par. 3.
29. Bacon, *Advancement of Learning*, bk II, p. 321.
30. Thomas Hobbes, *Leviathan*, ed. Richard E. Flathman and David Johnston (New York: W. W. Norton and Co., 1997), pp. 55f. Emphases added.
31. Gruner, *Theory and Power*, p. 55.
32. Aristotle, *Nicomachean Ethics* bk. VII, 1153b, line 33.
33. See Leo Strauss, "The Three Waves of Modernity," in *Political Philosophy: Six Essays by Leo Strauss*, ed. Hilail Gildin (New York: Pegasus, 1975), pp. 81-98.
34. Leon R. Kass, "The New Biology: What Price the Relief of Man's Estate?" in *Science, Technology and Freedom*, ed. Willis H. Truitt and T. W. Graham Solomons (Boston: Houghton Mifflin Co., 1974), p. 164.
35. Warren Winiarski, "Niccolò Machiavelli," in *History of Political Philosophy*, ed. Leo Strauss and Joseph Cropsey (Chicago: Rand McNally, 1963), p. 273.
36. By using "Man," I am agreeing with the feminist argument that the modern world is essentially a creation of the male.
37. Fredric Jameson, *Postmodernism, or, the Cultural Logic of Late Capitalism* (Durham: Duke University Press, 1999), p. 273.

# Chapter Two

# Religion, Risk, and the Technological Society

CONRAD G. BRUNK

Western society is preoccupied with risk and safety. This preoccupation may be explained in great measure by the simple fact that we have become accustomed to living with the significant reduction in the risks to health and impoverishment that modern technology has provided. The dramatic increase in life expectancy in the past century is a direct consequence of health care technologies as well as those that provide clean water, cheap food, and safe disposal of waste. As a consequence, we who live in technological societies expect to live longer and suffer less the ravages of ill health and poverty. We have devised means of manipulating the natural and social environments in ways that insulate us from the radical discontinuities that can make life poor, miserable, and short in pretechnological societies. Perhaps, having become accustomed to the reduction of these risks, we demand ever higher levels of safety.

That, however, is not the only, or even the most, profound way Western society is preoccupied with risk. It is preoccupied in a way that reflects an increasing impoverishment and narrowing of the range of the values by which we live and by which we formulate the social policies governing our collective lives. The concern about risk is first and foremost concern about the likelihood and the magnitude of harms, and safety is primarily about reducing these risks of harm to levels we are willing to accept.[1] Avoidance or reduction of harm, especially physical and psychological harm, is a value shared by nearly everyone, regardless of the other values they hold, however idiosyncratic. Hence, prevention and reduction of harm are among the fundamental goods of liberal, "secular" societies, and the science of risk assessment and the politics of risk management are among its most essential forms of expertise and its most reliable tools for public decision-making.

The preoccupation with risk and safety is both a product of modern technology and a powerful reinforcer of it. Technology has created the expectations of greater security, and these expectations in turn create pressures for ever more powerful technological solutions to perceived security problems. Consider how frequently the drive for technological innovation is rationalized by contemporary corporate and public institutions in the name of economic, food, and health or political "security." Technological innovations usually pose new risks of their own—to the environment or to human health, for example—but the benefits they promise in return can be promoted most effectively if they are characterized as "risk reduction." So, we can fully expect to see the old proposals for eugenic "improvement" to the human species, so discredited during the excesses of the World War II period (not only among the Nazis), recommence with full energy as new genetic engineering tools are refined. However, they will be rationalized this time, not as species "improvement" but as individual "risk reduction"—the reduction of the risks of growing old, of having children with unpalatable physical and behavioral traits, and so on. Everyone seems to agree on the value of avoiding "harm," and it is around this value that the technological amelioration of the human condition is most effectively pursued.

This chapter will explore how this emphasis on harm avoidance, as well as the technological approaches to assessing and managing the risks of harm, eclipses many other fundamental moral values, especially those rooted firmly in religious and broader philosophical understandings of the world. It excludes them from serious consideration in the forum of debate about public policy, including most importantly debate about the regulation of technology itself. As a consequence, public policy is formulated without regard for some of the most significant values that even a significant portion of the population in a society might hold. The case of the current debate about the regulation of biotechnology will be used as an example of this dynamic.

## The Biotechnology Debate

Recent advances in genetic engineering have stirred vigorous public debate over the extent to which genetic technologies should be limited. Success in the cloning of animals has raised the question of how, if at all, such technology can be used, especially in the case of human beings. Successes in the mapping of the human genome and new reproductive technologies have raised questions about the extent to which we should engage in the design and redesign of our children and future generations. Recent advances in stem cell research promise stunning new therapeutic techniques, while also resurrecting old debates about the use of human embryos. Success in the production of transgenic plants and animals has raised questions not only about their long-term human and environmental health effects, but also more deeply metaphysical questions about the moral limits to our redesign of nature (including human nature) itself.

Public resistance to new biotechnologies ranges across a wide spectrum of issues. Some of it is based on concerns about human health and safety—that is, traditional concerns about toxicological, immunological, and allergenic effects of modified foods on consumers. Some of it is based on concerns about the impacts of new bioengineered plants and animals on the natural environment—on ecosystem health or integrity. These are the concerns on which the regulatory system focuses its attention because of its commitment to "risk-based decision-making," which puts the question of harm in the forefront of concern. Public concerns in this area stem largely from suspicions about the adequacy of the safety studies to which industry and government regulators subject these products. However, a significant portion of this opposition is based on ethical concerns that go well beyond issues of health and safety. They involve worries that certain applications of the technology are *in themselves* morally inappropriate, that certain products are morally otiose, or that the technology will undermine the framework of human moral consciousness itself.

A significant aspect of this debate is that the concerns about new biotechnologies seem to be more intense and involve a wider range of issues among the lay public than among those who are responsible for the regulation of these technologies in government and international bodies and, certainly, in industry. They are also generally more intense among the public than among even the professional ethicists, who tend either to share the preoccupation with risk and safety issues as the only legitimate concerns or to speak with diverse and uncertain voices about many genetic engineering issues. This is not to claim that there is anything approaching a consensus, even a general convergence, on these matters in the public forum—far from it. What does seem to be emerging, however, is a widespread view among the public that certain actual or potential applications of biotechnology go beyond the limits of moral acceptability. What is at issue here, at least in the wider public debate, is not the moral acceptability of biotechnology per se, but only of certain applications of it—that is, of its *moral limits*.

This situation raises an important question: Is it possible that the "professional" assessments of these new technologies simply fail to take account of the ethical values underlying the public concerns about them? I propose that they do fail in this way because the usual methods by which some of the most important ethical aspects of technologies are discussed and public policy actually formulated tend to discount or discredit the fundamental ethical impulses underlying public attitudes toward them. This dynamic is inherent in the typical analyses employed by professionalized decision-makers, including many scientists, philosophers, and ethicists—those who exercise the greatest influence on public policy regulating technology development. If this kind of discounting of public moral attitudes actually occurs, the potential result is that some of the most significant moral attitudes actually held within the society are systematically factored out of public policy.

A broader understanding of ethical assessment is needed in the area of technology development—one capable of engaging the deep-seated moral and religious attitudes that tend to be ruled out of the public policy debate because they do not fit the accepted canons of analysis. Like many public attitudes toward technology, these attitudes are dismissed as irrelevant to public policy because they are based on metaphysical or moral assumptions that are nonrational, sectarian, or otherwise unsupportable by the reigning standards of ethical theory.

Indeed, one of the most widely recognized aspects of the biotechnology debate is that it, probably more than any other technology, raises questions of a fundamentally metaphysical and religious nature. This is inherent in the fact that the technology involves the power to redesign species and natural systems as well as what is perceived as "human nature" itself. In addition, perhaps more than any technology (except perhaps nuclear technology, which raises similar questions), its impacts are potentially enormous, extending far into the human and planetary future. Thus, it poses unprecedented, almost mythic, questions about the place of human power and intelligence in the world. As Hans Jonas,[2] along with many others, has argued, the standard approaches to ethical analysis are not conceptually adequate for handling these questions. Thus, it is not surprising that when these fundamental metaphysical/religious assumptions are expressed in public attitudes toward biotechnology, they are neutralized in the public debate by the standard "expert" formulas of ethical discourse. Increasingly, these "expert" formulas are dominated by considerations of harm and the risk of harm that are most amenable to the quantifiable, empirical methods of analysis that are most favored by the technological mind itself.[3]

### The Emerging Global Value: "Acceptable Risk"

The management of popular concerns about technology is simply one aspect of the larger problem of how ethical considerations can (or should) be incorporated into public policy, especially in pluralistic, liberal societies. Ethical values, especially those asserted most stridently in the public arena, are widely considered to be subjective, nonrational (if not *irrational*), and relative to religious, ethnic, or cultural traditions—that is, they are *sectarian*. Since, by definition, these sectarian values do not represent a broad-based value consensus, shaping public policy by reference to them runs counter to fundamental liberal principles of respect for plurality of values, and neutrality with respect to them.

The "globalization" of the economies of the world has intensified this problem, making it difficult even for societies with relatively homogeneous value orientations or nonliberal social and political cultures to apply their own values to the products that trading partners wish to export into their markets. Under current World Trade Organization interpretations of trade agreements such as the Sanitary and Phytosanitary (SPS) Agreement, any member country's exclusion of an imported food and plant product based on ethical concerns about its engineered genetic character would very likely be judged a "nontariff trade barrier" in violation of the WTO rules. The only permissible basis for the exclusion of such products is a credible scientific showing that the imported product poses "unacceptable risks" to human, animal, or plant health, narrowly defined.

Even the clearly normative criteria of "unacceptable risk" are increasingly narrowly defined, as part of the frenetic drive among trade partners for "harmonization" of safety standards (i.e., everyone adopts the same normative standards of risk acceptability—namely, the *lowest* ones). "Risk-based decision-making" has become the new mantra of industry, governments, and adjudicators in the free trade arena, because it is seen as providing at least a quasiscientific (and therefore value-neutral) basis for public policy decisions. This makes it increasingly difficult for any country to place explicit moral limits on technology development. In the case of biotechnology, this produces a situation in which, despite a great deal of public ethical concern and debate, there is nevertheless little systematic application of ethical principles and values behind these concerns to the public policies governing its development and application.

These pressures from the regime of globalized free trade are reinforced not only by the imperatives within technology itself, but also by the norms of the liberal democratic cultures in which these technologies flourish. The fundamental norms underlying liberal[4] societies are commonly recognized as (1) beneficence/nonmaleficence (maximize good/avoid harm); (2) individual autonomy; and (3) equality or fairness.[5] Further, liberalism assumes that *only* these values can be assumed to be shared across the society regardless of what other values may be held by individuals or groups within the society. Public policies, especially those regulating technologies, are guided almost exclusively by these values. If a technology poses any significant risk of physical or psychological harm to persons, or if its implementation poses a threat to personal freedom or privacy, then liberal societies are willing to place at least provisional restrictions or moratoria on its development. In these societies, appeals to risk or autonomy are fully accepted as "public" values, and generally trump all other values asserted in the debate.

The recommendations of the U.S. National Bioethics Advisory Commission and the Canadian National Commission on New Reproductive Technologies placing moratoria on the cloning of human beings graphically illustrate this restricted moral framework. For example, the former body recommended a moratorium on human somatic cell nuclear transfer cloning on grounds that the technique "is not safe to use in humans at this time" and would "involve unacceptable risks to the fetus and/or potential child."[6] The risks referred to here were clearly risks of physical or psychological harm.

However, it is interesting to note that the U.S. Commission added that there remain "other serious ethical concerns . . . which require much more widespread and careful public deliberation before this technology is used." But it did not identify what these other ethical concerns might be or how they might influence public policy. It did include a further, very important, recommendation—that, because of the diverse and conflicting ethical and religious concerns about cloning humans, the government and interested parties should encourage "widespread and continuing deliberation on these issues in order to further our understanding of the ethical and social implications of this technology and to enable society to produce appropriate long-term policies regarding this technology should the time come when present concerns about safety have been addressed."[7] Thus, the U.S. Advisory Commission recognized that many additional ethical issues posed by biotechnology remain on the moral landscape, but it clearly did not know how to identify them or take them into account.

It is easy to see, then, that the only real basis for deciding whether and how this particular technology should be deployed was the consideration of harm. The "experts" on this question become those who have the methodological tools for assessing the risks of harms, and the harms they will undoubtedly consider will be those that are empirically defined and quantitatively measured. They will most likely be the potential harms to physical health, and perhaps, but more scientifically dubious, psychological health. Harms of a more explicitly "moral" character—such as how this technology might influence the way individual persons are valued in society or what the impact might be on the concept of human dignity itself—will not likely be a part of the risk assessment.


### The "Technologization" of Professionalized Ethical Discourse

I have suggested that many of the most significant concerns being raised in the public debate about biotechnology get factored out of the actual decision-making process by which the technology is developed and regulated.

The narrow "technologization" of this decision-making process has a profound impact even on the way professionalized ethical discourse is carried out in relation to these technologies. By "professionalized ethical discourse" I refer to the discussion of ethics that takes place within the academic profession of (primarily philosophical and theological) ethics, as well as within the newly emerging research and consulting institutes that employ largely the graduates of the academies. It includes the cadres of persons who label themselves variously as "applied ethicists," "bio-ethicists," "environmental ethicists," and so on, who carry on their discussions in scholarly books and journals and whose professional competence is judged by their academic peers rather than by the lay public. These persons typically represent the "ethics perspective" on government commissions, ethics review boards, and other think tanks that recommend and implement regulatory standards for technology in most developed countries. They are the ones interviewed and cited in the media as the "experts" on the ethical aspects of these issues, and through this exposure they frame the public ethical debate on technology— they set the parameters of the "legitimate" ethical issues.

As would be expected, professionalized ethical discussion of technology typically takes place not only within the boundaries of the reigning "paradigms" of ethical theory within the profession, but, more importantly, within the boundaries of what is permissible in the public forum. And as I have argued, what is permissible within the public forum is strongly constrained by the narrow range of technologically acceptable values—those related to the efficient management of benefits and risks. To be credible with their peers, professionalized ethicists always have to be careful to respect the constraints on ethical claims imposed by the critical ethical, as well as scientific, texts of the day. Consequently, moral claims and arguments based on naive assumptions about the fact–value distinction, about essentialist views of self, human nature, or the world, or on religious or metaphysical assumptions—which usually fail to pass standard epistemological requirements—are not likely to be advanced or even explored seriously. They certainly are not likely to be advanced as credible bases for the formulation of public policy. While this critical and analytic role may be appropriate for scholarship in the academy, it is less clear how well it serves as a basis for the formulation of public policy involving the serious ethical and religious questions.

One of the striking characteristics of the moral debate about biotechnology among the lay (non-expert) public, however, is the way it invokes references to just the kinds of ethical and religious assumptions of which professionalized ethical discourse is most skeptical. Because the technology involves the power to manipulate and replicate genetic codes, permitting the intentional design and redesign of any life form outside normal biological and ecological processes and constraints, it goes to the heart of people's convictions about the order of nature and their fundamental religious or metaphysical conceptions of "the natural." For many laypeople, especially those within the great world religious traditions, the concept of "the natural" carries enormous normative weight.

In the lay, as opposed to the "expert," debates about the ethics of biotechnology, the most important concerns tend to focus around this issue of "the natural." These include concerns that certain biotech products, involving genes spliced across species, kingdom, or the plant/animal barriers, violate the natural order in some fundamentally egregious way. They include concerns that genetic alterations of human beings (somatic or germline) might change the way we perceive and hence *value* particular human beings relative to others, or value human life and human personality generally. This risk is posed by eugenic as well as certain therapeutic genetic engineering of humans. It is also raised by the prospect of cloning human individuals, when this is posed not as a risk to the physical health of the cloned individual (if things go wrong), but the risk to the moral status of persons (if things go right). They include concerns that the engineering of transgenic animals or plants will undermine our concept of nature and the "world" in ways that are detrimental to human, animal, or plant well-being in the future. For example, it may reduce the world to the status of purely human artifact, rendering it more amenable to exploitation, and undermine human experience of the sacredness of the earth or its status as divine creation. They include concerns that genetic engineering of humans will undermine future commitment to traditional moral values (e.g., human "dignity" or "sanctity," equality) or virtues (e.g., humility, reverence, Buddhist "letting go," etc.). They also include concerns about the potential of the technology to affect unforeseen, potentially catastrophic changes in the long-term future of the planet, raising questions about the appropriate moral limits to this power, and the ethics of risk taking. This latter type of concern is frequently expressed in the language of the human right to "play God."[8]

## Taking Nontechnological Values Seriously

Is it appropriate in a democratic society for moral attitudes that lie outside the terms of the narrow framework of technologized and professionalized ethics to be filtered out of the public debate? If they should not be, how should they be taken into account in the formulation of public policy? In a democratic society, should not the values that inform public policy be in some way representative of the values people in the society actually hold, not *only* those that pass muster in the professionalized ethical discourse of liberal technological society?

Determining just *how* they should be incorporated is, of course, the problem. There is a host of hurdles to be overcome in doing so effectively and democratically. To begin with, it is usually assumed that in pluralistic societies the nonliberal, nontechnological values are esoteric or "sectarian." They are shared, at most, among minority communities. There certainly is nothing approaching a social consensus around them, likely not even a majority. The population is likely to be spread out along a wide continuum of opinion. Further, it is assumed that even if there is a widespread (i.e., majority) opposition to a particular technological proposal (e.g., cloning humans for organ farming), the moral motivations behind the shared opposition would vary significantly. A further difficulty is posed by the fact that, even within traditional communities of value (e.g., religious, ethnic, and cultural traditions), one will find a wide difference of opinion about any given technological proposal. Not all opinions are equally informed or equally "considered," so should they all be given equal weight? These disparities and difficulties lead many public policy experts to conclude that there is no way to determine what "the public" thinks about the ethics of any particular technological development (or the ethics of almost anything else).

These are important questions, requiring politically feasible solutions. Here are a few observations about how we might address them. The first observation is that the assumptions generally held by people in modern societies about the widespread and incommensurable disparities in basic moral values are widely untested. At one level there clearly is wide diversity of opinion about many applications of biotechnology. But moral assessment of any action or state of affairs is a product not just of the moral values of the assessors, but of their factual and conceptual beliefs about it as well. In a relatively free society, where the public is exposed to a wide spectrum of factual claims and conceptual frameworks for these claims, producing an equally wide spectrum of moral opinion, it is erroneous to infer an equally wide diversity of underlying moral values. The only way to know what the underlying moral values are is to look methodically behind the judgments about individual cases. This requires ethical research of an empirical nature—descriptive or anthropological ethics.

But, second, there is no need to assume any convergence of basic moral values around the issues posed by the possibilities inherent in a given technology.[9] Taking the de facto moral judgments of a democratic public seriously does not require anything approaching a value consensus within that public. Democratic institutions do not assume that the only valid public policies are those expressing a public consensus. They do not even necessarily assume a majoritarian consensus in all decision-making. What they do assume is equality of participation in the processes of decision-making. Democratic decision-making is usually a complicated and murky process of public participation in which representatives of differing viewpoints nego- tiate among themselves to arrive at the decision most are willing to accept even if it is not the first choice of a majority. Participation in the *process* of decision-making is more constitutive of democracy than is majority rule.

It is increasingly recognized in democratic societies that public policy, especially policy governing the regulation of technologies affecting people's lives, needs to strike a reasonable balance between "expert" scientific and technological judgment and "non-expert" lay opinion. The idea that objec- tive mechanisms, like various forms of regulatory science, can provide tools for public policy formation that are neutral vis-à-vis the pluralistic values of the community they govern has turned out to be an illusion. It is an illusion for several reasons: first, because the issues are inherently value-laden, and subjecting them to quasiscientific mechanisms of resolution merely hides the values being appealed to by those who apply the science; and second, because failure to take into account the actual attitudes and values of those affected by the regulation is doomed to political failure as effective regula- tory policy.[10]

As we have seen, risk analysis (risk assessment, risk management, and risk communication) has become the preferred approach to decision- making in the area of technology regulation. This methodology, which focuses on assessing the potential harmful impacts of technology, has come under increasing criticism in recent years for its failure to recognize that the critical issues in the successful management of technological risks are not primarily related to the accurate scientific assessment of the "objective" risks, but rather to the accurate assessment of social *perceptions* of the risks, especially their *acceptability* (as opposed to their quantifiable magni- tude).[11] Part of this critique lies in the recognition that simple reliance on objective algorithms of risk acceptability, such as risk-benefit equations, while appealing to expert risk analysts and bureaucrats, often results in increased public suspicion of the risk management experts and decreasing acceptance of the risks. Any politically successful regulation of technologi- cal risks must take seriously into account aspects of public perceptions having to do with complex moral aspects of the risk—such as the percep- tion of the distribution of the benefits and risks, the voluntariness of the risk by the risk-bearer, and nuances about the characteristics of the popu- lations at risk (e.g., children, the elderly, the poor, the sick) or of the risks themselves (e.g., certain risks are "dreaded" more than others).

Often these nuances are viewed by risk experts as nonrational, idio- syncratic, even superstitious and irrational—just as professionalized ethi- cists view many of the moral attitudes toward biotechnology. The increasingly fashionable words for this among risk management experts are "dread" or "stigma." A stigma, it is claimed, is an irrational fear that becomes attached to certain risks (e.g., nuclear power, GM foods, mad cow disease, agricultural pesticides), which renders them unacceptable to people. It is a stigma insofar as the rejection of the risk is said to be based on either ignorance or mistaken assumptions about the probabilities and magnitudes of the risk, or of its offsetting benefits. A stigma is, in effect, any rejection of a risk based on a set of considerations that fall outside the standard expert algorithms for determining its acceptability.

Nevertheless, the failure to take so-called irrational stigmas seriously as significant aspects of the public acceptability of the risk can be politically disastrous, for both the producers and the regulators of new technologies. For this reason a vital part of "risk communication" theory must involve taking careful stock of stakeholder perceptions of risk problems, so that risk managers regulate the risks that people are actually concerned about, not only those that concern the scientific and technological experts. A careful reflection on the very concept of "risk acceptability"—the usual definition of "safe"—should make the necessity of this task obvious. If the risk of death by cancer, for example, carries a particular dread for most people that far exceeds their fear of dying in auto accidents (which is clearly the case in many developed societies), an objective risk-benefit algorithm that counts each type of death equally—failing to account for the actual social preference—will simply not give an accurate reading of the real (even objective?) *acceptability* of the risk. Those experts who consider the dread of cancer "irrational" (by what standard of rationality it is not clear), and thus discount it when setting the standards for maximum chemical residue limits in food products, will be perplexed by public mistrust of expert claims that pesticide-sprayed food is "safe." They don't understand that real people do not care only about *whether*, or even *when*, they die, but also *how* they die. These preferences are rooted in very profound religious and philosophical presuppositions about the meaning of life and death.

There is a series of values critical to public perceptions of risk that are routinely missed by the standard quantitative algorithms of risk acceptability. Magnitude and probability of risks, as well as their offsetting benefits, turn out to be relatively low in risk acceptability. Distribution of risks and benefits and the voluntariness of the risk taking are much more important. But among the most important are such things as controllability of the risk (often confused with voluntariness), potential for irremediable human or environmental harm, and probably most important, the trustworthiness of those who manage the risk.

Matters of controllability, irremediability, and trustworthiness all involve moral issues that are difficult to capture in expert paradigms of risk acceptability—thus the tendency to relegate them to the category of irrational "dread" or "stigma." Some of them, like the concern about irremediabilty of environmental harm, are especially suspect because they are based on deep-seated, but somewhat inchoate, essentialist (often religious) assumptions about the "natural" state of things. Rational or not, these perceptions are critical to the acceptance of new technologies in society, and they must be taken into account in design and marketing strategies. From the point of view of a truly democratic regulatory policy they *ought not to* be discounted simply because they are grounded in religious, sectarian, or other metaphysical assumptions on which there is no social consensus and that go beyond the liberal political values of nonharm, autonomy, and beneficence.

A helpful way to think about this question of "public ethics" is to think about ethical issues as matters of "moral risk." That is, just as we recognize that a technology may pose certain risks of harms to persons, animals, plants, and the environment, so also it may pose certain risks to the moral and religious values by which people live their lives, and that are threatened by the changes wrought by that technology. This is particularly true of biotechnology, since one of the major *ethical* issues it poses for people is precisely the possibility that changes to human beings in the future, and to the structure of the natural reality itself in which they will live, will radically alter the values by which these human beings relate to each other and to the world. People wish to protect the moral framework they consider essential to such things as "being human." What biotechnology places "at risk" in at least some of its potential implementations are *ethical and religious values themselves*, or perhaps even, for some, *ethical and religious consciousness itself*. Social perceptions of the acceptability of these "moral risks" are as central to the concept of the "public acceptability" of biotechnology, as social perceptions of risks of physical, psychological, and economic harm are to the concept of the "safety" of technologies generally.

This means that the ethical regulation of biotechnology requires the recognition and incorporation of the actual values people espouse. Part of the ethical task in the arena of public policy regulating biotechnology is that of *descriptive ethics*, or *ethical and religious anthropology*. What is needed is good empirical research into the ways different "value communities" in our societies conceptualize and evaluate the issues posed by technology. What are those values they perceive to be placed "at risk" by certain technological possibilities? In short, perhaps in addition to the mapping of the human genome, which science is currently celebrating, we also need new methods for "mapping" the moral values of the different value communities, religious and secular, that constitute modern societies, so that we better understand what values actually shape public attitudes toward technologies.

## Notes

1. William Lowrance, *Of Acceptable Risk: Science and the Determination of Safety* (Los Altos: W. Kaufman, 1976); Deborah G. May and Rachelle D. Hollander, *Acceptable Evidence: Science and Values in Risk Management* (New York: Oxford University Press, 1991).

2. Hans Jonas, *The Imperative of Responsibility: In Search of an Ethics for the Technological Age* (Chicago: University of Chicago Press, 1984).

3. See Jacques Ellul, *The Technological Society* (New York: Knopf, 1964); and George Grant, *Technology and Empire* (Toronto: House of Anansi, 1969).

4. I use the term "liberal" here in its classical sense in Western political theory—referring to the emphasis upon individual rights to liberty and autonomy acting as constraints on the power of government.

5. John Rawls, *A Theory of Justice* (Cambridge: Harvard University Press, 1971).

6. Quoted in Ronald Cole Turner, ed., *Human Cloning: Religious Responses* (Louisville: Westminster/John Knox Press, 1997), p. 133.

7. Turner, *Human Cloning*, p. 135.

8. As illustrated by Prince Charles' comment in a letter to the *Daily Telegraph*, reprinted in *The Ecologist*: "I happen to believe that this kind of genetic modification takes mankind into realms that belong to God and to God alone." HRH The Prince of Wales, "Seeds of Disaster," *The Ecologist* 28, no. 5 (1988): 252.

9. I am not assuming anything like the "Convergence Hypothesis" put forward by Bryan Norton, which argues that environmentalists "of all stripes" (e.g., anthropocentrists and non-anthropocentrists) would actually agree about environmental policies if certain assumptions are made about the facts, and certain constraints applied to the dialogue. Bryan Norton, *Toward Unity Among Environmentalists* (New York: Oxford University Press, 1991); and also "Convergence and Contextualism: Some Clarifications and a Reply to Steverson," *Environmental Ethics* 19 (1977): 87–100. Norton's hypothesis has been challenged, explicitly using the case of the biotechnology debate, in a recent Master of Arts thesis by Marc A. Saner, "Environmental Ethics and Biotechnology: A Test of Norton's Convergence Hypothesis" (M.A. thesis, Carleton University, 1999). Saner argues that certain features of the biotechnology debate show that a convergence of opinion is not, and could not be, achieved under Norton's conditions.

10. For a full discussion of these issues in the context of risk regulation, see Conrad Brunk, Lawrence Haworth, and Brenda Lee, *Value Assump-*

*tions in Risk Assessment: A Case Study of the Alachlor Controversy* (Waterloo: Wilfrid Laurier University Press, 1991).

11. See, for example, K. S. Shrader-Frachette, *Risk and Rationality: Philosophical Foundations for Populist Reforms* (Berkeley: University of California Press, 1991).

CHAPTER THREE

# Nature and Community
# in the Global Market

ROSEMARY E. OMMER

In confronting a threatening future, the only advantage we
have over the dodo is a dynamic consciousness to match a
changing environment. That is the great gift that offers us
our chance to shape our institutions to the realities of a
new age.
—Barnett and Müller, *Global Reach*

If the misery of our poor be caused, not by the laws of
nature, but by our institutions, great is our sin.
—Charles Darwin, *Voyage of the Beagle*

Why is it that Newfoundland fishers, whose livelihood depended on the
codfish of the northwest Atlantic, should have caught them all? Why
is it that the forests of the Amazon are being decimated in part by the local
people whose whole culture and way of life has depended on those forests
for generations without number? Why is it that resource-based communities across the globe look like willing parties in a drive to extract their own
economic bases until there is nothing left? Why is it that national governments seem powerless to stop this folly? It is the task of this chapter to
examine these problems of nature and community in the light of their relationship to the "gods" of advanced capitalism—Technology and the
Market.[1] I take "nature," in this context, to be the physical world that is
our planetary home, in particular those parts of it that we use in our global
and local economies. "Community" has many meanings, but there is
always an implication of sharing and communication. Here I refer to the

multitude of small social organizations of this nation (and the world) that are found in places that have been home for generations, which are rural, often remote, and whose people are usually neither politically nor economically powerful. This, then, is a discussion about social and economic exclusion, and the survival of the local in a world increasingly organized at the global level. It is therefore an examination of national and global economics and power.[2]

## The Global Market

Western economic and political orthodoxy today applauds globalization. Why this should be so is straightforward at the level of the business firm, but it is much less obvious at the level of the state. The "catechism" of *business* contains two apparently opposing tenets in the regular rhetoric of the firm: the importance of risk and competition; and the importance of security for business to flourish. The goal of business, however, is certainty, and the tension between competition and the drive to monopoly (the ultimate certainty) is based on the need for security. The risks of competition may be the only way to get there, but the purpose of winning the competition is to eliminate competitors.[3] Globalization is the best way to increase business certainty, because it helps to secure both inputs and outputs—resources and markets, supply and demand. What, however, does the "catechism" of the *state* teach? The state needs to secure the welfare and safety of its citizens, protect its borders, and find the wherewithal to do that from its revenues. Therefore, for it, too, globalization means trade. For the firm, trade is the securing of supply and demand to ensure viability and profitability; for the nation-state, it is the securing of necessary inputs to the national economy, growth in productivity, and an outlet for increasing numbers of products, so that the national economy can grow and provide a decent way of life for its citizenry. This is what Adam Smith meant by the "wealth of nations."[4]

The nation's interest in supply and demand is not, however, identical to that of the firm. The business of the state can be thought of as the *coordinated* sum of the businesses in the nation, businesses that would not, for their own individual purposes, require much coordination inter alia. With the advent of mass production at the onset of the First (U.K.) Industrial Revolution, government integration of disparate regional economies realized the full potential of an industrial state, making it possible to move inputs from regions of plenty to those of scarcity and to achieve a wider circulation of outputs (the mass market). National economies were run by the state, because only the state had the power to "oil the wheels of commerce" for the country *as a whole*. They were built on coherent overall national (not firm) production, for which both inputs and markets were needed. That is why trade has been important to both the firm and the state.

Trade is hard to control, however, because it is inherently international, potentially global, and hence open to influences beyond the control of the individual state, let alone the firm. The state was, until recently, the natural arena for internation agreements, and it remains so today to some degree, as governmental travel for purposes of trade and business promotion demonstrates. When Adam Smith rejected state interference in business, he was speaking of a mercantilist world, in which the state had required merchant companies to be under state controls on monetary supplies, as well as duties of various kinds designed to produce and protect state revenues. Such policies, Smith argued, hampered companies in terms of their ability to function efficiently in international commerce. With industrialization, however, the state, as well as the firm, had a new weapon for trade dominance: the technologies of an industrial age. Vastly more efficient means of production meant that technological dominance became the way to secure the necessary flow of goods for Britain's economic growth and to wipe out competitors (vide India's domestic cotton industry before the Industrial Revolution).

It is no coincidence that *free* trade ("laissez-faire") started when the First (U.K.) Industrial Revolution was well in hand, its legal basis being established incrementally between 1825 and 1850. By 1860, the first global trading system was in place. Industrial development and its associated trade dominance in the United Kingdom was by then so far ahead of the rest of the world that an opening of the global marketplace benefited Britain's search for natural resources but did not produce serious competition for her manufactures. That is, the "freedom" of trade was more apparent than real—the British technological edge protected Britain from serious competition for quite some time. It is important, then, when considering the free trade ideology of the present day, to remember that free trade was created by government intervention. Polanyi pointed this out a long time ago, observing that the "road to the free market was opened and kept open by an enormous increase in continuous, centrally organized and controlled interventionism."[5]

In the twentieth century, technological dominance in the marketplace, essential to successful competition, led to a new situation. The economic benefits won by technological success began to give such great market dominance to a relatively small number of very large business corporations that national economies became more and more dependent on those corporations' well-being. Since these firms were still concerned with making supply and demand secure and profits high, they had to increase trade to match their increasing productivity. One way this was done was by creating "branch plants" in other countries. These subsidiaries were able to take advantage of cheaper inputs (either goods or workers) and avoid tariff barriers by claiming local status. Multinational corporations (MNCs as those firms that had operations in more than one country were called) were welcomed by governments and local authorities because they increased revenue and employment and held out the promise of introducing higher technology into countries, such as Canada, whose research and development funds were slight.[6]

As technology advanced, industrial nations concentrated on developing those trade sectors in which they had a comparative technological advantage. Trade between industrialized nations expanded.[7] The more mature (non-high-tech) domestic industries were left to falter in a globalizing economy where they were unable to compete with those developed by the MNCs in the non-industrial world, with its vast pool of natural resources, cheap labor, and permissive legislation. Much of this activity took place in the guise of "Third-World development," for MNCs did well in the years after World War II, and especially during the 1950s and 1960s, when United Nations–led industrial aid programs for the less-developed world were flourishing.[8] Those countries were resource-rich but lacked the finance, infrastructure, and skills to become producers in the industrial world, while the MNCs had the finance capital and technology with which to build infrastructure and develop industrial plant. Thus, they were able to construct what the United Nations hoped would become nodes out of which indigenous development would grow. It did not work. Instead, what resulted were "industrial enclaves" in otherwise undeveloped regions of the world—the "dual economy" so typical of most underdeveloped nations and regions today. For the international corporation, however, the benefits were enormous: secure "resource inputs" (both material and human) at bargain-basement prices, the support of the industrial nations' trading expertise, and passive local governments that were willing to welcome any firm that could swell their coffers and help deal with massive problems of international debt.

By the 1970s, it was becoming more appropriate to speak of *trans-national corporations* (TNCs) rather than merely multinational ones—an important shift in terminology because, when business goes transnational, it moves away, in significant part, from the orbit of the home state. It leaves home, and becomes "footloose" in the sense that, if it doesn't like the situation in any one place, it is free to go elsewhere. "Globalization," as Rotstein and Duncan remark, "creates an accelerated pace of footloose economic activity. Goods, services, currency, and capital move out of their traditional moorings among nation states, regional authorities, and international supervisory bodies, and travel in wider and faster circuits beholden to no one."[9] From the business perspective, "the boundaries that separate one nation from another are no more real than the equator. They are merely convenient demarcations of ethnic, linguistic and cultural entities," was the arrogant and dismissive explanation of the then president of the IBM World Trade Corporation in the 1970s.[10]

As a result, the much-touted state benefits from the transnational corporate economy (higher wages, higher employment, better standards of living, and thus higher revenues for the state's coffers) have so far been honored more in the breach than the observance. In order, says the TNC, to stay globally competitive, it needs fewer workers and cheaper labor (or else it will move to the less-developed countries where labor can still be exploited), a guaranteed supply of cheap natural resource inputs where applicable (or it will move to a place where environmental conditions are more favorable) lower taxes (or else it will move to a place where there are more favorable corporate taxation laws), and less government intervention (or else it will move to where there is a more favorable business environment). Moreover, it also claims to need more government investment in it (or else it will not be able to help the parent country perform competitively in the global marketplace and thus reap the benefits of the global economy).

An additional argument against control of business in recent years has been the subversion of Darwin's theory of evolution ("descent by modification" was his preferred terminology) to bolster corporate need for noninterventionist state policies. Business, it is argued, is *by nature* competitive: it (and, indeed, the whole economy) functions through the fundamental principle of "survival of the fittest," as has the human race itself. Firms must therefore be given free rein ("laissez-faire," again) if the nation is to evolve globally. This is the ideological basis of global corporate capitalism and—as with the way in which laissez-faire is used—the argument, and the understanding of the intellectual basis from which it is drawn, are wrong. Biological evolution works on "hard" transmission. Children inherit genes that are exact copies of those of their parents. There is rarely change during this transmission and, if there is, it is usually lethal. Adaptation results from differential survival of some genes relative to others across generations. For social systems, however, information transfer is by language, not by genes. The transmission is "soft" in that the information is often altered in transmission, and it is without lethal consequences, there being no destruction of either the message or the recipient. Strictly speaking, Darwin's mechanism will not apply to soft transmission: many biologists consider social and economic Darwinism a perversion that fails to remember that biological evolution produces *cooperative* adaptations (flowers, anthills) as well as *competitive* outcomes (antlers in deer, infanticide in rats).[11]

Those who make evolutionary arguments for competition forget that business collaborates on such occasions as the creation of combines, when certainty has to take precedence over competition. The argument that competition weeds out the weaknesses in an economy, and fosters the survival of the fittest, has, however, been treated seriously and actually promoted by industrial states in the last twenty years. Consequently, we have seen major withdrawals by the state from its role as a regulator of capitalist enterprises. More than that, many nations now apply this business approach to other parts of their mandates, including social policies. Efficient government has become equated with good governance, "efficiency" being defined in narrow economic terms, and many social programs have suffered major cutbacks in the process.

## Globalization and the Developing World

How has this non-interventionist approach to business, the drive to globalization, and the application of business methods to government programs affected small communities and their relationship to nature? Resource-based communities can be thought of as embedded in their environments, in the sense that they have been, and many still are, profoundly dependent on them for their way of life, including their economies. As trade has liberalized under globalization, the discrepancy between the "have" and "have-not" countries and regions has intensified. However, while the exports of the underdeveloped world have grown as a percentage share of world exports,[12] these countries have remained primarily resource producers, providing inputs to the manufactures of the developed world and its TNCs. They have not moved from export-dependent growth into local diversification and increased self-sufficiency. The global implications of this pattern of trade for small resource-based communities and the environment are serious because they are caught in a catch-22. They are damned if they do exploit all their resources to decimation point. They are damned if they do not, because then their local economies, which have become enmeshed in the global corporate search for resources, will fail, having now become dependent on the vagaries of the world market.

What are the global forces in which the small communities of the developing countries are now caught, and from which they were once relatively isolated? Consider, for example, the well-known (but nevertheless not dealt with) complex of causes that has rendered the wholesale destruction of Amazonian rain forests an apparently intractable problem. Rain forests are both fragile and environmentally, economically, and culturally important. They are major carbon "sinks," which absorb carbon dioxide in large quantities, thereby cleaning the atmosphere. They contain many medicinal plants that are vital to the transnational pharmaceutical industry, and they are replete with valuable timber. They have also been home, for thousands of years, to small indigenous communities whose way of life is being rapidly eroded as modern medical and mechanical technology allows economic "development"[13] (read resource exploitation) of the once-impenetrable jungles of the vast Amazon basin. We have known of the Amazon rain forest problem and its ultimate consequences for at least fifteen years, as we have known about many others that are similar in terms of their legacy of environmental and community destruction. As long ago as 1988, "The Worldwatch Institute, which publishes an annual report on the state of the global environment, noted . . . that eight million acres of forest burned in the Amazon in 1987."[14] That same report warned of the devastating effects of desertification, holes in the ozone layer, toxic wastes, soil degradation, groundwater contamination from pesticides, extensive global deforestation. The World Summit on Sustainable Development, held in Johannesburg in August 2002, discussed such problems at length, but acknowledged that it cannot hope to solve them: international agreement seems unreachable on such fundamentals as greenhouse gas emissions, never mind poverty and disease.[15]

The problem, according to the Brundtland Report,[16] is the unbalanced growth of the world economy, and the uneven distribution of income that has resulted. It follows that, since the largest single share of global production and consumption rests in the hands of the top TNCs,[17] they must bear major responsibility here. In the example of the Amazon forests, and many others, the problem boils down to a combination of low primary product commodity prices, which affect the underdeveloped country's ability to improve its lot, and low production costs, which serve the interests of the TNCs and make it worth their while to operate in these regions. So do such things as lower safeguards on pollution and other weak environmental and health controls in developing nations. The end result is to force increased production of natural resources in the developing world in order to increase export income and the employment that goes with it in the short term. This is despite the long-term negative consequences to both the environment and jobs, since the burden of foreign debt repayment for these nations makes a longer-term perspective untenable.[18] In case after case, the pattern is the same, and the long-term outcomes sadly predictable. In the short term, however, the developed world is benefiting from this combination of exploitative international fiscal and corporate policies.

## Globalization, Community, and Development: The Case of Canada

It is not, however, only in the underdeveloped world that we find such negative effects of globalization. Even in Canada, where rural resource-based settler communities were never completely independent of global forces, there has been a serious loss of environmental (resource) and socioeconomic resilience in recent years. The small communities of Canada used to be its lifeblood. In a very real sense, they made the Canadian economy, because that economy started, in the colonial era, with the production of essential inputs into the British economy. Now rural Canada, with its continuing dependence on its resource base, shows the effects of globalization very clearly. The problem has been building for a very long time. It can fruitfully be thought of as the end point in a continuing history of extraction of primary products that have been needed as inputs to the metropolitan economy: by Britain in the eighteenth and nineteenth centuries, and increasingly by central Canada in the late nineteenth and throughout the twentieth century.[19] Rural Canada helped to fuel imperial trade and, indeed, to transport it in vessels built of Canadian timber.[20] Newfoundland was built on fish. New Brunswick and Quebec were "Great Britain's Woodyard." After timber, Ontario grew wheat. The Prairies followed; British Columbia provided furs and, later, gold, coal, and timber as part of the periphery of the new continental economy based in the (also new) industrial heartland of Ontario and Quebec, all of this bound together by the steel bands of the railroad.[21]

In the century that followed, Canada created itself, grew, achieved Dominion status, and developed an industrial heartland in southern Ontario, with a manufacturing base that has produced rather less economic independence than was once hoped, not least because of the emergence of a branch plant economy in the Canadian heartland, in the twentieth century.[22] Growth on the Canadian periphery was fragile—vulnerable to shifting commodity prices and the vagaries of world markets—and, by the last quarter of the twentieth century, the features of the small, open Canadian economy were set. It has a small "high-tech" sector, a large and increasingly vulnerable manufacturing sector, much of it in the form of U.S. subsidiaries (e.g., the auto industry) located in a few large centers mostly in Quebec and Ontario, and a semicircle of rural peripheries that produce raw or semi-processed natural products (fish, timber, oil, and gas) for manufacture by large and increasingly transnational corporations in either central Canada or, more often, the United States.

This is remarkably like the profile of an underdeveloped nation, with a strong suggestion of a dual economy, and yet that is not the case. Despite chronic complaints about have and have-not provinces over the years, the nation as a whole benefited from the terms of Confederation and the subsequent renegotiations that took place around them. There was put in place a set of policies that were designed to redress the revenues lost by the provinces at Confederation and then to balance by redistribution some of the wealth from the richer parts of Canada to its less advantaged provinces. Major improvements were made in the years between 1960 and 1973, expressly to meet the principle of equalization and to help with education and health costs as well as the infrastructural costs that are of benefit to the nation as a whole. They were a remarkable exercise in national equity.

Until 1974, the Canadian economy as a whole did well. But there were serious underlying concerns about structural weakness, including the growing strength of the branch plants in the country, the continuation of an export-led and natural resource-based basis for most of the nation's economic well-being, and increasing foreign direct investment as the means of financing expansion.[23] However, if seen in regional as well as national terms, the good times were not reflected uniformly across the country, although the west boomed in the wake of potash and oil development. But the east flagged as efforts to decentralize industry proved inadequate. Technology in the Newfoundland fisheries improved, but this helped the fishing firms, which were developing international components, rather than the rural inshore fishing communities.[24] Social programs like Medicare helped rural areas, but income and regional disparities remained intransigent, despite a series of policy innovations expressly designed to address them.

The break came in 1974 with recession, exacerbated by the rise in oil prices brought about by the formation of OPEC (the Organization of Petroleum Exporting Countries) and the U.S. departure from the gold exchange standard. This was, in effect, the final demise of both the Bretton-Woods system and the postwar boom. It marked the end of genuinely coordinated international monetary policy and heralded increasing instability in world financial matters. The reverberations were felt around the globe, including Canada, where inflation and the fiscal policies created to fight it resulted in depression.[25] Canadian responses distinguished between global and national factors:

> The obvious external factor was the dramatic success of Japan . . . and the appearance of a whole set of Japan imitators. . . . Japan appeared to have cornered the high-technology end of the market, while the other countries had taken over the production of standard-technology items. . . . Many felt that Canada's historical advantage in natural resource industries was ending as it cut the last of the virgin timber, mined the last of the high-quality ore, moved to the Arctic and offshore for its petroleum, and witnessed the salinization of its soils.[26]

Externally, the overexploitation of natural resources was highly lucrative, in the short term, for the TNCs who controlled the staple industries of the nation; in the longer term they could move elsewhere. Internally, the problem was seen by some as related to the underdevelopment of Canadian manufacturing (with its overreliance on the branch plants of TNCs and its underinvestment in Canadian R&D), and by others as the result of overly generous policy interventions in the economy (such as the Unemployment Insurance increases of 1971, high minimum wages, rent controls, regional development incentive grants, and so on). The policy argument won and social policies were retrenched. By 1982, in the teeth of a range of seemingly intractable problems both domestic and international, the era of the postwar search for national equity faded. In 1984, with the election of a government headed by Brian Mulroney, a former TNC director, market solutions became the order of the day: free trade and deregulation, being examples. Interest rates were raised, and unemployment increased. The wider structural problems resulting from the underdevelopment of manufacturing, and the associated overreliance on staple production, were left in abeyance. Likewise, the international situation that had generated the crisis was, to all intents and purposes, forgotten. The problem was seen as boiling down to a long-overdue reduction of federal debts and deficits, and the language of the time was replete with business aphorisms about good management and the need to live within one's means. The business of government was to become efficient, and efficiency meant serious cutbacks. Depression followed.

Worst hit were those places least able to cope. "Short-term pain for long-term gain" had little meaning in places like Newfoundland and Labrador, no stranger to international currency problems or the "decay of trade,"[27] where the pain had been around for a long time. In 1986, the Newfoundland provincial government struck a Royal Commission on Employment and Unemployment, whose task it was to find a path to a brighter economic future for a region reeling from unemployment and collapsing staple industries (fish, hydro, mining, and forestry). Attempts by the premier to "modernize" the province after it entered Confederation in 1949 had been marred by bad judgment. There was an influx of corporate adventurers into the province, bringing with them modern industries like petrochemicals. There was a misguided sale of Labrador hydroelectricity to Quebec, which left the province without the revenues that could have otherwise flowed to provincial coffers in hard times. There was the "resettlement" of people from their traditional outport communities to central places where modern jobs, goods, and services were to be more readily available for them, had they ever materialized. There was the drive to technological innovation in the fisheries, which served to concentrate capital in the hands of a few large firms, while marginalizing the small-boat inshore fishers who would have benefited more from a policy of appropriate small-scale innovation and diversification. In the international realm, there was increasing evidence of overfishing by foreign fleets until the introduction of the Canadian 200-mile limit, which merely altered the nationality of the fleets and allowed major depredation by Canadian offshore high-tech TNCs.

The Royal Commission argued against this way of operating, urging instead that the province "build on its strengths,"[28] pointing to the traditional strengths of outport life, including a rich informal economy that operated as a flexible strategy for survival in hard times and could be developed to create local small-scale business and diversification of an enduring nature. It also strongly argued for improved affordable secondary and post-secondary education and a guaranteed annual income (an idea that had been debated at the federal level for years, but was never activated). Regional development boards and innovation malls were recommended also; indeed, the Commission was advocating a "small is beautiful" approach to the development of the province.

It did not happen, despite considerable interest in the report. What did happen was that in 1991 the codfish stocks of the northwest Atlantic, which were the basis of the province's historic fishery, were found to be seriously depleted. This was the result of a combination of factors that, taken with the massive overfishing by high-tech Canadian and foreign fleets alike, resulted in the biological collapse of the stocks and the imposition in 1992 of a moratorium on groundfish that is still in place. The inshore fishery went into crisis; communities experienced as much as one hundred percent unemployment, and a rescue package was put in place temporarily to alleviate the immediate impact of the situation and give people time to adjust.[29]

The story is tragic in and of itself, but what is even worse is that the lessons that might have been learned seem to have been ignored. While the province's inshore fishers struggled to adjust, the fishing corporations merely sailed off to other waters and continued to fish as before. Indeed, Fishery Products International reported its largest profits ever in the years following the moratorium. At home, Newfoundlanders turned to other species, as they had to do to survive, and overfished those, too. Capelin, crab, and shrimp are now vulnerable, much as was the codfish. Nor was the problem confined to that province. In British Columbia, the salmon stocks were also showing signs of depletion by the late 1990s, and again the policy response was to protect the large companies' revenues rather than seek solutions for the small communities.[30]

What's happening in communities? Wherever one looks in rural Canada today, small communities are in serious trouble, facing collapsing primary production industries, whether mining, agriculture, ranching, fishing, or forestry. There also appears to be, on occasion and among some people, a weakening of the communalistic ethos of country life, to be replaced by an individualistic (capitalist) ethos. A striking example of this occurred recently in the face of the drought in central Alberta that had left ranchers without feed for their cattle—while some hay farmers across the country offered hay free, others increased their prices to take advantage of the high demand and scarcity, saying that that is just the way business goes. The problem is both one of global commodity prices and of environmental distress: the same syndrome that is manifest in the underdeveloped world. It is not so severe only because there are "safety nets" (social policies) in place in the developed world to cushion the blow, but they are no solution to what is clearly a structural problem of global dimensions. Moreover, governments seem to be at a loss as to what to do.

### Future Directions

Are there any solutions? Perhaps, since in contrast to the capitalist hay farmers previously mentioned, there is also evidence that primary producers (fishers, farmers, and loggers) are becoming increasingly aware of the environmental damage that their industries have created and are taking what steps they can, at the local level, to address these concerns. They are aware that TNCs are pragmatists, and vulnerable to public opinion, though they try to shape it more and more as they take over either ownership or control of more of the world's communication channels.

Sometimes, however, events come together in a combination that allows local pressures to have an effect on major resource companies. There are moves afoot to change things: small, local, but they might be a beginning, if only because other things at the international level are shifting as the United States becomes increasingly protectionist of her own natural resources. An example reported in the *Vancouver Sun* is instructive.[31] It tells of a new framework for agreement that is being discussed by loggers, First Nations, and a transnational timber company on the Queen Charlotte Islands (Haida Gwaii) of British Columbia that "could change the face of logging in B.C.," said the article's author, Gordon Hamilton. Faced with constant fears of layoffs, long-distance employers, and provincial regulations that fail to protect the forests and ensure a sustainable harvest, loggers have thrown in their lot with the Haida Nation, who have lived on the islands for thousands of years and are becoming increasingly powerful as First Nations land claims meet with increasing success in the courts. The Haida want more control of their forests, and the company, facing a remarkable alliance of loggers and First Nations, says it is willing to cut its harvest on Haida Gwaii by half, even though the provincial government has set the harvest at almost twice that amount. The chief forester for British Columbia says the company proposal is novel and "may require some cabinet-level sanction. It may require some changes to legislation. . . . Whenever big business and communities, native or non-native, have ways of solving some of the social tensions that are out there, government would be ill-advised not to pay attention to it."

Nor is this only a local issue. The timber also supports jobs in the southwest of the province, adding millions of dollars to provincial revenues. Moreover, if the company maximizes employment for local residents as a sign of its goodwill, that will be resented by the international union, who represents labor on the whole coast and needs to protect the contract principle of "layoff by seniority, not residence." However, the company recognizes that the industry has to restructure. Loggers and the Haida say the harvest level is unsustainable (the David Suzuki Foundation supports them in this), and their jobs will go when there is no timber left.

The example is instructive because it brings together all the forces at work, and usually in opposition, in resource-based transnational industries and shows that there can sometimes occur a concatenation of events that may (it remains to be seen in this case) effect genuine change. First Nations' voices are very powerful here. Their time frames of reference are very long, and they are ecologically sensitive, even more than other small-scale "traditional" societies, because the environment is part of their spiritual sense of themselves. The time for small-scale development may finally be approaching, as local people begin to take more responsibility for what happens to their communities and their resources, in the wake of governmental inability to do that.[32]

As things stand, however, equity and efficiency, environment and productivity are at war globally. The TNC is the most efficient business organization yet created from a business point of view. But from the perspective of local development, of equity, and of environment (which works itself out in the vagaries of local conditions), it is a disaster, at least as currently structured. We need to ask ourselves whether people are at the service of the economy, or the economy at the service of the people—because at present society and nature are in distress, while business goes global and national governments hasten to follow suit. It is time we looked hard at the actions and vocabulary of government and business. Is it "efficient" to fish out all the fish, log all the forests, pollute the atmosphere? Is it "efficient" to end up eating plankton soup because there are no fish left? The corporate answer is "yes," unless the marketplace (i.e., consumers—ordinary people) refuses to go along with them.

## Conclusion

Industrial technology started as control of the means of production and developed as an instrument of wider (global) economic dominance and power for the industrial state. In the 1950s and 1960s it became increasingly the means by which corporations wielded both national and international dominance of a global marketplace—which is how they think of the world. It is important here to make a distinction between the legitimate function of business and that of government. The business of business is profit, not for people or a citizenry, but for the firm and its shareholders. The business of the state is to ensure that the nation benefits from the success of its firms. But today's industrial state finds itself in a curious position in which really large corporations (on whose economic health the state is convinced it depends for high employment, higher standards of living, technological development, trade revenues, and so on) have a much larger lobbying voice than those who belong in other parts of the state's mandate. This has happened despite the fact that the duty of the state, for which its governments are elected and from which they draw their legitimacy, is to *all* its people in a civil democratic society. Its duty to its corporations is part of that mandate, not its entire obligation. The serious erosion of trust in government in recent years, and the concomitant increase in cynicism (which politicians bewail), is not really surprising, when government speaks to its citizens in business jargon, when its departments talk about their "clients" and politicians talk of "productivity," "efficiency," "competitiveness." Citizens are not clients of the state. Government is at the service of its people, not the reverse. Moreover, the national economy is designed *in principle* to be at the service of people—not the reverse—and national economic policy is supposed to be the handmaiden of the state, not of its corporations, despite current practice. The relationship between a citizenry and business is not identical to the relationship between that citizenry and its government that serves it: all of it, not just the business sector. We do not vote for our corporations, but we do vote for our governments, who enter thereby into a contractual relationship with us to represent us and *all* our interests, social and cultural as well as economic.

There is no such contractual arrangement with our corporations. If there were, we would be voting for them, and choosing between them, and they would be required to solicit our votes, offer us incentives—make a contract with us, at the national level, for the fulfillment of which they could be held accountable. Those transnational corporate chief executives who say that the TNC is better able to run the world than the United Nations is or any other combination of governments forget that there is *and should be* more to governing than managing the books in a democratic humane civil society. The distinct realms of business and government should never be conflated, although that has happened in much political rhetoric, just as, in the days leading up to perestroika, there was a tendency to conflate the concepts of "free world" and "free market." Now, however, with the collapse of the U.S.S.R., corporations no longer need to justify themselves through a subtle elision of the ideas of the free market (capitalism) and the free world and the concomitant implicit suggestion that capitalism is morally superior to other economic systems. Capitalism without the requirement, however spurious, to demonstrate moral superiority is left free to justify itself in purely economic terms: profits, productivity, efficiency, and competitiveness. It is also able to disempower the nation-state of which it now, diplomatically speaking, has little need. The rules of the game have changed since 1990, and it is not clear what the world of business and of nation-states will look like in the years to come. It is not even clear whether or not nation-states will have any real global power or influence in future when compared to that of the transnational megacorporations.

In 1984, the Bruntland Report warned of an impending global environmental crisis, and there have been many similar warnings since. In 2002, President George W. Bush rejected the Kyoto Accord on Climate Change, saying that it was against the "national interest" for the United States to meet emissions targets. These are two voices speaking past one another, proclaiming two different truths. It is now vitally necessary to seek the intellectual basis to create a debate out of what has become a collision of ideologies. But that is the nature (and problem) of dogma: it requires faith in a worldview that, by becoming framed in dogmatic terms, can no longer be debated. Such confrontations always fail to move us on, and yet move on we must—but not on the trajectory of the last 150 years, which has generated such violence both to people and to the environment, and such huge global disparities. That way is demonstrably unsustainable, and its promised rewards unrealized. For it is now very clear that the requirements of most of the world's citizenry for a clean and safe environment, a decent standard of living, enough work to put food on the table, affordable health care, and an adequate education are not being met.

Advanced (including transnational) capitalism, unless it reforms itself, is also now proving to be ultimately unsustainable in the environmental sense, and we are beginning to see that its arrogance can make it careless, and hence more vulnerable. In 2002, a wave of investment accounting scandals followed the September 11, 2001, terrorist attacks on the Pentagon and the World Trade Center (arguably the most powerful symbols of the arrogance of the heartland of global capitalism as expressed in its aggressive and defensive modes). These events raise serious moral and political questions about the fruits of global capitalism, but anyone in the United

States who has broached them in recent times has had to face accusations of traitorship and betrayal. We would do well to remember that the society that cannot see its faults, falls—as have the global empires of Rome, Britain, and the U.S.S.R. and the global corporate empires of ENRON and WORLDCOM. How much more violence, how many more tragedies, how large a global crisis do we need before the arrogance of those officially or unofficially in power is shaken, and government and industry are forced to rethink?

## Notes

The author wishes to thank Rusty Bittermann, Bob Cecill, Greg Kealey, Ian Perry, and Eric Sager for their comments on earlier drafts of this chapter.

1.  "The utopian vision of the marketplace offers . . . an enthralling religion, a self-satisfied belief system that attracts fervent and influential adherents. . . . Abstracted from human reality, the market's intricate mechanisms convey an entrancing sense of perfection, logical and self-correcting. Many intelligent people have come to worship these market principles, like a spiritual code that will resolve all the larger questions for us, social and moral and otherwise, so long as no one interferes with its authority. In this modern secular age, many who think of themselves as rational and urbane have put their faith in this idea of the self-regulating market as piously as others put their trust in God." William Greider, *One World, Ready or Not* (New York: Simon & Schuster, 1997), p. 473.

2.  There is a huge literature. For a range of perspectives see, for example, the work of Samir Amin, *Class and Nation, Historically and in the Current Crisis* (New York: Monthly Review Press, 1980); W. Keith Bryant, *The Economic Organization of the Household* (Cambridge: Cambridge University Press, 1990); Peter F. Drucker, *Post-Capitalist Society* (New York: Harper Business, 1994); Daniel R. Fusfield, *The Age of the Economist* (Glenview, Ill.: Scott, Foresman/Little, Brown Higher Education, 1990); John Kenneth Galbraith, *The Culture of Contentment* (Boston: Houghton Mifflin, 1992); David Harvey, *The Limits to Capital* (Oxford: Basil Blackwell, 1984); Jane Jacobs, *The Nature of Economies* (Toronto: Random House, 2000); Harold James, *The End of Globalization: Lessons from the Great Depression* (Cambridge, Mass.: Harvard University Press, 2001); David S. Landes, *The Wealth and Poverty of Nations: Why Some Are So Rich and Some So Poor* (New York: W.W. Norton, 1998); E. F. Schumacher, *Small Is*

*Beautiful: Economics As If People Mattered* (New York: Harper & Rowe, 1973).

3. Firms will collude with one another, rather than compete, when it serves their collective interest, unless adequate antitrust legislation is in place. For the Canadian story, see Christopher Armstrong and H. V. Nelles, *Monopoly's Moment: The Organization and Regulation of Canadian Utilities, 1830–1930* (Philadelphia: Temple University Press, 1986).

4. There is a vast literature covering the history of the world economy. Essential reading is, in the first instance, Adam Smith, *An Inquiry into the Nature and Causes of the Wealth of Nations* (New York: P. F. Collier & Sons, 1909), whom too many cite without reading what he actually said, and the context in which he said it. A few accessible books on the subject, from a range of perspectives, are: Fernand Braudel, *The Wheels of Commerce: Civilization and Capitalism, 15th–18th Century*, Vol. 2 (New York: Harper and Row, 1982); John Kenneth Galbraith, *A Journey through Economic Time: A Firsthand View* (New York: Houghton Mifflin, 1994), and his classic *The New Industrial State* (New York: Houghton Mifflin, 1971); E. K. Hunt, *Property and Prophets: The Evolution of Economic Institutions and Ideologies* (New York: Harper and Row, 1990), as well as works cited elsewhere in this chapter.

5. Karl Polanyi, *The Great Transformation: The Political and Economic Origins of Our Time* (Boston: Beacon Press, 1957), p. 140.

6. John N. H. Britton and James M. Gilmour, *The Weakest Link: A Technological Perspective on Canadian Industrial Underdevelopment*, Science Council of Canada, Background Study 43 (Ottawa: Supply and Services Canada, 1978).

7. A. G. Kenwood and A. L. Lougheed, *The Growth of the International Economy, 1820–1900* (London: Routledge, 1992), pp. 288–289.

8. The story is long and complex. The Bretton Woods agreement, which aimed to get the world back on its feet after the destructive war years, was the first step in an international effort to rebuild multilateral trade, which included the World Trade Organization, the International Monetary Fund, and the General Agreement on Tariffs and Trade. For the industrial countries of the world, it worked well; for the "underdeveloped world" it was the means of penetration by the MNCs into economies that desperately needed capital, infrastructure, medicine, and education. Short-run benefits led to long-term loss of control, and OPEC was the first organized resistance to Western penetration of "Third World economies." For a standard account of this period, see Kenwood and Lougheed, *The Growth of the International Economy*, pp. 244–259.

9.  Abraham Rotstein and Colin A. M. Duncan, "For a Second Economy," in *The New Era of Global Competition, State Policy and Market Power*, ed. Daniel Drache and Meric S. Gertler (Kingston: McGill-Queens University Press, 1991), p. 415.

10. Richard J. Barnett and Ronald E. Müller, *Global Reach: The Power of the Multinational Corporations* (New York: Simon and Schuster, 1974), p. 14.

11. I am grateful to Dr. David Schneider, marine biologist, Memorial University of Newfoundland, for this careful explanation of the incorrect nature of economic Darwinism.

12. Kenwood and Lougheed, *The Growth of the International Economy*, p. 287, Table 25.

13. The word "development" has meant different things at different times in the past fifty years. There used to be an important distinction between "growth" and "development," in which the former meant simply increments in output, whereas the latter referred to growth that produced economic diversification and therefore set a region on the path to being genuinely developed. See, for example, Harold Brookfield, *Interdependent Development* (Pittsburgh: Methuen, 1975). Now, the latter meaning has been lost, and growth and development are spoken of as if they were the same thing. The implication here may be that attempts at diversification are now thought of as failed, or perhaps passé. At any rate we are now seeing a further entrenchment of what André Gunder Frank referred to as "the development of underdevelopment": André Gunder Frank, "The Development of Underdevelopment," *Monthly Review* 18, no. 4 (1966).

14. Frank J. Tester, "Canada and the Global Crisis in Resource Development," in Drache and Gertler, eds., *The New Era*, p. 399.

15. Significantly, a CBC report on August 29 (*CBC Newsworld*, Eve Savery reporting) observed that there was a much greater chance of success with very small low-tech projects supported *at the local level*, and showed one cooperative in South Africa that was flourishing.

16. World Commission on Environment and Development, *Our Common Future* (New York: Oxford University Press, 1987). The commission was chaired by Gro Harlem Brundtland, and its mandate was to provide strategies for environmentally sound development for the new millennium.

17. Tester, "Canada and the Global Crisis," p. 400, citing the UNCTAD *Review* of Winter 1982. The situation has worsened since then.

18. For a detailed critique of this complex of forces, see Tester, "Canada and the Global Crisis," pp. 399–414.

19. There is a vast, if now dated, literature on core-periphery and metropolis-hinterland approaches to Canadian economic development, most

of it from the 1970s and early 1980s. The roots of this analysis are found in the classic works of Harold Innis, A. R. M. Lower, and others. See, for example, Harold A. Innis, *The Fur Trade in Canada: An Introduction to Canadian Economic History*, rev. ed. (Toronto: University of Toronto Press, 1956), and *The Cod Fisheries: The History of an International Economy*, rev. ed. (Toronto: University of Toronto Press, 1954); Donald Creighton, *The Empire of the St. Lawrence* (Toronto: Macmillan, 1956); A. R. M. Lower, *Great Britain's Woodyard: British America and the Timber Trade, 1763–1867* (Montreal: McGill-Queens Press, 1973); Graeme Wynn, *Timber Colony* (Toronto: University of Toronto Press, 1981).

20. Lewis R. Fischer and Eric W. Sager, eds., *The Enterprising Canadians* (St. John's: Memorial University of Newfoundland, 1979).

21. The literature is considerable, starting with the seminal work of Canada's first economic historian, Harold Innis. For those who want to pursue it, the basic teaching texts are W. T. Easterbrook and Hugh G. J. Aitken, *Canadian Economic History* (Toronto: University of Toronto Press, 1988); Kenneth Norrie and Douglas Owram, *A History of the Canadian Economy*, 2nd ed. (Toronto: Harcourt, Brace, 1996); William L. Marr and Donald G. Paterson, *Canada: An Economic History* (Toronto: Gage, 1980). There are debates, of course, including that around the staples thesis in its many forms, but the undisputed bare bones of the story are as I have them here.

22. George Grant, *Lament for a Nation* (Toronto: McClelland and Stewart, 1965); Britton and Gilmour, *The Weakest Link*; Mel Watkins, *Innovation in a Cold Climate: The Dilemma of Canadian Manufacturing*, Science Council of Canada, Report No. 15 (Ottawa: Supply and Services Canada, 1971); Kari Levitt, *Silent Surrender* (Toronto: Macmillan, 1970); D. M. Ray, *Regional Aspects of Foreign Ownership of Manufacturing in Canada*, Report (University of Waterloo, 1967, mimeograph); his "The Location of United States Manufacturing Subsidiaries in Canada," *Economic Geography*, 1971, pp. 389–400; and many others. There is a long history: see the still useful, though dated, annotated bibliography of historical work by Anne T. Ostrye, *Foreign Investment in the American and Canadian West, 1870–1914* (Metuchen, New Jersey: Scarecrow Press, 1986).

23. For statistics, see Norrie and Owram, *A History of the Canadian Economy*, pp. 417–419.

24. There is a large literature. See in particular the recent work of Miriam Wright, *A Fishery for Modern Times* (Oxford: Oxford University Press, 2001), and my own essay in Harold Coward, Rosemary Ommer, and Tony Pitcher, eds., *Just Fish: Ethics and Canadian Marine Fisheries* (St John's: ISER Books, 2000). The works of David Alexander are also

key readings, including his book on the fish trade, *The Decay of Trade: An Economic History of the Newfoundland Saltfish Trade, 1935–1965* (St John's: ISER Books, 1977).

25. Norrie and Owram, *A History of the Canadian Economy*, p. 439.
26. Norrie and Owram, *A History of the Canadian Economy*, pp.440–441.
27. David Alexander, *The Decay of Trade*, especially pp. 39–65 and pp. 128–157.
28. Government of Newfoundland and Labrador, *Building on Our Strengths: Final Report of the Royal Commission on Employment and Unemployment* (St. John's: Queen's Printer, 1986).
29. See Rosemary E. Ommer, "The Final Report of the Eco-Research Project of Memorial University" (St. John's: ISER Books, 1998), and the subsequent volume, Rosemary E. Ommer, ed., *The Resilient Outport: Ecology , Economy and Society in Rural Newfoundland* (St John's: ISER Books, 2002), for details.
30. Rosemary E. Ommer, "The Ethical Implications of Property Concepts in a Fishery," in Coward et al., *Just Fish*, pp. 117–139.
31. *Vancouver Sun*, Thursday, July 25, 2002, in "Business BC," p. C8, cited by ghamilton@pacpress.southam.ca.
32. There is a strong case to be made for low and intermediate technology to be introduced with aid from the developed world, rather than high technology, which merely imports TNC technology and does not lead to import substitution. In developed-world rural communities, inter-mediate technologies have been tried with success in some places. See discussions in Schumacher, *Small Is Beautiful*, and the Government of Newfoundland and Labrador Royal Commission on Employment and Unemployment, *Building on Our Strengths*.

# Chapter Four

# Media Technology and the Future of Religions

## JAY NEWMAN

Those who are devoutly convinced of the central importance of religion to culture—and who also may be convinced that there are culture-transcending dimensions of religion—have had disparate views on the cultural relevance of new media technologies for religion.[1] This broad observation may bring to mind the very latest media technologies: the newest and most exciting "high-tech" devices being anxiously scrutinized at this moment by technophiles, technophobes, and stock market speculators. Or it may bring to mind fairly new media technologies—such as the Internet or even television—with which our grandparents may have been familiar but certainly not their own grandparents. But for those given to taking a wider view, the observation may spontaneously be taken to be an historical one that applies not only to modern media technologies but to ancient and medieval media technologies that were indeed new in their own time and were once at least as enchanting, encouraging, terrifying, disorienting, and transforming—to both individuals and cultures—as any media technologies that have emerged in the last hundred years or are likely to emerge in the next hundred.

Humanistic and social-scientific scholars routinely remind their students, readers, and listeners that to understand recent cultural changes, it is generally wise and prudent to give considerable thought to comparable cultural changes that occurred in the past—even the distant past. But these scholars themselves sometimes forget that the traditional media technologies that they so much revere, such as the written and printed word, were once viewed as suspiciously by some of their distant ancestors as are certain

79

new media technologies that they themselves may regard as dehumanizing and culturally subversive.[2]

A keen sensitivity to pattern and meaning in history has benefited such constructively provocative explicators of the importance of changes in media technology as Harold Innis, Walter J. Ong, and Marshall McLuhan—all of whom, perhaps not coincidentally, have had some intimate interest in religion as a form of experience and culture. Besides providing us with insights into comparatively new media technologies and the cultural changes leading up to and ensuing upon their integration into our own culture, these thinkers—who have generally distanced themselves from one-dimensional antitechnological and protechnological agendas—have emphasized the value of fully appreciating that media technologies that we now take for granted were once new and unfamiliar to those who first appropriated them, have both transformed and been transformed by other media technologies and other forms of culture with which they have interacted in the long course of their development, and must continue to change to some extent if they are to survive. These points also apply to technologies normally not regarded specifically as media technologies and even to more general forms of culture, including religion. That said, it may also be worth considering that conceptual distinctions commonly made between media, technology, culture, and even religion itself may not be as precise, as definitive, or as useful as has often been believed.[3] Yet it is not hard to understand why those who are new to media studies are still rather perplexed when on opening McLuhan's *Understanding Media* for the first time, they find that in addition to discussing the printed word, telephone, and radio, McLuhan also considers the electric light bulb, clothing, money, and clocks.[4] Something easier to grasp initially is McLuhan's proposal that to understand the far-reaching significance of the transition from the mechanical age to the electronic age, it is exceedingly helpful to reflect on earlier epochal transitions in media culture.

Much religious cultural criticism of new media technologies has taken the form of homiletical (and occasionally hysterical) diatribe. This encompasses pious rhetoric about how the disruptive technology itself, or its immoral or amoral content, or the corrupt coterie that controls it, is undermining the lofty spiritual program of traditional, mainstream religion as well as respect for the universal values that the world's great faiths have conceivably done more than any other cultural institutions to promote. Probably nowhere has this form of religious cultural criticism been louder and more persistent in recent years than in criticisms directed by religionists at television, television programming, and those responsible for television programming.[5] This is a specialized version not only of religious criticism of new media technology but of religious criticism of new technology in general.[6] On further reflection it can be seen as an application to a particular object of cultural criticism a general and classical type of religious criticism of a rival form of culture. For example, many attacks by religious reactionaries against television basically conform to a pattern already evident in classical reactionary religious criticism of new forms of rational, philosophical, and scientific inquiry.[7] Even more generally, such attacks to some extent represent a universal pattern of competition between representatives or promoters of rival forms of culture.[8]

However, even while joining their fellow religious cultural critics in lamenting and decrying the spiritually subversive cultural influences of new media technologies, many dynamic and resourceful religionists have focused on the utilitarian possibilities of these new media technologies for promoting traditional religious objectives. These individuals see new media technologies as blessings—if undeniably mixed ones—in representing remarkably effective tools for carrying out age-old religious missions of educating, civilizing, and even procuring salvation for unprecedentedly large numbers of people. In recent years, the most conspicuous expression and consequence of this recognition has been in the growth of televangelism and closely related forms of electronic religious communication;[9] and we find that in line with a classical historical pattern, televangelism has elicited negative responses not only from those who object to what it preaches but also from many who in large part approve of what it preaches.[10] Televangelism, to be sure, is an easy mark for the intellectually sophisticated cultural critic—religious or secular. But even when electronic religious communication is at its most refined, most profound, and most compassionate, it remains open to the suspicions not only of technophobes and dogmatic secularists but of those who have deeply considered anxieties about the transformative influence of new media technologies on the very form of culture that is ostensibly being served by their specifically religious application.

Some of these anxieties arise from a genuine awareness and understanding of what is truly distinctive about a new media technology; and not only do electronic forms of mass communication differ significantly, as such, from non-electronic forms, but more recently developed forms of electronic communications such as the Internet differ significantly from earlier developed forms such as radio and television. But some of these anxieties are classical anxieties. They are not entirely different in spirit or significance from the anxieties that once troubled many religionists first encountering such new media technologies as the book or the written word, or indeed first encountering one of the diverse new forms of inquiry and understanding communicated in philosophy, astronomy, biology, sociology, and hermeneutics. These classical anxieties are not necessarily more important than the more specific and more contemporary ones, but they are of greater philosophical interest.


## Harold Coward on the Written Word

In the concluding chapter of his comparative study of scripture in world religions, *Sacred Word and Sacred Text*,[11] Harold Coward offers some stimulating philosophical reflections on the rise of a new media technology far more influential on the development of religion than any we are likely to encounter in our own lifetime. That new media technology is the written word; and Coward's study of scripture in six world religions—Judaism, Christianity, Islam, Hinduism, Sikhism, and Buddhism—has led him to reflect at length on the importance of appreciating the complexity of the cultural relations between written scripture and an oral scripture that it has not entirely superseded. Coward is not only an historian of religion and a sociologist of religion but something of a philosopher of religion. It is partly his philosophical inclination that leads him to pursue a kind of comparative analysis that is currently somewhat out of fashion among religious studies scholars. Coward is scrupulously careful to avoid a largely obsolete form of "comparative religion" that has been biased and to some extent invidious; but he remains convinced that promoting appreciation of both the common and the distinctive elements of world religions is an important project for religious studies scholars, not only for philosophical reasons but for practical reasons relating to interfaith dialogue and cooperation. Coward has also stressed, however, that philosophers of religion stand to benefit greatly from closer familiarity with a broad range of world religions. Moreover, Coward is a scholar widely respected for his work on the relation of religion to a wide range of contemporary technological issues. Like Innis, Ong, and McLuhan, he distances himself from the technophiles and technophobes and focuses on concrete theoretical and practical concerns.

Accordingly, serious students of the relations of religion and media technology can hardly avoid being impressed when on the basis of his detailed and comprehensive analysis of scripture in six world religions, Coward concludes that what is most impressive to him is "the primacy of the oral."[12] And Coward's observation in this regard appears to be more than merely descriptive, for though his respect for the importance of written scripture is evident in the concluding chapter, as indeed throughout his entire study, he does not conceal what is in effect, in Innis' words, "a plea for consideration of the role of the oral tradition."[13] In Coward's view, such consideration is required if we are to attain a fuller philosophical and practical understanding of religious scripture and of religion in general; but it is also valuable in understanding the future of religions[14] and the prospects for civilization generally.

The normative thrust of Coward's position is indicated by his decision to open the concluding chapter of his study with a lengthy quotation from Ong:

> Early man had a true, if at the same time confused, sense of the mystery, power, and holiness of the word. . . . Today the oral word, the original word, is still with us, as it will be for good. But to know it for what it is, we must deliberately reflect on it. The spoken word, center of human life, is overgrown with its own excrescences—script, print, electronic verbalism—valuable in themselves but, as is generally the case with human accomplishments, not unmixed blessings. One of the reasons for reflection on the spoken word, the word as sound, is of course not to reject the later media but to understand them, too, better.[15]

While recognizing the "provocative" nature[16] of Ong's suggestion that the original spoken word has become "overgrown with its own excrescences," Coward is clearly sympathetic to Ong's point, which he sees as connected with related points made by Plato and other great thinkers throughout history[17] and in harmony with his own comparative analysis of scripture in six world religions. Those religionists who have anxieties about the transformative influence of modern media technologies on religion specifically, and on culture generally, may well find confirmation of their conviction in Coward's insistence on the primacy of the oral, not only because of Coward's demonstration of the practical relevance of this point to the future of religions[18] but because Coward recognizes, with Ong, that the latest "excrescences" to be confronted—and those that may call for the most urgent action—are not script and print but those involved in the electronic media.

Coward is no more a technophobe than Ong is, and he cautiously balances his emphasis on the primacy of the oral with a discussion of "the need for the written":[19] "Although the world religions begin with oral scripture as primary, all at some point experience the need for a written text."[20] Still, "even then the written text dominantly functions as a script for oral performance."[21] After examining the historical and future relations of oral and written scripture in three areas—worship, education, and private devotion—Coward concludes his entire comparative analysis by observing:

> [B]oth the written and the oral experience of scripture have been shown to have importance. The modern bias toward the written, however, has the tendency of shifting contemporary practice away

from the traditional predominance of the oral word. Our analysis suggests that the traditional approach of emphasizing the oral experience of scripture in early education and then continuing to nourish that early experience through repeated oral practice in adult worship and devotion is essential if scripture is to continue to have transforming power in human lives.[22]

Coward's implicit traditionalism regarding religion and media technology is at once more incisive, more balanced, more theoretical, more historical, more empirical, and more practical than that of most other religionists who have expressed classical anxieties about the impact of new media technologies on religion as a form of experience and culture. His conception of the modern bias toward the written—in all its proliferating "excrescences"—is no mere expression of a temperamental conservatism. Rather it is the outcome, at least in part, of a meticulous comparative analysis of the historical development of scripture in six major world religions that reveals what may reasonably be taken to be some of the "primary" roles played by religious scripture and religion generally in positively transforming the human condition. Moreover, Coward does not merely accept new media technologies grudgingly or stoically; he underscores "the need for the written" in religion and not merely the need to *accommodate* a secondary media technology or the utilitarian value of applying such a technology. In this regard, Coward leaves a place in his theoretical and practical analyses for the need for future media technologies in religion. But Coward's response to the classical anxieties that he has so temperately expressed is unequivocally traditionalist. It is based on a hierarchical model that sees progress in religion as essentially to be judged in relation to the "primary" roles of religion that are revealed to us by the comparative historical and social-scientific analysis of world religions.

Much is to be gained by attending to Coward's counsel that we endeavor to overcome any bias that prevents us from better appreciating the historical and continuing value of an older, more traditional, and more fundamental form of media technology in religion and in culture generally. This counsel is, in fact, at the core of the most thoughtful polemics of those religious cultural critics who express their classical anxieties about the contemporary bias toward the latest and trendiest excrescences of the oral word, and indeed of earlier forms of the written word such as script and print. All such biases are well worth overcoming, for practical as well as theoretical reasons; but the progressivist serves us well here, as in so many other areas of cultural debate, by cautioning us regarding the dangers of traditionalist biases.

For one thing, we should be careful not to identify too closely what is historically or temporally "primary" with what is normatively or practically primary at the present stage of civilization. A conscientious scholar like Coward can make a reasonable case for the continuing importance of an historically primary form of media technology in religious culture; and a reasonable case can also be made for the continuing importance for religion and culture of script, print, and other such technologies which are too often undervalued in the electronic age. But sometimes it is not enough for the cultural traditionalist simply to acknowledge that there is a need for new media technologies. It is also wise to recognize the possibility that new media technologies will continue to enable religion, as they have in the past, to perform better and indeed clearer roles than religions have performed in the earliest known stages of their development. Coward draws attention to Plato's Socratic anxieties about the personal and cultural risks involved in shifting from the spoken to the written word;[23] but certainly no less important is Plato's confidence in the power of the written word—and the forms of rationality it makes possible—to free traditional religion and culture from the superstition, emotionalism, and blind faith that have corrupted and vitiated them.[24] If Plato is very much a traditionalist, he is also a critical one, constantly mindful of the limitations of primitivism and of so many prephilosophical religious and cultural conceptions, customs, and institutions.[25] In their formative stages prior to the emergence of literacy, the ancient world religions and cultures may have been purer in some ways than they later became; but even a diehard religiocultural conservative will allow that in its most primitive forms, religion as a form of culture is imbued with what must now be regarded as a barely comprehensible savagery.

New media technologies have been responsible in no small measure for the ability of humanity not only to refine religion but to constructively *reconceive* it. One may consider in this regard the enormous impact of the printed word: it is plain from even a cursory consideration of the history of early modern ideas that Gutenberg's new media technology did much to make possible the religious and other cultural reforms of the Renaissance and Age of Reason that enabled the Western world to leave behind it some of the most lamentable features of medieval life. This consideration is all the more important for contemporary society if one is prepared to accept Pamela McCorduck's proposal that the computer is the "emblematic machine" of our time in much the same way as Gutenberg's printing press was the emblematic machine of the fifteenth century.[26] As Western religion after the rise of Greek philosophy was something essentially more profound than it had been earlier, and Western religion after the Renaissance and Age of Reason was something essentially more profound than it had been earlier, it may well turn out in time that Western religion in the future will be essentially more profound than it is today. Progress in religious culture may perhaps involve discarding more than preserving the historically primary features of religion, especially if what is ultimately worth preserving

in traditional religion—as, say, morality, compassion, and contemplation—
can be conceived independently of religion as such.

Here the very question of what is normatively or practically "primary"
in religious culture can be seen to be exceedingly complex. In his own analysis, Coward properly indicates that he is focusing in his project only on particular aspects of religious culture (scripture, worship, education, and
private devotion) and on a particular development of media technology in
religious culture (the emergence of the written word); and he explicitly
leaves a place in his analysis for the need for new media technologies in religion. Yet despite his estimable effort to avoid the technophobia of many
other religious traditionalists with classical anxieties about new media technologies, even Coward may be open to the criticism that his emphasis on
the traditional in religious communication involves a traditionalist bias
against later forms of religious communication—including future ones—
with a constructively transformative power that may be far more pertinent
to contemporary life and the future of civilization than any available to
those who have been confined to oral communication alone.

At the same time, Coward indirectly exposes a crucial weakness in the
argument of less sophisticated religious traditionalists who bemoan at
length the influence of recently developed (and developing) media technologies. For in offering us his own distinctive plea for consideration of the
role of the oral tradition, Coward is not so much challenging the forms of
electronic religious and secular communication that disturb so many contemporary religious cultural critics as he is challenging the bias toward the
written that those very cultural critics themselves have routinely exhibited.
Here Coward stands with Innis, McLuhan, and Ong, who have all recognized that even when electronic media such as radio and television have
offered us "verbalism," it is more often an oral, spoken verbalism than a
written one. (And, of course, the electronic media offer listeners and viewers much more than words.) In this regard, electronic media technologies
have done much to restore the primacy of the oral (and indeed of the non-
verbal) in religious and secular culture and, ironically, to help liberate us
from an age-old preoccupation with written scripture and its more
unwholesome "excrescences."

## The Perspective of Philosophical Theology

This last point is an invitation to consider some of the salient issues from
the perspective of philosophical theology. Conservative critics of religious
media and technology, in the classical tradition of conservative religionists
generally, often complain about the latest forms of "idolatry." And while

the ancient scriptures of world religions have nothing directly to say about modern media technologies such as the cinema and the Internet, they indeed have much to say that may render it appropriate for their professed champions to wonder aloud about whether fashionable new media technologies—and the larger part of the imagery that those technologies parade before us and impose on our conscious and subconscious mind—represent, to some extent, the latest in an apparently unending line of "idols" that divert our attention from the divine and generally from the worthiest objects of human attention and devotion. There is a significant case to be made here, particularly by those who can rise above reactionary petulance and an irrational fear and hatred of cultural novelty and progress. But our reflection on several of Coward's points is a useful stimulus to our considering the latest of any such "idolatry" in relation to some of its historical prototypes. Our modern problems are, for the most part, not merely problems arising from modernity; they are also classical problems. That is why they elicit classical anxieties among others. Contemporary critics of religious culture do well to consider the latest forms of "idolatry" in relation to modernism and the distinctive acids of modernity, but sometimes they can benefit from a wider historical, philosophical, or theological view.[27]

On this occasion, in light of Coward's consideration of scripture, it is particularly fitting to consider bibliolatry. A particularly suitable image for us to reflect on is that of the televangelist—making sophisticated use of the medium of television—theatrically waving his copy of written scripture while denouncing the false god of television and all of the faithlessness and immorality that this false god has engendered. Many a religionist will share the view of the secularist that this image properly elicits our revulsion and derision. The typical religionist, after all, is at least as likely to be sensitive to hypocrisy as the typical secularist, for hypocrisy receives proportionately much more attention in religious teaching than in secular teaching, and with good reason.[28] Still, a religionist's reaction cannot be precisely the same here as a secularist's; and, of course, different religionists, even among those who nominally share the bible-waving televangelist's faith, will react negatively for somewhat different reasons.

There are religionists who are so technophobic as to believe that religion should have as little to do with new media technologies as possible. While they may grant that the electronic media have sometimes impressively served traditional religious objectives, and can continue to do so, they will insist that the dominant influence of the electronic media on religion has been—and will ultimately be—corruptive. For such religionists, the corruption of a hypocritical televangelist is largely to be expected, as he serves two masters.[29] Religious technophiles, on the other hand, may be incensed when a co-religionist hypocritically or even wholeheartedly launches into a tirade against new media technologies that he misunderstands and fails to appreciate. And some religionists who are neither technophobes nor technophiles may simply be perturbed by the televangelist's appeal to his audience's indignation and alienation. But I propose that many of the televangelist's nominal co-religionists may be bothered above all else by the televangelist's waving of the bible. While the medium of television may be seen as inviting such a misuse of written scripture, the principal idol here is not the *new* medium but the old. It is not mainly television that has replaced God here but the written scripture itself, the supposed repository of God's word. Progressive religious thinkers have railed against bibliolatry from the age of the Hebrew prophets to our own day.

It is mainly the peculiar literalism of so many televangelists—and not their utilization of an electronic medium—that irritates many religious and secularist critics of televangelism. These critics, who are normally well aware that it was not the electronic media that gave rise to biblical literalism, can usually be heard on occasion to praise something in the electronic mass media that qualifies in their estimation as "serious" religious programming, whether it be in the form of a sober documentary or professorial discussion. Some of these critics would endorse the view of the Protestant theologian Paul Tillich:

> Literalism deprives God of his ultimacy and, religiously speaking, of his majesty. It draws him down to the level of that which is not ultimate, the finite and conditional. In the last analysis it is not rational criticism of the myth which is decisive but the inner religious criticism. Faith, if it takes its symbols literally, becomes idolatrous! It calls something ultimate which is less than ultimate. Faith, conscious of the symbolic character of its symbols, gives God the honor which is due him.[30]

Tillich, of course, is not deploring the cultural influence of scripture as such, or even written scripture; rather, he decries a misapplication and profanation of scripture. Television, in fact, effectively exposes such misuse to some viewers by focusing their attention on such gestures of the literalist televangelist as his bible waving and bible thumping. Yet where a theologian like Tillich sees bibliolatry, a hostile secularist may instead be struck by the corruptive cultural influence of scripture itself and of institutional religion in general.

A religionist with authentic reverence for scripture (and a broadminded secularist with respect for the constructive cultural value of scripture) will know better than to put the blame here squarely on any of the various media technologies involved in this religious communication: the television transmitting the televangelist's performance, the book being waved, the written word making a written scripture possible, or the historically primary oral word of the ancient message that the televangelist seems to be endeavoring to impart. Though in a certain sense it may be the case that the medium is the message,[31] we ultimately cannot afford to undervalue the responsibility of the reflective beings who create and appropriate media as cultural products to impart, interpret, transmit, and receive messages.[32]

For the religious mind, the divine must somehow be reckoned with as the ultimate inspiration for all cultural processes, including those by which new media technologies have emerged, developed, been constructively employed, and even been misused.[33] Yet even the religionist who professes commitment to an austere form of theological determinism knows better than to blame the divine rather than place trust in the divine. Cultural creations differ from other natural or divine creations precisely because of the role played by human thought in their creation and development.[34] When human beings worship what they have created, as extreme technophiles risk doing, then from a theological perspective they are undoubtedly guilty of idolatry. But it is only by means of the fundamental forms of human culture and technology, especially language itself,[35] that ordinary human beings— those not gifted with certain mystical or miraculous experiences—are capable of conceiving and understanding the divine. (Even a prophet must rely on those forms of culture and technology to communicate with humanity.) The religious mind thus must acknowledge that while language and the proliferating media technologies that grow out from it may result in the creation of idols, they represent the essential means by which most mortals can conceive and understand the divine.

New media technologies provoke misgivings partly because of their potential, often realized, to contribute to barbarism by obscuring traditional wisdom. But a religionist is rather more obligated than a materialist to have confidence that new media technologies, wisely employed, can continue to contribute—as they have done on countless occasions in the past— to cultural progress and civilization, not least by elevating human conceptions of the divine. Judging on the basis of extrapolation from the historical cultural contributions of the book—the printed word, the written word, and indeed the oral word itself—we have some reason to believe that new media technologies are ultimately likely to foster more than retard civilization. It must be acknowledged, however, that major advances in civilization almost invariably carry with them the potential for more sophisticated and more extreme forms of barbarous reaction.[36]

Some reactionary religious thinkers remain convinced that civilization has been largely in decline since the Renaissance, or the High Middle Ages, or the Patristic period, or some other ancient theophany. To such thinkers, the very expression "modern civilization" is virtually an oxymoron. While many reflective individuals are impressed by the conceptual and moral power—the lucidity, intelligence, integrity, and hopefulness—of so much contemporary philosophical and theological discourse in a wide variety of media, these reactionary thinkers tend to regard most of that discourse as representing one or another form of vanity. Such being their "faith," they are not likely to be persuaded by an account of cultural advances in the modern world. But perhaps the characterization of humanity—or indeed the characterization of the divine—that has been preserved for us in ancient literature, in written scripture as well as secular writings, should serve as a caveat to us to avoid any temptation to idealize even the noblest worldviews of the distant past.

## Conclusion

It is not only reactionary religious thinkers who find it exceedingly difficult to believe that the newest media technologies can conceivably elevate our religious conceptions in a way comparable to that in which the written word and printed word elevated ancient and medieval religious conceptions. Traditionalist biases and the bias toward the written remain strong and widespread; comparison in this case may be invidious and unhelpful, since it is not unreasonable to assume that advances in the earliest stages of the civilizing process are more influential than later ones. In any case, little is to be gained from the effort to show that there is a "need" for television or the Internet comparable to "the need for the written" that Coward has described. Still, we should not be hasty to dismiss the testimony of those who insist that a depiction of the divine in even a film comedy[37] or a television cartoon program[38] has enriched their religious experience.

Contemporary religionists who harbor classical anxieties about new media technologies may properly observe that Internet Web sites devoted to serious religious subject matter, though certainly numerous, are to some extent engulfed by a great deal of rubbish; and it can hardly be denied that the proportion of radio and television programming devoted to profound spiritual concerns is not conspicuously large. But our often habitual association of literature with great literature—a product largely of formal education and its selective emphasis on classics and other edifying works—leads us to forget that great literature, too, is to some extent engulfed by a great deal of inconsequential or unwholesome literature. (A visit to the typical bookstore in a shopping mall is revealing here, but the problem is an old one; and it was not entirely with self-serving motives that medieval ecclesiastics fretted about the rise of literacy among the general population.) This point applies to the spoken word as well, and our appreciation of Ong's point about early humanity's sense of the mystery, power, and holiness of the word should not lead us to infer that the primal uses of speech are largely religious. In any case, the substantial proportion of conversation that even learned philosophers and theologians devote to mindless gossip no longer astonishes me.

Nevertheless, it must be granted that modernity in the Western world has brought with it increasing secularization, and that the pace of this secularization has increased exponentially with every major phase of religious liberalization from the Age of Reason and the Enlightenment to the present day.[39] This increasing secularization should not be attributed primarily to new media technologies, but the advances in media technology that have contributed significantly to the exchange of old conceptions of the divine for new ones have also contributed significantly to increasing loss or abandonment of any conception of the divine. Consequently, we witness not so much the idolization of media technologies themselves—for television and the Internet almost surely invoke less of a sense of awe than the word did for early humanity—as a heightened suspicion that the human activity on which the media are largely focused may be the most important creative activity in the cosmos. That granted, despite scientific advances in futurology, we cannot prophesy with a great deal of confidence what the long-term influence of the latest media technologies will be for religion and culture. Despair, cynicism, and pessimism remain generally less suitable options for the authentic religionist than for the materialist.

## Notes

1. Jay Newman, *Inauthentic Culture and Its Philosophical Critics* (Montreal: McGill-Queen's University Press, 1997), pp. 69–76. Cf. H. Richard Niebuhr, *Christ and Culture* (New York: Harper and Row, 1951).

2. Jay Newman, *Religion and Technology* (Westport, Conn.: Praeger, 1997), ch. 1.

3. Newman, *Religion and Technology*, chap. 5.

4. Marshall McLuhan, *Understanding Media: The Extensions of Man* (New York: New American Library, 1964).

5. Jay Newman, *Religion vs. Television: Competitors in Cultural Conflict, Media and Society Series* (Westport, Conn.: Praeger, 1996), chaps. 1–2.

6. Newman, *Religion and Technology*, chap. 1.

7. Newman, *Religion vs. Television*, chap. 4, esp. pp. 123–132.
8. Jay Newman, *Competition in Religious Life*, Editions SR (Waterloo, Ont.: Wilfrid Laurier University Press, 1989), pp. 48–52, 192–198.
9. Newman, *Religion vs. Television*, pp. 81–98.
10. Newman, *Religion vs. Television*, pp. 84–85.
11. Harold Coward, *Sacred Word and Sacred Text: Scripture in World Religions* (Maryknoll, N.Y.: Orbis Books, 1988), chap. 7.
12. Coward, *Sacred Word and Sacred Text*, p. 161.
13. Harold Innis, "Minerva's Owl," in *The Bias of Communication* (Toronto: University of Toronto Press, 1951), p. 32. This paper was Innis' 1947 presidential address to the Royal Society of Canada.
14. Cf. the title of the concluding chapter: "Scripture and the Future of Religions."
15. Walter J. Ong, *The Presence of the Word* (New Haven, Conn.: Yale University Press, 1967), p. 314. The passage is cited in Coward, *Sacred Word and Sacred Text*, p. 159.
16. Coward, *Sacred Word and Sacred Text*, p. 159.
17. Coward, *Sacred Word and Sacred Text*, pp. 159–160.
18. Coward, *Sacred Word and Sacred Text*, pp. 182–189.
19. Coward, *Sacred Word and Sacred Text*, pp. 171–174.
20. Coward, *Sacred Word and Sacred Text*, p. 171.
21. Coward, *Sacred Word and Sacred Text*, p. 171.
22. Coward, *Sacred Word and Sacred Text*, p. 189.
23. Coward, *Sacred Word and Sacred Text*, p. 159. Cf. Plato, *Phaedrus*.
24. Cf. Jay Newman, *Biblical Religion and Family Values: A Problem in the Philosophy of Culture* (Westport, Conn.: Praeger, 2001), pp. 303–308; Newman, *Inauthentic Culture*, pp. 104–107, 177–182.
25. Alvin W. Gouldner, *Enter Plato: Classical Greece and the Origins of Social Theory* (New York: Basic Books, 1965), p. 194.
26. Pamela McCorduck, *The Universal Machine: Confessions of a Technological Optimist* (New York: McGraw-Hill, 1985), pp. 18–29. Cf. Newman, *Religion and Technology*, p. 56.
27. Walter Lippmann, *A Preface to Morals* (New York: Macmillan, 1929), esp. chap. 4.
28. Jay Newman, *Fanatics and Hypocrites* (Buffalo, N.Y.: Prometheus, 1986), esp. chap. 3.
29. Cf. Matthew 6:24.
30. Paul Tillich, *Dynamics of Faith* (New York: Harper and Row, 1957), p. 52.
31. McLuhan, *Understanding Media*, chap. 1.
32. Newman, *Inauthentic Culture*, chaps. 1–2.
33. Newman, *Inauthentic Culture*, pp. 68–72.

34. Newman, *Inauthentic Culture*, chaps. 1–2.

35. Ernst Cassirer, *An Essay on Man* (New York: Bantam Books, 1970; 1st ed. 1944), chap. 8.

36. Cassirer, *An Essay on Man*, pp. 65–67. Cf. R. G. Collingwood, *The New Leviathan, or, Man, Society, Civilization, and Barbarism*, ed. and intro. David Boucher (Oxford: Clarendon Press, 1992), chaps. 34–45.

37. Note, e.g., Rex Ingram's performance as De Lawd in *The Green Pastures* (Warner, 1936) and George Burns' turn as God in *O God!* (Warner, 1977).

38. The popular television series *The Simpsons* has received much attention in this regard.

39. Cf. Lippmann, *A Preface to Morals*, esp. chaps. 2–10.

# CHAPTER FIVE

# The West Against the Rest?

## A Buddhist Response to *The Clash of Civilizations*

DAVID R. LOY

> *The next world war, if there is one, will be a war between civilizations.*
> —Samuel S. Huntington, *The Clash of Civilizations?*
> *The Debate*

Has September 11 vindicated Samuel Huntington's claim in "The Clash of Civilizations" that the new battle lines today are the fault lines between the world's civilizations? Or is his argument becoming a self-fulfilling prophecy—because, for example, the U.S. response to 9/11 is deepening those fault lines?

The collapse of most communist states in 1989 and the end of the Cold War raised worldwide hopes that were short-lived. Francis Fukuyama claimed that we had reached "the end of history," but history did not seem to notice. Although neither the United States nor the Soviet Union needed to engage in proxy wars anymore, violent conflicts continued, even in the backyard of a paralyzed Europe that could not figure out how to respond to Yugoslavia's disintegration. Despite the preeminence of the United States, now unchallengeable as the only hyperpower, the world was not becoming any less messy. Other nations and peoples were not falling into line, not accepting their proper places in the *Pax Americana*. What was going on? What new description of the world could make sense of it all?

The Gulf War of 1991 gave a hint. Saddam Hussein is not much of a Muslim and Iraq is hardly an Islamic state, but the aggressive U.S. response to his attack against Kuwait aroused widespread support for his cause among other Muslim peoples (although less so among their more cautious governments). Few of them agreed that the sanctions afterwards imposed on Iraq, which caused widespread misery, including the deaths of over half a million Iraqi children, were "worth the cost," as U.S. Secretary of State Madeleine Albright famously put it. A civil war in eastern Europe had Christians fighting Muslims. In southern Asia there was more tension between Hindu India and Muslim Pakistan, and periodic battles in Kashmir. China, too, continued to be difficult, modernizing in its own way: a growing source of cheap labor, and occasionally a big market for Western products, but unwavering in its own political direction and suppression of all dissent.

## Samuel Huntington and "The Clash of Civilizations"

The penny dropped. When he wrote "The Clash of Civilizations," Samuel P. Huntington was the Eaton Professor of Government and Director of the Olin Institute for Strategic Studies at Harvard University. His now-famous (or infamous) essay was originally written for an Olin Institute project on "The Changing Security Environment and American National Interests," published in *Foreign Affairs* in 1993, and later expanded into a book. As this genesis suggests, what he offers us is not some impartial overview of global civilization but the postwar world as perceived by the U.S. foreign-policy elite—the "best and brightest" who previously gave us the Vietnam War and the "domino theory" that also rationalized U.S. support for Pinochet, the Shah of Iran, Marcos, Suharto, Mobutu, and many other dictators around the world. Huntington himself was a consultant for the State Department in 1967, when he wrote a long position paper that supported U.S. goals in Vietnam but criticized the military strategy for attaining them.

I mention this not to make an ad hominem attack on Huntington but to clarify the purpose of his essay: determining the new security needs of the United States in the post–Cold War world. This becomes apparent in its second half, which is more obviously concerned about defending "the values and interests of the West" against those of other civilizations. This national security subtext is not always explicit, yet it determines what Huntington sees and what he is unable to see.

What he sees is a new global paradigm that brings the new global mess into focus. The era of struggle between nation-states and rival ideologies is over. Democratic societies, in particular, do not go to war against each other. The new conflicts are between civilizations, which have different languages, histories, institutions, and—most important—different religions. Huntington lists seven or eight civilizations: Western, Confucian, Japanese, Islamic, Hindu, Slavic-Orthodox, Latin-American, "and possibly African."[1] We are told that the differences between them are more fundamental than the old differences between political regimes or ideologies. Huntington claims that increasing interaction among people of different civilizations is enhancing the historical "civilization-consciousness" of peoples in ways that "invigorate differences and animosities stretching or thought to stretch back deep into history."[2]

This challenges the common and more irenic perception that increasing contact tends to decrease tensions. Today, more than ever, people from different parts of the world not only buy each other's commodities but enjoy each other's music, films, and television shows, fashions and cuisines; when they have the opportunity, many are eager to travel to faraway countries, to meet other people, and occasionally even to intermarry. Is this growing contact and awareness increasing intercivilizational intolerance and strife or decreasing it? Or does that question miss the point because the effects of all this interaction are too complicated to generalize about in such a black-and-white way?

Civilizations, Huntington tells us, are the broadest level of cultural identity that people have, "short of that which distinguishes humans from other species."[3] Yet why such cultural differences should be emphasized more than our similarities as fellow humans is not immediately obvious, except perhaps for the unfortunate if widespread tendency to identify ourselves by distinguishing our own interests from those of some other "out group." This is no minor point, if the subtext of Huntington's argument—U.S. national security—itself exemplifies such an "in group" defending its own interests at the cost of others. United States relations with Latin America are an obvious example: history suggests that the Monroe Doctrine (1823) was promulgated not so much to protect Central and South American countries from European interference as to monopolize U.S. interference.

How are present global tensions viewed by those who are not part of the Western elite? What other perspectives are possible? Although a U.S. citizen, I have been living and traveling in Southeast Asia and East Asia since 1977; and although these regions are home to three or four of Huntington's civilizations, what I have been able to observe is something quite different from Huntington's clash between civilizations. While there are certainly clashes of values and interests, the predominant tensions are more readily understood as due to the efforts of a West "at the peak of its power"[4] to transform the rest of the globe in ways that suit the self-perceived interests of its own elites (especially U.S. corporate managers). From an Asian perspective, Western-led economic, political, technological, and cultural globalization is the main event of our times, and resistance to it is where the main fault lines have been forming.

Of course, globalization is not one development but a web of related processes, usually (although not always) augmenting each other. From this alternative perspective, the fissures that matter most today are not civilizational differences but the conflicting social forces promoting or challenging different aspects of globalization—resulting in various stresses, most obviously due to economic changes or pressures to change.

This is not a small point. Huntington's clash of civilizations assumes a pluralism of irreconcilable values and interests in the world, a perspective that paradoxically both implies value-relativism ("Since there is really no such thing as 'the best civilization'") and justifies Western ethnocentrism ("we should defend and promote our own values and interests"). If, however, the real issue is Western-sponsored globalization, then that globalization can and should be evaluated according to the ways it is changing societies, including Western ones.

For example, many of those who want more human rights and more consumer goods are also suspicious of the self-preoccupied individualism that seems to encourage social breakdown in so many developed countries (not all of them Western). Then the most important question becomes: who is entitled to decide which changes a society will embrace, and which to reject? The World Trade Organization? The International Monetary Fund? A West defending its own interests? Or the people most affected by those changes?

By no coincidence, the same fissures are deepening within the West as well. Huntington's West is more or less monolithic, yet if we do not focus so much on the differences between civilizations we can see the same tensions at home, especially in the United States. Internationally, globalization has been increasing the gap between rich and poor; the same thing is happening inside the United States, which now has more poor people than any other Western nation. Internationally, globalization is increasing corporate influence on governments, as well as corporate dominance of economies and natural resources; the same thing is happening in the United States. Internationally, an antiglobalization movement has sprung up to challenge these developments; a similar resistance has developed within the United States, the strongest domestic movement since the Vietnam War. Because the pressures of globalization tend to affect different civilizations in some similar ways, much the same tensions and ruptures are recurring within different civilizations.

### Religion and the "Clash of Civilizations"

One way to focus this point is by considering the role of religion in these struggles. Religion is crucial for Huntington. It is the most important way that civilizations differentiate themselves from each other. In his *Foreign Affairs* response to his critics, he claims that "in the modern world, religion is a central, perhaps the central force, that motivates and mobilizes people."[5] His original article quotes George Weigel—the "unsecularization of the world is one of the dominant social facts of life in the late twentieth century"—and emphasizes that this revival of religion serves as a basis for identity and commitment transcending nations and unifying civilizations.[6]

Religions unite civilizations by providing people with a common identity, which they are often willing to die and kill for. Religions are also the source and repository for our most cherished values—except perhaps in the modern West, where traditional religion has been losing a war of attrition with this-worldly values such as Enlightenment rationalism, secular nationalism, "moneytheism," and consumerism. For Huntington, the social scientist and foreign policy mandarin, what is most important about religion is that the identity it provides is irreconcilable with other religious identities. A Jew is a Jew, a Muslim is a Muslim, and ne'er the twain shall meet. That is why religious differences are at the heart of the civilizational clash.

Again, things look somewhat different from a perspective more sensitive to religious concerns than to "realist" foreign policy (i.e., nationalist) values. The struggle over globalization is, at its heart, not just a clash of identities but a clash of values: the different values that people of different cultures want to live by. To understand the contemporary conflicts that religions are involved in, we must also realize that modern Western culture does not really offer a secular alternative to religious values; rather, it offers this-worldly values that are still religious, in the most important sense of the term. Religion is notoriously difficult to define, yet if we understand it functionally—as teaching us what is really important about the world, and therefore how to live in it—modern identities such as secular nationalism and modern values such as consumerism are not so much alternatives to religion as *secular religions*. They offer this-worldly solutions to the problem of ultimate meaning in life: for example, patriotic identification with one's nation (a poor impersonal substitute for genuine community) or the promise of a more sensuous salvation in consumerism (the next thing I buy that will make me happy).

The Cold War victory of the West means that capitalism now reigns unchallenged and so has been able to remove its velvet gloves. Because capitalism evolved within a Christian culture, they have been able to make peace with each other, more or less, in the contemporary West. Christ's kingdom is not of this world, we should render to Caesar what is Caesar's, and as long as we go to church on Sunday we can devote the rest of the week to this-worldly pursuits. From more traditional religious perspectives, however, the values of globalizing capitalism appear more problematical.

Buddhism, for example, emphasizes that in order for us to become happy, our greed, ill will, and delusion must be transformed into generosity, compassion, and wisdom. Such a transformation is difficult to reconcile with an economic globalization that seems to encourage greed (producers never have enough profit, advertising ensures that consumers are never satisfied), ill will (a consequence of looking out for "number one"), and delusion (the world—our mother as well as our home—desacralized by commodifying everything into resources for buying and selling).

Buddhism provides other problems for Huntington's thesis, since it straddles the Indian, Chinese, and Japanese civilizations he identifies; and Buddhism is beginning to make significant inroads into the West as well, another phenomenon that does not quite fit into his paradigm of faults between civilizations. If religious identity provides the core of civilizations, why has Buddhism been so successful not only in India and other South Asian and Southeast Asian cultures, but also in China, Tibet, Korea, Japan, and so on? Why did many Chinese syncretically embrace Confucianism, Taoism, *and* Buddhism? Why do many Japanese celebrate birth at a Shinto shrine, wed with a Christian ceremony, and perform Buddhist funeral rites?

As the Buddhist example shows, it is too simple to say that tensions arise because of a clash of fissured, irreconcilable value systems, in which we need to focus on promoting our own. In the contemporary world all religions are under tremendous pressure to adapt to new circumstances, including new worldviews and new values, for globalization means that renegotiation with modern developments is constant. Fundamentalism—clinging to old verities and customs—is a common response, but the fact that some fundamentalists are willing to die and kill for their cause does not quite disguise the reality that the fundamentalist reaction to modernity is defensive, cramped, and in the long run untenable in a fast-shrinking world where all civilizations are increasingly interconnected.

This does not mean that religious beliefs and values are incompatible with globalization. It means that the tension between globalization and antiglobalization is in part an ongoing struggle between traditional religious concerns—most important, love of others and responsibility to something greater than our own individual egos—and the corrosive effects of a secular modernity that, when unchecked, tends to become nihilistic.

For either side to "win" this struggle would be disastrous. Traditional religions need the challenge of modernity to wake them from their dogmas and institutional sclerosis, to encourage them to ask again what is essential in their teachings and what is cultural baggage that can be shed. On the other side, the unrestrained dominance of corporate capitalism and its commodifying values would be catastrophic not only for human communities but for the entire biosphere.

## Islam and the "Clash of Civilizations"

The real test case for their negotiation is Islam. Huntington discusses many clashes between civilizations, and most of them involve Islam. "Islam has bloody borders."[7] Without Islam, it would be difficult for him to make his case; thanks to Islam, it is easy, since the Islamic world is having trouble getting along with any other world.

Or so it seems from a Western perspective. That perspective, however, is hardly an objective or a neutral one. For most of their histories, the Christian West and the Islamic world have been each other's chief rivals. At first Islam had the edge, culturally as well as militarily. Medieval Christian theology and philosophy were revived by the rediscovery of classical Greek texts preserved by Islamic scholars; European science developed on an Arabic foundation. That is part of Islam's burden today: in contrast to early Christianity, which had to endure centuries of Roman persecution, Islam was immediately triumphant, establishing a mythic legacy that makes eclipse (including colonial and now economic subordination) by the modern West all the more difficult to bear.

There are other ways in which Islam stands out from other missionary religions such as Christianity and Buddhism. Unlike Jesus and Shakyamuni, Muhammad was not only a spiritual teacher but a political and military leader, in ways that were usually quite progressive for his time. Some of them, however, have become more problematical as the world has changed. Because neither Jesus nor Shakyamuni provided a detailed political or economic program, it has been easier to adapt their teachings to radically different cultural conditions, including secular modernity. Today a Christian can pray in church on Sunday and more or less serve Mammon the rest of the week. A good Muslim prays five times a day and follows more than a few customs that were common in seventh-century Arabia, including studying and often memorizing the Koran in Arabic.

Partly as a result of these differences, Islam has remained more traditionalist than either Christianity or Buddhism. No religion is monolithic, and all major religions have deep fissures of their own, including an unavoidable one between more literal interpretations of scriptures and more flexible metaphorical readings. There have been rationalist movements in Islam, such as the Mutazilists in the ninth century and, more recently, many other attempts at modernist reform, yet they have generally been less successful than similar movements in Christianity and Buddhism. As a result, the contemporary image of Islam among most non-Muslims is of an extremely conservative, ritualistic, and literalistic faith. Among the major religions, Islam is having the most difficulty adjusting to the modern distinction between an enervated sacred sphere and a more dynamic secular sphere. There are also political problems due to the legacy of Western colonialism (including the imposition of a nation-state structure that evolved in Europe and has not often grafted well onto non-Western cultures) and economic problems due to the neocolonialism of Western-led globalization.

Yet there is another way to look at Muslim difficulties today. Of the world's missionary religions, Islam is the one most deeply concerned with social justice—and social justice is an increasingly important issue in the struggles over what kind of globalization we will have. That is the other side of Muhammad's legacy as a political leader as well as a spiritual one. This theme is missing in Huntington, but we cannot understand Islamic values and present concerns without it. That is why it is not enough simply to emphasize the fissure between Islam and the West, a clash between their values and ours. A demand for social justice has become essential in a world where, according to the United Nations Development Report for 1999, almost a billion people in seventy countries consume less today than they did twenty-five years ago; where the world's five hundred billionaires are worth more than the combined incomes of the poorest half of humanity (a gap that globalization is aggravating); where, as a result, a quarter of a million children die of malnutrition or infection every week, while hundreds of millions more survive in hunger and deteriorating health.

Allah is a merciful God, but He is also a God of justice and will judge us harshly if we do not accept personal and collective responsibility for the less fortunate. The third pillar of Islam is *zakat,* alms. *Zakat* is not so much charity as an essential expression of the compassion that all Muslims are called on to show to those who need it. Muslims believe that everything really belongs to God and that material things should be used as God wishes them to be used. This means not hoarding but sharing with others who need them. For example, the often-quoted *Surah* 102:1 of the Koran declares that "The mutual rivalry for piling up (the things of this world) diverts you (from more serious things)," and *Surah* 92:18 praises those who spend their wealth for increase in self-purification. That is why the capitalist idea of using capital to gain ever more capital—you can never have too much!—is foreign, even reprehensible, to many devout Muslims.

By adapting so well to the modern world of secular nationalism, capitalism, and consumerism, most Christians in the West have learned to finesse such concerns. The Bible tells us that the poor will always be among us, and in any case we must accept what the "social science" of economics tells us are laws of supply and demand, the importance of free trade, and so on. Admittedly, the main effect of transnational capitalism so far has been to make the rich richer, yet we must have faith that a rising tide of worldwide wealth will eventually lift all boats.

Islam is less willing to accept such equivocations, because it recognizes no God above Allah. The need to "have faith" that corporate globalization will eventually work to benefit almost everyone points to what is increasingly apparent: as Western culture has lost faith in any afterlife salvation, the West's economic system has also become its religion, because it now has to fulfill a religious function for us. Economics today is less a social science than the theology of that moneytheistic religion, and its god, the Market, and has become a vicious circle of ever-increasing production and consumption by promising us a this-worldly salvation. Western-led globalization means that the Market is becoming the first truly world religion, rapidly converting all corners of the globe to a worldview and set of values whose religious role we overlook only because they are not otherworldly.

Few people yet understand pro- versus antiglobalization struggles in such spiritual terms, but many instinctively feel what is at stake, in a way that Huntington does not. The clash of civilizations is a convenient paradigm for foreign-policy mandarins who take globalization for granted and who prefer to insulate the culture-specific values of different religions from each other. "Let them have their values, and we'll have ours!" For those who can see how the West is imposing new "religious" values on other civilizations in the economic guise of "free trade," Huntington's paradigm is a smokescreen that obscures more than it reveals about the ways the world is now groaning and travailing together.

## The "Clash of Civilizations" and Western Values

The issue of social justice also brings me to my final point: to a gaping fissure that runs right through the middle of Huntington's own essay. Although he concludes by calling on the West to develop a better appreciation of the religious and philosophical understandings of other civilizations, Huntington has more specific short-term recommendations for Western (read U.S.) foreign policy, including: to maintain Western military superiority, to exploit differences among Islamic and Confucian states (he is worried about a nascent Confucian–Islamic axis), to support non-Western groups that are "sympathetic to Western values and interests," and "to strengthen international institutions that reflect and legitimate Western interests and values."[8] Huntington the hard-headed realist has no illusions about a world community of civilizations, but his oft-repeated phrase "Western values and interests" deserves some attention for the way it elides one into the other.

In the only place where he identifies Western values, Huntington trots out the usual shibboleths: "individualism, liberalism, constitutionalism, human rights, equality, liberty, the rule of law, democracy, free markets, the separation of church and state"—which "often have little resonance" in other cultures. And what is the relationship between these Western *values* and Western *interests*? Huntington never addresses this uncomfortable question, perhaps because it is difficult to square these mostly commend-able ideals with the ways that the United States has actually treated other nations when its own short-term interests have been at stake.

The United States has supported constitutionalism, human rights, lib-erty, the rule of law, and democracy in other countries when those values have produced leaders amenable to our own national interests. Those same values evidently resonate less loudly for us when they produce leaders who have different ideas. In 1954, for example, the United States sponsored a coup against the democratically elected government of Guatemala, which over the following years led to the deaths of over one hundred thousand peasants. In 1965, the United States overthrew the government of the Dominican Republic and helped to kill some three thousand people in the process. In 1973, the United States sponsored a coup against the democratic government of Chile that murdered or "disappeared" several thousand people. In the 1980s, the United States sponsored a terrorist *contra* war against the government of Nicaragua, which led to the deaths of over thirty thousand innocent people and to a World Court declaration that the U.S. government was a war criminal for mining Nicaragua's harbors. Another U.S.-supported war in the 1980s against El Salvador resulted in the deaths of eighty thousand more innocent people. Lots of "collateral damage."

All those recent examples are from Latin America alone. Also in 1965, the United States sponsored or assisted a military coup in Indonesia that involved the deaths of over half a million people, leading to the military dic-tatorship of Suharto, who invited Western corporations back into the coun-try. When President Bush declares that Iran is part of a new "axis of evil," we should remember why many Iranians return the compliment, viewing the U.S. government as "the Great Satan." Why? When Western oil inter-ests were threatened, the CIA helped to sponsor a brutal coup that installed the widely detested Shah of Iran, whose notorious Savak secret service then proceeded to torture and kill over seventy thousand Iranians between 1952 and 1979.

Unfortunately, many more examples could be cited. Clearly, the prob-lem here is something more than not living up to our own ideals. Nor do we just keep making mistakes, such as innocently backing the wrong sort of people. Once can be a mistake, twice may be stupidity, but this pattern of repeated violations of our own self-declared values amounts to some-thing more sinister. "By their fruits shall you know them," as someone once put it. It is difficult to avoid the conclusion that our so-called values are not really our values, at least not when it comes to international relations. The basic problem is not a clash between our values and theirs, but between our (declared) values and our (short-term) interests.

Huntington admits that a world of clashing civilizations is inevitably a world of double standards,[9] but with such a clash between U.S. ideals and

U.S. interests, one need not look any further to understand why U.S. international goals so often meet resistance. Given how little most Americans know about the rest of the world, it is not surprising that other civilizations—on the receiving end of U.S. foreign policy—are more aware of this clash than we are. As long as our preeminent foreign policy value continues to be narrow and often brutal self-interest, we will not need a sophisticated new paradigm to explain why the new *Pax Americana* is not working.

Surely Huntington, a distinguished Ivy League professor of international relations, knows about these violations of the Western ideals he identifies. Why does he ignore such a gaping fissure between U.S. values and U.S. interests? Perhaps he regards such incidents as regrettable but unavoidable consequences of the Cold War, whereas the clash of civilizations is a post–Cold War paradigm. Yet such rationalizations won't do. If we were concerned with combatting communism in Latin America, we picked some of the worst ways to do it—ways that alienated many of the best people in those countries and made them more sympathetic to alternatives such as communism. No, the basic problem is that U.S. foreign policy has been more concerned with the best interests of the United Fruit Company, and so on, than with the best interests of Latin Americans.

And what about today? Even if we ignore recent military and more covert actions, in the year 2001 alone the United States refused to join 123 other nations in banning the use and production of antipersonnel bombs and mines (February); Bush declared the Kyoto global warming protocol "dead" and refused to participate in revising it, because that might harm the U.S. economy (March); the United States refused to participate in OECD-sponsored talks in Paris on ways to crack down on offshore tax and money-laundering havens (May); the United States was the only nation to oppose the U.N. Agreement to Curb the International Flow of Illicit Small Arms (July); and the United States withdrew from the landmark 1972 Antiballistic Missile Treaty, to the dismay of virtually every other country (December). In addition, the United States has not ratified the Comprehensive (Nuclear) Test Ban Treaty, signed by 164 nations but opposed by Bush; and the United States has rejected the Land Mine Treaty, concluded in Ottawa in December 1997 and signed by 122 countries, because the Pentagon finds land mines useful.

### Conclusion

Do these examples support a clash of civilizations or show that the United States is unwilling to work with other civilizations? As the only superpower, the United States cherishes its sovereignty because it wants to be free to do whatever it wants to do, regardless of what the rest of the world may think.

In that case, however, is the clash of civilizations a valid paradigm for understanding the world, or a self-fulfilling rationalization for self-serving behavior in the world?

Born and raised a U.S. citizen, I value most of the ideals that Huntington identifies as Western: liberalism, constitutionalism, human rights, equality, liberty, the rule of law, democracy, and so forth. As a convert to Buddhism—an intercivilizational religious traitor?—I also believe that a life lived in accordance with such ideals will nevertheless not be a happy one unless I also make efforts to transform my greed into generosity, my ill will into compassion, and my delusions into wisdom. Buddhism teaches me that this not only makes others happier but is even more important for my own happiness, because that is the only way to overcome the illusory duality between myself and other people.

Is the same also true collectively for the relations between peoples and cultures? If the answer is yes, there are immense consequences for United States relations with the rest of the world and for the Western relationship with other civilizations. Instead of dismissing such Buddhist ideals as foreign, by relativizing them as the attributes of an alien civilization, another option is to learn from them, and perhaps even assimilate some of them into our own culture, as China, Tibet, Korea, Japan, and other nations have done.

The rest of the world still has much to learn about such Western ideals as human rights, equality, liberty, the rule of law, and democracy; for that matter, so does the West. The West may also have much to gain from a more profound understanding of the basic religious and philosophical values underlying other civilizations—as Huntington perhaps implies in the last paragraph of his essay.

Any American who lives outside the United States for long cannot help but be reminded, repeatedly, how important the United States is for the rest of the world. It is not just that others enjoy our pop culture or crave our consumer goods. Most other nations look to the United States for international leadership, and they are repeatedly dismayed when a nation that is already by far the wealthiest and most powerful responds by promoting its own short-term interests at the cost of a larger good—and at the cost of its own long-term interests in an increasingly interdependent world. September 11 has shown us that this attitude is dangerous as well as selfish and arrogant.

### Notes

1. Samuel S. Huntington, *The Clash of Civilizations? The Debate* (New York: Foreign Affairs, 1996), p. 3.
2. Huntington, *The Clash of Civilizations*, p. 4.

3. Huntington, *The Clash of Civilizations*, p. 2.
4. Huntington, *The Clash of Civilizations*, p. 5.
5. Huntington, *The Clash of Civilizations*, p. 63.
6. Huntington, *The Clash of Civilizations*, p. 4.
7. Huntington, *The Clash of Civilizations*, p. 5.
8. Huntington, *The Clash of Civilizations*, pp. 24–25.
9. Huntington, *The Clash of Civilizations*, p. 13.

PART TWO

# Gods of War?

# CHAPTER SIX

# Terrorism

## Some Theological Reflections

### TIMOTHY GORRINGE

The words "terrorism" and "terrorist" entered the Western political vocabulary in the wake of the French revolution. Terrorism has a history, however, reaching back at least to the time of the Zealots in the time of Jesus, and to the Sicarii, or "knife men," whom one Roman commander took Paul to belong to (Acts 21.38). Crucifixion was a form of what today would be called counterterrorist practice, designed to repel terror by terror. That Christianity is organized around such a symbol ought at the very least to inform our understanding of this phenomenon.

In his *Reflections on the Revolution in France* Edmund Burke spoke of those "Thousands of Hell hounds called Terrorists . . . let loose upon the people." This has set the trend for reflection on terrorism ever since: terrorism is what those who are not in government, or those opposed to the status quo, do. In the past thirty years terrorism has even been identified with what non-Westerners do, as in Dobson and Payne's *Terror! The West Fights Back*,[1] Bruce Hoffman's *Inside Terrorism*, or even Adrian Guelke's more critical *The Age of Terrorism*.[2] Terrorism, we understand from the vast bulk of publications from experts on the subject, is something done by Communists, anarchists, and now by Muslims or separatists. Noam Chomsky is a lone voice in documenting what he calls *The Culture of Terrorism*, in a work not cited by either of these experts. Such understandings of terrorism run the risk of being self-serving and unself-critical justifications of Western, and especially of U.S., foreign policy.

## Defining Terrorism

After reviewing a number of accounts of terrorism that he considers inadequate, Hoffman gives his own definition as "the deliberate creation and
exploitation of fear through violence or the threat of violence in the pursuit
of political change." In his view terrorism has five hallmarks: it is
ineluctably political in aims and motives; violent; designed to have psychological repercussions beyond the immediate target; conducted by an organization with an identifiable chain of command or conspiratorial cell
structure; and perpetrated by a subnational group or nonstate entity.[3] This
account seems too tightly framed. The anarchist bombings of the 1890s, for
example, which were the theme of Conrad's *The Secret Agent*, expressed a
hatred of bourgeois society as a whole but were probably not motivated by
any clear idea of how political change might be effected, or what the desir-
able alternative might be. This seems to be true of the September 11 attacks:
they expressed hatred of the United States and its global pretensions; they
showed that the United States was not invulnerable. Beyond that, there
seems to have been very little clear idea of political change behind them.
Tying terrorism so tightly to political change invests it with a rationale it
may often not be worthy of. In our world, as in Conrad's, there is a
romance of the bomb and the gun that may take either criminal or terrorist forms. There is, as Robin Morgan argues, a sexuality of terrorism, which
finds a thrill, an erotic justification, in destruction and mayhem.[4] At the
same time, the two last elements of Hoffman's hallmarks of terrorism, in
putting it by definition beyond the realm of the state, leave us without a
vocabulary to discuss the vast majority of uses of terror in the twentieth
century. Hitler, Stalin, and Pol Pot are usually agreed to have worked
through terror, and the Latin American regimes supported by the United
States during the 1970s and 1980s, responsible for at least two hundred
thousand deaths, were similarly terrorist states. Lurking in the background
seems to be Weber's idea that the state is, by definition, that body that has
a monopoly on legitimate force. But because all power corrupts, all states,
even those most committed to democracy, are tempted to transgress the
legitimate means of democratic change—education, discussion, and debate.
In Britain, for example, the antinuclear campaigner Hilda Murrell was murdered, most probably by the state security forces, and the use of these forces
to assassinate opponents in Northern Ireland is well established. Under the
Reagan doctrine, wrote Chomsky of Nicaragua, "the United States has created something new in the annals of international terrorism: a lavishly
equipped army organized not for combat but for terror. . . . This achievement stands alongside the creation of a terrorist army dedicated to sup-
pressing the population by massive violence in El Salvador."[5] "Throughout

the world," said an Amnesty International Report in 1996, "on any given day, a man, woman or child is likely to be displaced, tortured, killed, or 'disappeared,' at the hands of governments or armed political groups. More often than not, the United States is to blame."[6] One can see the point of the distinction between terrorism and state terror, but unless we read them together we end up with a distorted understanding of our times. To refuse to speak of state terrorism except in connection with those states, like Libya, Iran, or Iraq, which supposedly sponsor terrorism, seems pedantic and, incidentally, helps explain the incomprehension that greeted the September 11 attacks.[7] It also deeply skews any understanding of what is happening in Palestine. I will define terrorism, therefore, as the use of violence by individuals, groups, or the state, to intimidate, to cause havoc, often but not always for political ends.

### Can Terrorism Be a Form of Just War?

Over the past thirty years we have got used to the cliché that one person's terrorist is another person's freedom fighter. Bruce Hoffman cites the spiritual leader of a Lebanese terrorist group who protests: "We don't see ourselves as terrorists because we don't believe in terrorism. We don't see resisting the occupier as a terrorist action. We see ourselves as *mujihadeen* who fight a Holy War for the people."[8] Similarly, both the Israeli *Irgun*, to which Ariel Sharon belonged, and Yasser Arafat deny that they are or were terrorists, though both have bombed and murdered. In their view they fight a just war against an oppressor. Before we dismiss this out of hand as specious let us recall that the Stauffenberg plot to assassinate Hitler in July 1944, in which Bonhoeffer was implicated, and for which he died, worked through planting a bomb, a normal terrorist tactic, and was treated as terrorism by the Nazi authorities. The Church now regards Bonhoeffer as a martyr—the same word used by the Hamas suicide bombers. Calvin, in the *Institutes*, allowed, with many hesitations and safeguards, that it might be right to assassinate a tyrant. Of course, there is an important strand of Christian reflection, stemming from Jesus himself, which argues that violence is self-defeating. I shall myself endorse that view. By and large, however, the Church has regarded this as a counsel of perfection and instead framed rules for what it has called a just war. So distinguished and radical a theologian as Karl Barth took something like this view with regard to the opposition to Hitler. Could it be applied to terrorism, understood, in another cliché of the past thirty years, as one of the "weapons of the weak"? Illegitimate states, it is argued, have the massive resources needed to support armies, air forces, and so on, and they use them mercilessly. To resist them the only alternative is to resort to terrorist tactics: good examples would be either the *Irgun* campaign against the British or the "battle of Algiers" waged against the government of France. In both cases these were successful to the extent that both the British Mandate and French colonial rule were ended relatively quickly.

Let us consider them in the light of the various criteria of the just war argument. This distinguished between reasons for engaging in conflict in the first place and then criteria for conduct in the course of the conflict. Those for engaging in conflict (*"jus ad bellum"*) were sixfold and went as follows:

1. There must be legitimate authority to wage war.
2. There must be a Just Cause.
3. The war must be motivated by Right Intention—the achievement of freedom, for instance, rather than simply amassing spoils of war.
4. It must be an act of Last Resort, after all attempts at negotiation were over.
5. It must have a reasonable hope of success.
6. It must have a reasonable expectation of doing more good than harm.

I shall compare the Israeli and Algerian examples with the bombing campaign of the Irish Republican Army (IRA) and September 11, looking also at the struggle of the African National Congress (ANC) in South Africa and the current wave of suicide bombings in Israel.

The first criterion is perhaps the most problematic for any terrorist struggle. When a government is in power, who is to define struggle against it as legitimate? Notoriously, the German Lutheran Church (*die Evangelische Kirche*) even found this a difficult issue in regard to Nazism. In the case of the British Mandate, this was originally vested by the League of Nations and therefore had the authority of an international body. Such authority, like that of the United Nations, is that of the "community of nations," but it is often not accepted—not least by the United States or Israel.[9] The authority of the United Nations is a form of democratic authority, although the veto enjoyed by some of the most powerful players calls the reality of democracy into question. When the Just War criteria were elaborated, of course, democracy was nothing but a faint historical record in the annals of Greece, and Aristotle's view that it was the worst form of government was taken as read. "Authority," in the Middle Ages, might be a papal command or the command of a prince or bishop, both speaking, as mullahs sometimes do today, as interpreters of the word of God. Legitimate authority, then, refers to ways of understanding God's command, which, in most religious traditions, will be through a mixture of reference to texts ("Scripture") and to the ongoing commentaries and discussion that constitute case law or tradition. Since the seventeenth century, however, and the reflections of Hobbes and Locke in the light of the English Civil War, it has been taken for granted that authority lies with "the people." This, too, is problematic. At any given historical moment it is likely that the majority of people in any population will be preoccupied with getting and spending, "the dull compulsion of the quotidian." In the Indian struggle against British imperialism it is probable that at no time were the bulk of the population resolutely committed to the freedom struggle. That struggle required conscientization by Gandhi and other activists, who spoke on behalf of the people. As we all know, discussion in homes, pubs, and clubs will often be deeply skeptical about the pretensions of such "tribunes of the people"—this applied even to Gandhi in his lifetime. Does this skepticism mean that the struggle is not justified? Since Fanon and Freire we have gotten used to the idea that people internalize their oppression and that education for conscientization is needed to make them aware of it. Consciousness-raising was a major part of the most important cultural movement of the twentieth century, second-wave feminism. It seems necessarily to involve the notion of vanguardism, made dubious for us by its association with Lenin and everything that followed in Russia. Any vanguard knows what the mass of the population do not know: that they are oppressed and in need of freedom. The source of this knowledge cannot be dismissed, as liberation theology sometimes unthinkingly does, as greater suffering and greater oppression. For as Freire shows, precisely this can be the cause of loss of a sense of bondage. It can induce a fatalism that believes nothing can be changed. It rests, then, on greater thought or on revelation: we are back to the medieval justifications for struggle. Many twentieth-century struggles, we know, look back through however many detours to Hegel's discussions of freedom. This was true of Lenin, and let us not forget that the Russian Revolution began (in 1905) with terrorism. At its root, then, is a philosophical conviction that human beings are made for freedom. Biblically we know that the exodus from slavery, the call to freedom, is the leitmotif of the whole scriptural narrative.

Let us consider this in relation to our specific examples. In the case of the *Irgun* in 1948 there was quite a unique emergency behind their actions—namely, the Holocaust. Though Zionism long predates that, and though the Mandate was set up when Hitler was nothing more than a (highly decorated) corporal, it was the "never again!" that was the moral mandate for *Irgun*'s atrocities. British actions in impounding or even turning back ships full of refugees take on an obvious horror in the light of what had happened, though in the view of the colonial administrators it could be argued that what they wanted to prevent was something like the present situation emerging. Nevertheless, with the Balfour Declaration in the background, it might be said that the authority behind *Irgun's* terrorism was that of desperation, of those with nowhere else to go, and moreover with a clear international commitment to appeal to.

None of this was the case with the FLN in Algeria, a struggle especially important for providing a role model for Yasser Arafat and the PLO. Their theorist, Abane, thought of terrorist bombs as "the poor man's air force" and quite deliberately targeted cafes and civilian centers, as Hamas is currently doing in Israel. For Abane this was no different from the aerial bombardment that had become a standard form of warfare since 1940, or perhaps even since Guernica. The bombing campaign was defeated by the ruthless tactics of the French army, which included systematic torture of all suspects. Ironically, this was the seed of ultimate French defeat. As Hoffman comments: "The brutality of the army's campaign . . . completely alienated the native Algerian Muslim community. Hitherto mostly passive, or apathetic, it was now driven into the arms of the FLN . . . increasing its popular support. Domestic public opinion in France was similarly outraged."10 What, however, of the authority for the FLN struggle? Abane was, like Fanon, an intellectual, and both of them believed in freedom as fundamental to human dignity and in self-determination as necessary to freedom. Of course, Gandhi shared something like the same view, but believed, more realistically (as I will argue), that it could only be achieved by nonviolence. We see clearly from the FLN both the role the vanguard plays (conscientization was only brought about by French terror) and the role of philosophical justification in the authority to engage in violence.

More problematic still is the bombing campaign of the Provisional IRA, still, according to Chomsky, not listed as a terrorist organization by the U.S. State Department.11 The rhetoric of the IRA was both socialist and anti-imperialist. In the name of a freedom struggle it carried out a bombing campaign both in Northern Ireland and on the British mainland that included, as with the Algerian bombings, pubs and clubs. The organization was funded in part by the Irish American lobby through NORAID, and indeed it is only the events of September 11 that have led Sinn Fein, in view of altered perceptions of terrorism in the United States, to "apologize" for civilian casualties in the campaign. Prior to that both Martin McGuiness and Gerry Adams have resolutely refused to condemn them. The problem with the legitimacy of the IRA campaign is the complication of the seventeenth-century Irish settlement. Ireland was settled with Protestants in that century to prevent its becoming a potential fifth column within the British state. Following the defeat of James II at the Battle of the Boyne, Protestant concentration in Ulster was particularly increased. The Irish freedom struggle that began in 1916—which, like the Algerian struggle, gained popular support because of the brutality of British response—culminated in a situation in which the overwhelming Protestant majority in the north opted to remain part of the United Kingdom. The object of the IRA was to complete the job of the liberation of Ireland from British rule, against the wishes of this rump of Unionists in the north. Demographics are changing the situation of which section of the community is the majority. But Sinn Fein is still far from able to win an outright democratic mandate for its policy of reunification. Given this difficulty, and in the face of the use of force from both an overwhelmingly Protestant police force and the British army, the IRA resorted to bombings, using tactics identical to those of Abane. Given the strength of the Unionist population in the north, and their clear political will not to live in a united Ireland, justifications in terms of freedom for self-determination cannot be applied in the same way. The authority for the IRA rested on a set of revolutionary doctrines indifferent to the actual situation of the population. The romance of the bomb and the gun—together with the romance of a history of Ireland that refused to come to terms with the fact of the Settlement having produced what is, in its own way, a distinctive version of Irish culture—took the place of such justifications.

The September 11 attacks are different again. Whether or not these were masterminded by the Taliban or al-Qaeda, it seems that the authority for the attacks must have been religious, expressing a widespread judgment on what is seen to be a corrupt and immoral West and its centers of power.[12] I will discuss this further under the heading of "religious terrorism" and the corrupting power of violence. Here it suffices to note that freedom and self-determination, the central ethical motive for terrorism in the twentieth century, are not the issue.

The two next criteria of just war theory—just cause and right intention—are obviously related to the issue of authority. Among my examples, the *Irgun* and the FLN, but also the PLO, have most by way of a just cause. In terms of right intention, the September 11 attackers have the least, followed by the IRA.

Very few terrorists bother to invoke the criterion of last resort. Famously, Nelson Mandela did so in his trial, arguing that every attempt at suasion had failed. All the other groups we have considered, with the exception of the September 11 attackers, who form a special case, adopted this line; they considered violence as the necessary precursor to discussion, a way of softening the enemy up, or getting them to pay attention.[13]

The last two criteria speak of doing more good than harm and of having a reasonable prospect of success. Freedom movements that achieve their aims show that they have the latter. The question of doing more good than harm is much more difficult to evaluate. On the one hand, memories of defeats and injustices can rankle for centuries and fester into profound sores, as in Bosnia or Northern Ireland; on the other hand, in many societies memory fades quickly. For all the contemporary interest in World War I the horror of it is not felt as it was by the generation that went through it. In Britain the Birmingham bombings of 1974 are not an issue of current reflection. Terrorists of the Abane variety might measure the loss of a few hundred lives against the achievement of freedom and consider this cheap at the price. On the other hand, the disintegration of Algerian society in the past decade may owe something to the avowal of violence thirty-five years ago. I return to this question later.

After the discussion of reasons for going to war, the medieval ethicists set out two broad criteria for behavior in war (*jus in bello*). These were noncombatant immunity and proportionality. Violence inflicted had to be proportional to the goods achieved. Of course, these criteria were elaborated in respect to atrocities in the first place and were never properly followed. Nevertheless, they represented an attempt to regulate conflict in a way that anticipates the Geneva conventions.[14] As we have seen, most terrorist groups disregard the idea of noncombatant immunity, perhaps in the light of the change in warfare initiated by Fascist Spain and Germany but most terribly at Hiroshima and Nagasaki. Terrorists have simply followed this general logic. Douglas Lummis makes this point very effectively. Speaking of the Gulf War of 1991 he wrote:

> Air bombardment is state terrorism, the terrorism of the rich. It has burned up and blasted apart more innocents in the past six decades than have all the antistate terrorists who ever lived. Something has benumbed our consciousness against this reality. In the United States we would not consider for the presidency a man who had once thrown a bomb into a crowded restaurant, but we are happy to elect a man who once dropped bombs from airplanes that destroyed not only restaurants but the buildings that contained them and the neighbourhoods that surrounded them.[15]

Air bombardment raises the question of proportionality still more starkly than conventional terrorism.

Violence has been used as a deterrent by the state at least since Roman times, and probably much earlier. To that extent it may be said to have been vested with an educational purpose. Hoffman points to the writings of the Italian revolutionary Carlo Pisacane as arguing that violence was a proper form of education, drawing attention to a cause and rallying support.[16] The Russian revolutionaries at the end of the nineteenth century were scrupulous about using violence only against high-profile figures like the Tsar and shedding "not one drop of superfluous blood."[17] It was Lenin, however, who urged the use of mass terror to push through the revolution, a tactic in which he was followed first by the Fascists and then by one military regime after another in the wake of World War II. The understanding of violence as a didactic tool is part and parcel of the understanding of war as a means to an end, and in this respect does not differ from it.

Let me conclude this section: can terrorism, as conventionally under-stood as the work of small disaffected groups, be regarded as a form of just war? My answer is that it is no different than wars undertaken by the state in this regard. That is, there are wars undertaken by states that are, as the new Anglican Archbishop described the proposal to bomb Iraq, "illegal and immoral," and there are wars, of which the attempt to defeat Hitler is the paradigm, that may be considered necessary evils. I will argue that terror-ism is never the most effective way to conduct a freedom struggle, but, if we are to allow the criteria of just war, then, as Nelson Mandela argued, "ter-rorism" may be the description by an illegal state of the attempt to attain that freedom. If it is objected that its targets are random and often civilian, then, as Lummis points out, just so is this the case in all modern warfare.

I turn now to the question of religiously motivated terrorism.

### Religiously Motivated Terrorism

"Religion," wrote Burke of the violence of the French revolution, "morals, laws, prerogatives, privileges, liberties, rights of men, are the *pretexts*. The pretexts are always found in some specious appearance of a real good."[18] Common sense tells us this is so, but there is much evidence that religion may rather be a direct cause of violence. Bruce Hoffman cites the young Jewish extremist who assassinated Yitzak Rabin "on orders from God," Hamas and other Muslim groups, the Aum Shinrikyo sect in Japan, and the American Christian Patriots. Some of the American religious right believe that "the righteous" "are called by God's law to exercise a holy 'violence' against certain of the wicked, thereby manifesting God's wrath."[19] Perhaps we could add to these instances the various Ulster Protestant terrorist groups, which seem to be closer to their own version of Christianity than the IRA are to theirs. As Hoffman points out, the progenitors of this kind of terrorism were the Zealots, among whom Judas Iscariot may have been one. Following David Rapoport, he argues that religion was the only justi-fication for terrorism until the nineteenth century.[20] For the religious ter-rorist violence is a sacramental act or duty. He goes on: "Terrorism thus assumes a transcendental dimension, and its perpetrators are consequently unconstrained by the political, moral or practical constraints that may affect other terrorists."[21] Religiously motivated terrorists, he believes, may engage in larger-scale killing than others. Empirically this claim seems questionable, especially if we consider Lummis' "terrorism of the rich" as part of the picture. What distinguishes religiously motivated terrorism is twofold. First, there is often a connection between territory and God's command—whether it is Southern Africa, gifted by God to the Boers, greater Serbia, or greater Israel. Yigal Amir assassinated Rabin because he believed Rabin was compromising God's plan for greater Israel, and the Torah commanded death for such a person. Orthodox settlements on the West Bank roundly identified with the assassin.[22] Second, what we are seeing in the Muslim suicide missions at the moment is that a belief in a martyr's crown can make a person supremely indifferent to life here on earth. It needs to be emphasized that this is not a peculiarity of Islam. We find it in the Maccabean struggle and in zealotry. It was part of crusading ideology (though most crusading reality was a much more cynical affair), and secular ideologies beget their own indifference to death by making history transcendent.

Theologically, there are two points to be made in relation to the whole question of such terrorism. First, it is part of the dehumanizing side of religion that Karl Barth set out in words of fire in his two commentaries on St. Paul's Letter to the Romans, and which Bonhoeffer then developed a little in his prison letters. A German Jesuit of my acquaintance once remarked that the most important political text in Scripture was 1 Pt 5.8: "Be on your guard, for your adversary the Devil roams about, seeking whom he may devour." He applied this to his experience in the thirties in Germany, but we can equally apply it to the corrupting power of religious absolutism. If God is *for* us, then anyone who is against us is also against God—unless we have a self-critique, or a critique of power, or of the difference between faith and religious knowledge, or all three. Because religious knowledge, and the power it confers, is so absolute, it is the most deeply corrupting of all. The old flogging line used to be: *castigo te, non sed odio, sed te amo*: (I beat you not because I hate you but because I love you). Some such sentiment underlay the burning of heretics in the Middle Ages. It is true that there are alienating forms of love: we do need to reprove, discipline, and punish in human relations and human society, but as Barth spelled out in his profound reflections on education, we do so only as those under the same schooling, in the same school of discipleship.[23] Alienating forms of love, however, do not extend to murder and maiming. As soon as we are sure that we and God are on one side—and Satan and those with whom we disagree on the other—the Devil (to use the terms of the letter of Peter) has us in his clutches.[24] Absolute belief in the rightness of our cause, of which identity between our cause and the cause of God is the ultimate symbolic expression, accounts for the supreme disregard for the lives of those not directly involved in the conflict symbolized particularly dramatically by the hijacking of the airliners on September 11. At the same time, such belief characterizes all terrorism: it was a hallmark of the IRA campaign, which was in no sense religious, and it characterizes the "counterterrorist" agency of Massu in Algeria and that of the death squads in Latin America.

This brings us back to Burke: religiously motivated terrorism clothes fanaticism in the stolen robes of faith. It is an example of what Kosuke Koyama calls false center symbolism, a kind of idolatry that puts my ego, in the guise of my faith, my creed, or my country, at the center of things and pushes others beyond the margins.[25] Theologically, then, we have to characterize terrorism as a product of idolatry. It is a hallmark of idols (as opposed to the God of life) that they kill people. Where "God" means death for those who do not agree, we know we are in the presence of idols.

Second, we have to learn from Walter Wink about the ancient connection between religion and violence. As Wink points out, the Babylonian Marduk epic was a story of redemption through violence, and he shows how this continues to the present day. He describes the myth of redemptive violence as the true religion of the United States.[26] The Christian scriptures are full of violence, and South American Indians have reminded us that they read the story of Exodus from the Canaanite point of view. Their ancestors were the Amalekites: those whom the god YHWH put under the ban, requiring genocide, according to the terrible story in 1 Sm 15. On these grounds Charles Raven, when Professor of Theology at Cambridge, advocated that the Church abandon the Old Testament as an unchristian book. Here, apart from manifesting the kind of ignorance for which Protestants are notorious about the way in which tradition functions, Raven was being naive, for much Christian doctrine has internalized violence, as René Girard has above all helped us to see. The idea that God redeems us by requiring the death of God's Son has—despite oceans of theological ink insisting that Christ's death is a gracious gift, one for all and once for all—always underwritten the idea that violent death is the response to sin. "The non-violent God of Jesus comes to be depicted as a God of unequalled violence, since God not only allegedly demands the blood of the victim who is closest and most precious to him, but also holds the whole of humanity accountable for a death that God both anticipated and required."[27] When we hear Ian Paisley preach we hear the rhetoric that inspires the Ulster Defence Force. The song writer Leon Rosselson concludes his great song, 'Stand Up for Judas": "Two thousand cruel years have shown the way that Jesus led." The Church has a long way to go before facing up to its own inner violence. We are only just beginning to realize that, as Wink puts it, "the God whom Jesus reveals refrains from all forms of reprisal and demands no victims.

God does not endorse holy wars or just wars or religions of violence. Only by being driven out by violence could God signal to humanity that the divine is non-violent and is antithetical to the Kingdom of Violence."[28]

## The Psychology of Terror

The English word "terror" comes directly from the Latin, and terror, in the Roman empire, was part of policy. It was used to maintain the *pax Romana*. A key instrument of this policy was crucifixion: both Cicero and Livy speak of the *terror crucis*. Crucifixion was the punishment for slaves and rebels because savagery was necessary to prevent the social fabric from disintegrating, to keep slaves in their place. It was a punishment, says Martin Hengel, in which the caprice and sadism of the executioners were given full rein. He quotes Josephus' account of the Jewish war: "The soldiers, out of rage and hatred they bore the prisoners, nailed those they caught, in different postures, to the cross by way of jest, and their number was so great that there was not enough room for the crosses and not enough crosses for the bodies."[29] Fear of the threat of danger from slaves aroused hate and cruelty that found expression in the use of crucifixion, which was supposed to be a supremely effective deterrent.[30] Not only that, however, but it satisfied the primitive lust for revenge and the sadistic cruelty of individual rulers and of the masses. Hengel makes connections with the present day:

> Crucifixion is thus a specific expression of the inhumanity dormant within men which these days is expressed, for example, in the call for the death penalty. . . . It is a manifestation of transsubjective evil, a form of execution which manifests the demonic character of human cruelty and bestiality. . . . This form of execution, more than any other, had associations with the idea of human sacrifice, which was never completely suppressed in antiquity. The sacrifice of countless hordes of people in our century to national idols or to "correct" political views show that the irrational demand for human sacrifice can be found even today.[31]

We cannot read these words, I believe, without thinking of the demonic tortures used by the military governments of Videla, Pinochet, Duarte, and many others in Latin America, in which people were sawn apart by electric saws, had their tongues cut out, eyes gouged, electric torture applied to their genitals, and so on and so forth, all in the name of protecting freedom and democracy.[32] Wink speaks of a spirituality of violence as characterizing our age. He suggests that redemptive violence gives way to violence as an end in itself, "a religion in which violence has become the ultimate concern, an elixir, sheer titillation, an addictive high, a substitute for relationships."[33] To return to Burke's suggestion that religion is primarily a pretext, I believe that, behind the undoubted belief of the suicide bombers, there lies also a love affair with death, violence as elixir. The romanticization of terrorist martyrdom argues this to be the case.

Contrary to Hoffman's exclusive emphasis on the political motivation of the use of terror, therefore, I believe we have to follow Hengel and seek to understand the sadism, hatred, and cruelty involved in it, whether administered by state security forces, armies, or the small cells Hoffman acknowledges as terrorists. Terror in any form is indifferent to the value of human life. This may be because the cause is supposed to override such value. But also involved, as Hengel and Wink help us to see, is cruelty toward—and a wish to obliterate—our repressed other. The terrorist sees in the other the one he or she cannot acknowledge as fully human without questioning his or her whole moral universe. The "other" must then be dirt, filth, subhuman, so that it does not matter if they are blown apart, crucified, sawn up, mutilated. There is an analogy, I believe, between terrorism and torture; and, as we know, the two are often mutually implicated. As William Cavanaugh has argued, the purpose of torture is not to obtain information but to manifest "the other" as filth. He cites Admiral Merino, a member of the Chilean Junta, justifying repression by referring to Marxists as "humanoids."[34] Exactly the same applies to the al-Qaeda suspects, held without trial in Guantanamo Bay, or to Israel's vision of Hamas, or of Hamas' vision of Israel. "Resistance to evil . . . constellates in our own depths whatever is similar to the outer evil we oppose. Our very resistance feeds the inner shadow. The very shrillness of our opposition may indicate that a part of us secretly desires to emulate what we oppose."[35]

The Genesis narrator's commentary on the growth of urban civilization, which followed hard on the expulsion from Eden and the first murder, was that "the earth was corrupt and full of violence" (Gn 6.11). On the most radical estimates this perception of the connection between violence and the corruption of culture goes back more than two and a half millennia. Violence corrupts. It not only destroys lives but destroys cultures, communities, and souls. It does this, as Wink argues, by turning us into the people we hate. "Since our hate is usually a direct response to an evil done to us, our hate almost invariably causes us to respond in the terms already laid down by the enemy. Unaware of what is happening, we turn into the very thing we oppose." We see this in the racism and militarism that have taken shape in Israel, and in the way an Algeria formed through violence has now collapsed into it. It is worth pausing and asking how this applies, or will apply, to those groups, which we now call collectively al-Qaeda, in relation to United States culture, or to Muslim critics of British culture. The shrillness of their denunciations evidences their fascination, and we can recall Brian Keenan's account of his four-and-a-half-year captivity in Lebanon, in which, he says, his kidnappers were obsessed by ideas of Western promiscuity, an obsession that was lust by default.[36] By the same token, as spokesmen in the United States and Britain came out with the conventional Marduk theology of the war of good against evil after September 11 we can recall Chomsky's words, written over a decade earlier, that "the United States is a lawless and violent state and must remain so, independently of such nonsense as international law, the World Court, the United Nations, or other international institutions."[37] We become what we hate, and this law destroys us.

Sadism and religion easily go together, but it goes without saying that they should not be simply identified. I wish to argue that what Hengel calls the "manifestation of trans-subjective evil," the surrender of human beings to cruelty and sadism, is involved even in religiously motivated terrorism and that there is no terrorism completely without it. Terrorism means an intent to cause terror—fear, panic, dismay, dread (the meanings of the Latin word)—by setting aside the normal means of human decency. It is, in other words, a form of lust. Even in the asceticism of suicide-bombing there is not the purity of religious intention but the lust for destruction of "the other." Terror, therefore—in which I include many forms of war urged by the state—is a pathology. Is there an alternative?

### Nonviolent Militancy

Part of the current tragedy of the Palestinian situation is the political stupidity of both sides in the conflict, fuelled by religion in each case. Had the Palestinians adopted Gandhian methods thirty years ago there is little doubt that Israel would be out of the West Bank by now. Israel, in turn, adopts no response other than ratcheting up the violence, while both sides adopt the nauseous "terrorist speak" perfected by the IRA, of refusing to condemn the violence of their own side while blaming the other. In his important study of the relation between religion and atrocity, *Unholy Alliance*, Marc Ellis records how Martin Buber argued with Ben Gurion for a binational state on the Swiss model, invoking the most ancient of Jewish arguments: "You too were strangers in the land of Egypt." Nothing more perfectly illustrates the corruption effected by violence than the Palestinian situation. The binational model, also advocated by Hannah Arendt, and a model that is certain to become increasingly common in a multicultural world, cannot be heard. This is because one lesson of the Holocaust has seemed to be that violence must be met by violence. Like the biblical Joseph, Martin Buber has been rejected by his brethren as "that dreamer." Richard Rubenstein once argued that the Holocaust teaches that those who lack the power to defend themselves must be prepared for any obscenity to be inflicted on them. Thus, he spoke of Buber as a man whose "thought had so little relevance to the concrete experience of his own time and people that it was of no continuing relevance."[38] Neither of the participants in this struggle could be expected to look to Christianity for inspiration, but it is tragic that they have been unable to look further East to learn from a man who, like Rabin, was assassinated by a co-religionist for trying to make peace with Muslims, Mahatma Gandhi. In contemporary Muslim writing *jihad* is often described as primarily inner struggle; but there is, alas, very little evidence of a widespread understanding of that sense of the word. The group that calls itself Islamic Jihad is, on the contrary, committed to terrorism. What Gandhi learned from the Christ of the Beatitudes, and from Tolstoy, and then lived out in a way Tolstoy never could have done, is that violence is always counterproductive; it always destroys itself, but that the alternative is not passive compliance with what is happening. On the contrary, *satyagraha* was militant and steely action for the truth, thought conducted by peaceful means. As Wink puts it, in terms of the Gospel, "Turning the cheek, stripping naked, carrying the soldier's pack the second mile do not at all mean acquiescing passively to evil . . . but a studied and deliberate way of seizing the initiative and overthrowing evil by the force of its own momentum . . . . What Jesus distilled from the long experience of his people in violent and nonviolent resistance was a way of opposing evil without becoming evil in the process."[39] Far from being unrealistic, it is, in fact, the only form of realism, the only practical form of policy that does not end in self-destruction. It is the ultimate practical politics.

Freedom fighters or terrorists? I have argued that the medieval understanding of just war could be applied to some terrorist activity but that all violence, whether of the state or of terrorist cells, ultimately destroys us. "Do not fear those who can kill the body but not the soul," says Jesus. "Fear those who can kill both body and soul in hell"(Mt 10.28). "Hell" is the creation of the culture of violence. Terrorist violence, whether of the CIA or of al-Qaeda, is to be deprecated—not just because all violence is pathological, but because it finally rots the foundations of any culture. No culture is immune from this rule. The story of the flood, beginning with the perception that the earth was corrupt and full of violence, is a mythic expression of the need for a new start founded on principles of peace rather than of demonization and hatred. The people who wrote it knew that the first terrorist states—Sumer, Ur—were literally dead and buried. They

consistently predicted the same for the terrorist states of their own day—
Assyria and Babylon, and later Rome. And they were right. Can we learn
from them? It is bad news for us if we cannot, for the lessons they taught
still hold.

## Notes

1. C. Dobson and R. Payne, *Terror! The West Fights Back* (London: Macmillan, 1982).
2. B. Hoffman, *Inside Terrorism* (New York: Columbia University Press, 1998); A Guelke, *The Age of Terrorism and the International Political System* (London: Tauris, 1998). This is unfortunately also true of George Weigel's repristination of Just War theory after September 11, unaware that "mass murder for evil political ends" has ever been perpetrated by Western governments. "The Just War Tradition and the World after September 11th," *Logos* 5, no. 3 (2002): 13-43.
3. Hoffman, *Inside Terrorism*, p. 43.
4. R. Morgan, *The Demon Lover: On the Sexuality of Terrorism* (London: Methuen, 1989).
5. N. Chomsky, *The Culture of Terrorism* (London: Pluto, 1989), p. 43.
6. Washington Office of Amnesty International, *Human Rights and US Security Assistance* (Washington, D.C.: Office of Amnesty International, 1996), p. 1.
7. Hoffman argues that terrorism sponsored by Iran, Iraq, and so on constitutes a kind of covert or surrogate warfare "whereby weaker states could confront larger, more powerful rivals without the risk of retribution" (*Inside Terrorism*, p. 27). The argument of Chomsky and Blum, on the other hand, is that the United States is also involved in this kind of surrogate warfare, so the argument about weaker states would not follow.
8. Hoffman, *Inside Terrorism*, p. 31.
9. Chomsky, *Culture of Terrorism*, p. 80.
10. Hoffman, *Inside Terrorism*, p. 64.
11. N. Chomsky, *9–11* (New York: Open Media, 2001), p. 120.
12. For example, see Z. Sardar, *Postmodernism and the Other* (London: Pluto, 1998) and cf. his post-September 11 article in *New Internationalist* 345 (May 2002). Kalim Siddiqui, writing in the *Guardian*, speaks of "the corrupt bogland of western culture and supposed 'civilization'" and of the need for Muslim morals to mark themselves off as distinctive. Cited in Newbigin et al., *Faith and Power* (London: SCM, 1998), p. 109. It is, of course, an ironic reversal of the eighteenth-century

European perception of the Ottoman Empire as corrupt and sexually dissolute.

13. Weigel's (see note 2) enthusiasm for war as a way of dealing with those with whom we disagree, or who attack us, is in my view, completely sub-Christian, as indicated by his endorsement of R. Kaplan's *Warrior Politics* and its pagan ethos. The argument would have made sense to the Third Reich.

14. Burke argued that "the new school of murder and barbarism, set up in Paris, having destroyed all the other manners and principles which have hitherto civilized Europe, will destroy also the mode of civilized war, which more than anything else, has distinguished the christian world." Letter to a Member of the National Assembly, 1791, cited by Connor Cruise O'Brien in his introduction to Burke's *Reflections on the Revolution in France* (Harmondsworth: Penguin, 1986), p. 62. Burke must have been entirely ignorant of the Thirty Years War and atrocities like the sack of Magdeburg.

15. Cited in W. Blum, *Rogue State* (London: Zed, 2002), p. 92.

16. Hoffman, *Inside Terrorism*, p. 17.

17. Hoffman, *Inside Terrorism*, p. 18.

18. Burke, *Reflections*, p. 248.

19. W. Wink, *Engaging the Powers* (Minneapolis: Fortess, 1992), p. 28.

20. D. Rapoport, "Fear and Trembling: Terrorism in Three Religious Traditions," *American Political Science Review* 78, no 3 (September 1984).

21. Hoffman, *Inside Terrorism*, p. 94.

22. M. Ellis, *Unholy Alliance: Religion and Atrocity in Our Time* (London: SCM, 1997), p. 41.

23. K. Barth, *Ethics* (Edinburgh: T & T Clark, 1981), pp. 363ff.

24. Something like this perception is expressed by Madeline Albright in her claim that "The United States is good. We try to do our best everywhere." *Washington Post*, October 23, 1999, p. 17.

25. K. Koyama, *Mount Fuji and Mount Sinai* (London: SCM, 1984).

26. W. Wink, *Engaging*, p. 13.

27. Wink, *Engaging*, p. 149.

28. Wink, *Engaging*, p. 149.

29. M. Hengel, *The Cross of the Son of God* (London: SCM, 1986), pp. 117, 118.

30. Hengel, *Cross of the Son of God*, p. 146.

31. Hengel, *Cross of the Son of God*, p. 179.

32. These tortures, as Chomsky and William Blum remind us, were endorsed by the United States. Those who administered them were trained in the School of Americas and used U.S. equipment. See W. Blum, *Rogue State* (London: Zed, 2002), pp. 38–91.

33. Wink, *Engaging*, p. 25.
34. W. Cavanaugh, *Torture and Eucharist* (Oxford: Blackwell, 1998), p. 31. Compare the statement of White House spokesman Marlin Fitzwater, after the killing of many hundreds of civilians in an air raid shelter in Iraq, that "Saddam Hussein does not share our value for the sanctity of human life." Cited in Blum, *Rogue State*, p. 8.
35. Wink, *Engaging*, p. 206.
36. B. Keenan, *An Evil Cradling* (London: Vintage, 1992).
37. Chomsky, *Culture of Terrorism*, p. 69.
38. Ellis, *Unholy Alliance*, pp. 18, 19.
39. Wink, *Engaging*, p. 127.

# CHAPTER SEVEN

# Islam and the Politics of Violence

## Defining the Muslim Community

ANDREW RIPPIN

B iographies of Muhammad from the earliest times down to today convey a fundamental Muslim assumption. W. Montgomery Watt's contemporary popular account, *Muhammad, Prophet and Statesman*,[1] for example, expresses the thought and the theory perfectly on every level from its title through its contents. From the time the Muslim community came into being, the year of the migration (*hijra*) from Mecca to Medina (622 C.E., year 1 in the Muslim calendar), Muhammad combined the roles of prophet and political/military commander. The synthesis of politics and religion was perfect during this era. This is reflected in early documents that portray Muhammad's authority to solve problems between conflicting tribes in Medina as grounded in the authority that God has given him. The "Constitution of Medina," the agreement put in place to legitimate the role of Muhammad when he moved to Medina,[2] commences by saying:

> In the name of God, the Merciful, the Compassionate. This is a document dictated by Muhammad, the prophet, between the believers and Muslims from Quraysh and Yathrib (Medina), and those who followed and joined them and strove with them. They are one community, distinct from all others. The immigrants from Quraysh, according to their established customs, are bound together and shall ransom their prisoners with the kindness and justice common among believers.

Further, it suggests, "Whenever a dispute or controversy likely to cause trouble arises among the people of this document, it shall be referred to God and to Muhammad, the apostle of God. God is the guarantor of the pious observance of what is in this document."

The continuing authority of Muhammad is solidified through the notion of the *sunna*, a source of law that suggests in its basic conception that whatever Muhammad did in his life is worthy of emulation because the individual actions of his life are the perfect manifestation of the will of God. Muhammad's actions, as documented in the tradition (*hadith*) material, are viewed as working out the interpretation of the Qur'an in the practicalities of daily life; Muhammad's actions are thus the ultimate expression of God's will for human behavior.

The death of Muhammad was the event that caused the issue of authority in the community to become pressing for individual Muslims. From that point down until today, the Muslim community debated the mode and method by which the authority of Muhammad may be implemented. Clearly, it was important to have a defined sense of authority for the community to remain unified. However, closely linked to that question of authority was the matter of community membership. Accepting authority is, of course, a measure of membership; but what of the situation where there are competing conceptions of authority? In the Muslim view, when Muhammad was alive, there could be no divergence because he was the living authority. Disputes are referred to God and Muhammad, as the Constitution of Medina puts it. However, after he died, accepting authority was no longer a clear-cut matter.

Even more pressing for day-to-day life than the issue of competing conceptions of authority was the more immediately relevant question of how to judge whether somebody was actually accepting the source of authority. The predicament is clear. Some people say they are Muslims, but somebody else looks at their behavior and evaluates that as not meeting the standards set by the source of authority that is accepted by (a portion of) the community. What then?

This question was discussed extensively by Muslims using the model of a crucial historical event that occurred in the development of the early empire—the assassination of the third caliph of the expanding Muslim empire, Uthman ibn Affan. The event is paradigmatic rather than necessarily historical. Fundamentally, the question of community membership was approached by asking, "Was Uthman justly killed?" Were Uthman's sins such as to have placed him outside the community of Islam and thus not deserving of the protection of his contemporaries? Another implication was that those responsible for Uthman's death need not be pursued and justice need not be sought if Uthman was, in fact, a non-Muslim. From the sources available to us today, this one question emerges as so significant that it may have provided the stimulus toward developed theological writing in Islam as a whole.

The historical background for the discussion of this issue in terms of the assassination of Uthman may well have derived from substantially later disputes over succession within the Arab ruling groups. Whether Ali, the fourth leader of the Arabs after Muhammad, had the responsibility for avenging the death of his assassinated predecessor, Uthman had a significance to later Shi'ite groups well beyond the theological issue. Likewise, the descendants of the clan of Uthman, pictured as being led by Mu'awiya, championed the claims of their kinsman in order to legitimate the rule of the Umayyad dynasty. They suggested that Ali had lost his rightful claim to rule because of his failure to follow up on the obligation to pursue Uthman's killers.

Theological questions were discussed within the framework of these events. Do one's actions affect one's status as a Muslim? Answers varied, but for most Muslims, the response was a pragmatic one. If a person claims to be a Muslim, then that person must be treated as a Muslim. Only God truly knows the status in faith of the individual, and thus, on a legal plane, the individual's rights and privileges of membership in the community of Islam must be honored. Most discussions revolved around how to understand the Muslim who sinned. Was such a person "less" of a Muslim, as some suggested, or was such a person to be declared a "hypocrite," as others suggested; or was it a matter that would only have implications after death as reflected in the level of reward and punishment in the hereafter?

The trends within the theological debates may be separated into four major streams.[3] The Murji'a adopted a position dedicated to preserving the status quo. They argued that those who appeared not to be following the outward precepts of Islam must still be accepted as Muslims; only God truly knows their religious state. A profession of faith along with an inward assent to Islam was all that was required to confirm community membership; faith (*iman*) is "of the heart and of the tongue." Thus, decisions on the questions related to Uthman and Ali and their status as Muslims must be left to God. As a theological position, this stance holds that works are not a part of faith; as long as a person professes belief in Islam (through the single act of confession of faith), then that person is a Muslim. The actual performance of the ritual acts of Islam is not a criterion for membership in the community. This position was supported in the view of the Murji'a by the notion that, in the Qur'an, God used the word "believers" to refer to those who had confessed their faith (and that alone). The position of the

Murji'a is associated especially with Abu Hanifa (d. 767), who argued that good works will be rewarded primarily in the hereafter. In the here and now, any increase in faith as manifested in pious works is really only an increase in conviction on the part of the individual. The discussion frequently invoked an interpretation of the Qur'an that was historical in nature. People were declared Muslims within the Qur'an prior to the revelation of the ritual requirements of Islam; thus, it is argued, one's status as a Muslim depends only upon inner assent and not on outward performance. The doctrine thus had the practical and pragmatic result of easing conversion to Islam and became the dominant position of the theological school associated with al-Maturidi (d. 944). Other Muslims, however, felt that such a position did not provide the moral motivation that believers needed. As a position associated with Ahmad ibn Hanbal (d. 855), it was argued that there are degrees of "being Muslim." Works do count toward one's status in the community, although one can still be a believer and commit sin. There are, therefore, degrees of faith. This position is found as the fundamental thread in the later books of *hadith*, and it became the position associated with the theological school of al-Ash'ari, which dominated classical Islam. The position is summarized in a statement attributed to Ibn Hanbal that "faith consists in verbal assent, deeds and intention, and adherence to the *sunna*. Faith increases and decreases."[4]

Yet another position in the overall debate became attached to those known as the Qadariyya, associated with theological statements ascribed to al-Hasan al-Basri (d. 728). As with the Murji'a, a person who professes faith in Islam is considered a member of the community. However, those who can be observed not to be following the requirements of Islam are to be considered neither believers nor unbelievers, but somewhere in between; they are hypocrites. The end result in practical terms is the same as that of the Murji'a, but the claim is made that it is, in fact, possible to have an opinion about the status of a believer's adherence to Islam. The position does not distinguish, however, between levels of faith as does that of Ibn Hanbal.

Finally, one group took an activist position that proved disruptive to the early Muslim community. The legacy of the movement and the theological position has lingered until today. The group is known as the Kharijites;[5] in their most extreme form, they claim that all those who fall short of total adherence to the Islamic precepts are unbelievers. Any of those who might happen to slip are thus rendered targets for the Islamic *jihad* against all nonbelievers; membership in the community, at the very least, provides protection from such attacks.[6] The duty of rebellion against what might be declared an illegitimate government is seen as an absolute.[7]

The Kharijites were, in many ways, a marginal group when viewed within the overall context of Islamic history. As a group, their significance faded. However, the tendency displayed in their thought has always provided a tension in Islam. These demands for judgment of adherence—always varying in their intensity and their precise theological motivation, certainly—provided a constant threat to the unity of the community, yet those threats existed under the guise of making the demand for that very unity that was considered possible only with a strict implementation of a single code of Islam. Such an approach to Islam became prominent at times of community stress. A perceived threat from the outside to the integrity of the Muslim community has, throughout history, provided the stimulus for a retreat to a more closely defined conception of Islam and a greater call for a judgment on fellow Muslims as to the acceptability of the practice of their Islam.[8] The most famous enunciator of this position in Muslim history was the Hanbalite jurist Ibn Taymiyya (d. 1328), whose defense of the concept of Islam in the decades following the Mongol invasion of Baghdad in 1258 has become the inspiration and the intellectual grounding for all later thinkers facing a similar situation. Ibn Taymiyya's reputation in the modern Islamic world as a defender of the faith is unrivaled.

Muhammad Ibn Abd al-Wahhab in the eighteenth century is especially prominent for his continuation of this line of thought. Ibn Abd al-Wahhab (d. 1792) was a prolific writer and the founder-figurehead of the Wahhabi movement, the underlying ideology of modern Saudi Islam.[9] Among his many tracts is one called *Nawaqid al-Islam*, "the things which nullify Islam." This tract sets out, in point form, the limits to what a Muslim may believe or do and still maintain membership in the community. The text appears to be a distillation of many of the central points of Ibn Abd al-Wahhab's most famous and emblematic text, his *Kitab al-Tawhid*, "The Book of Unity." For modern readers, an update of that document (although the relationship between the two texts is not made apparent) composed by the Saudi cleric Shaikh Abdul Aziz ibn Abdullah ibn Baz is of special interest.[10] Ibn Baz was born in 1912 in Riyadh, Saudi Arabia; although blind from the age of twenty, he was appointed as Vice-Chancellor of the Islamic University of Medina in 1961 and Chancellor of the University of Medina in 1970. In 1992, he was appointed the official Mufti (expounder of Islamic law and provider of *fatwa*s, legal opinions). Ibn Baz was also appointed to the presidency of the Committee of Senior Scholars and the presidency of the Administration for Scientific Research and Legal Rulings. He continued to hold other posts until his death in 1999.

The document *Nawaqid al-Islam* needs to be viewed within the context of Muslim discussions of defining community membership with a view to understanding the political ramifications of theological issues. Such discussions show a remarkable evolution through time, adapting to the situation of the writer and, in doing so, reflecting the perceptions of the social and political pressures of the day. A comparison of the versions of the text from Ibn Abd al-Wahhab and Ibn Baz illustrates this point quite clearly. The situation is somewhat complex from a scholarly point of view because of some instability in the textual tradition of the documents themselves. For the purposes of this discussion I will simply present them in the form in which I have them in front of me and leave further textual analysis to a future study. It may well be that other versions of the same texts exist; certainly the English translations available on the Web appear to conflate the two Arabic documents on occasion in various minor ways.

An "official" translation of Ibn Baz is available at http://www.fatwa-online.com/ under "Fatwa Categories—Creed—Shirk" [September 11, 2002] or directly at http://www.fatwa-online.com/fataawa/creed/shirk/9991120_1.htm [September 11, 2002]; the Arabic text that I have used is found at http://www.khayma.com/hazem/naqd.html [September 11, 2002]. The text of Ibn Abd al-Wahhab is found in his *Mu'allafat al-Shaykh al-Iman Muhammad ibn Abd al-Wahhab*, Riyad 1398 A.H., volume 5, pp. 212–214;[11] an English translation of a version of the text is available at http://islamicweb.com/beliefs/creed/what_negates_Islam.htm. The following translation follows the Arabic text of Ibn Abd al-Wahhab in italics. This is then interspersed, in commentary format, with the version of Ibn Baz, with special attention drawn to each basic point within the overall structure of the "ten things."

> *Know that the greatest matters which nullify your Islam are ten:*
> 1. *Ascribing partners (shirk) in the worship of the one God who has no partners. The indication of that is in His saying: "God does not forgive setting up partners with Him but He forgives whom He pleases for sins other than that" (Qur'an 4/116). This includes slaughtering animals in the name of someone other than God, as in slaughtering the name of the jinn or graves.*

Ibn Baz uses a different proof text with a more apocalyptic tone and changes the examples, taking the emphasis away from the ritual of animal slaughter by restating the point as follows: "'Truly, whosoever sets up partners with Allah, then Allah has forbidden the Garden for him, and the Fire will be his abode. And for the wrongdoers there are no helpers' (Qur'an 5/72). Calling upon the dead, asking their help, or offering them gifts or sacrifices are all forms of *shirk*."

*2. Setting up intermediaries between oneself and God, making supplication to them, or asking their intercession with God is unbelief (kufr) by the consensus of the community.*

Ibn Baz adds three Qur'anic proof texts, "Have they taken others as intercessors besides God? Say: Is that so, even if they have no power over anything and know nothing? Say: To God belongs all intercession!" (Qur'an 39/43–4); "Fear the day when people will not help one another at all, nor will intercession be accepted from them" (Qur'an 2/48); "Indeed you have come to Us alone just as We created you for the first time. You have left behind you all that We bestowed on you. We do not see your intercessors, whom you claimed to be partners, with you" (Qur'an 6/94).

*3. Anyone who does not consider the polytheists (mushrikun) to be unbelievers, or who has doubts concerning their unbelief, or considers their way to be correct, is an unbeliever (kafir) by consensus.*

Ibn Baz glosses "polytheist" with "among the Jews, the Christians, etc." in line with (but without citing) Qur'an 98/1 ("Those who disbelieve among the people of the book and the polytheists") and then adds "or believes that it is possible that they will enter paradise." The text then goes into an extended discussion of the status of Jews and Christians that results from their disbelief in Muhammad, citing the Catholic and Protestant view of the doctrine of the trinity that is contrary to the explicit statement of Qur'an 5/73 ("Those who say that God is the third of three and not that of gods there is only the one God, disbelieve"), and the Orthodox view of the divinity of Jesus deemed contrary to Qur'an 5/72 ("Those who say that the messiah, the son of Mary, is God, disbelieve"). The Jews already declared their nonbelief by rejecting Jesus, as reflected in Qur'an 3/52 ("When Jesus came to know of their disbelief, he said, 'Who will be my helpers towards God?' The disciples said, 'We are the helpers of God. We believe in God and we bear witness that we have submitted [become Muslims]'"). Ibn Baz is obviously far more concerned with the Euro-American-Israeli threat than Ibn Abd al-Wahhab. Notably, this extended passage on the errors of the Jews and Christians is absent from the English translations of Ibn Baz's document widely available on the Internet.

*4. Anyone who believes any guidance to be more perfect that the prophet's, or a decision other than his to be better, is an unbeliever. This is like those who prefer the rule of evil (taghut) to his rule.*

Ibn Baz extends this matter extensively by citing three examples (listed as a, b, and c below):

> (a) To believe that systems and laws made by human beings are better than the *shari'a* of Islam; for example, saying that the Islamic system is not suitable for the twentieth century; or that Islam is the cause of the backwardness of the Muslims; or that Islam is a relationship between God and the Muslim that should not interfere in other aspects of life.

All of the specific examples listed under this point have been common refrains of modernists in Islam since the nineteenth century. The rejection of the privatization of Islam in the Protestant Christian mode is especially telling and represents a rejection not only of modern tendencies and debates over civil society, but also of the heritage of *taqiyya*, a doctrine associated with Shi'i Islam that allows for the hiding of the outward manifestation of one's religion in face of oppression.[12]

> (b) To say that enforcing the punishments prescribed by Allah, such as cutting off the hand of the thief or the stoning of an adulterer, is not suitable for this day and age.
>
> (c) To believe that it is permissible to give a rule based on something God did not reveal when dealing with commercial transactions or matters of law, punishments, or other affairs. Although one may not believe such things to be superior to the *shari'a*, in effect such a stance is affirmed by declaring a thing which God has prohibited, such as adultery, drinking alcohol, or usury, to be permissible. According to the consensus of the Muslims, one who declares such things to be permissible is an unbeliever (*kafir*).

> 5. *Anyone who hates any part of what the messenger of God has brought, even though he may act in accordance with it, is an unbeliever by consensus. God has said: 'This is because they hate what God has sent down, so He has made their deeds fruitless" (Qur'an 47/9).*

Ibn Baz states this notion of hypocrisy more concisely, omitting "even though he may act in accordance with it, is an unbeliever by consensus."

> 6. *Anyone who ridicules any aspect of the religion of God, or any of its rewards or punishments, is an unbeliever. The indication*

> *of that is in God's saying: "Say: Was it God, and His signs and His Messenger that you were mocking? Make no excuse; you have disbelieved after you had believed" (Qur'an 9/65–66) .*

Ibn Baz speaks of making fun of God, Muhammad, any aspect of the law (including trimming beards, wearing full-length clothes, wearing the *burqa*, protecting women from exposure to other men, using a *siwak* as a toothbrush), or those who uphold the traditions of Islam. These explanations do not appear in the Internet English translations once again.

> 7. *The practice of magic. Included in this, for example, is causing a rift between a husband and wife by turning his love for her into hatred, or tempting a person to do things he dislikes using black arts. One who engages in such a thing or is pleased with it is outside the fold of Islam. God said, "But neither of these two [angels, Harut and Marut] taught anyone magic until they had said, Indeed, we are a trial; then do not disbelieve" (Qur'an 2/102).*

Ibn Baz adds that magic includes soothsayers, those who claim to have knowledge of the unseen, reading tea leaves, using astrology, making horoscopes, or trusting blue amulets.

> 8. *Supporting and aiding polytheists against the Muslims. The indication of that is God saying: "Whoever among you who takes them as allies is surely one of them. Truly, Allah does not guide the wrongdoers" (Qur'an 5/51).*

Ibn Baz repeats this verbatim.

> 9. *Anyone who believes that some people are not required to follow Muhammad is an unbeliever and that leaving its shari'a is possible just as al-Khidr left the shari'a of Moses is an unbeliever.*

Ibn Baz expresses this differently: "Anyone who believes that it is possible for people to leave the religion Islam is an unbeliever. God has said, 'And whoever seeks a religion other than Islam, it will not be accepted of him, and in the hereafter he will be from among the losers'" (Qur'an 3/85).

> 10. *To turn completely away from the religion of God neither learning its precepts nor acting upon it. The indication of that*

> *is God's saying: "And who does greater wrong than he who is reminded of the revelations of his Lord and turns aside there from. Truly, We shall exact retribution from the guilty"* (Qur'an 32/22).
> *It makes no difference whether such violations are committed as a joke, in seriousness or out of fear, except when done under compulsion (i.e., from threat of loss of life). We seek refuge in God from such deeds as entail His wrath and severe punishment.*

Ibn Baz does not include the second paragraph of item ten.

Ibn Baz has updated Ibn Abd al-Wahhab. The concerns of the late twentieth century according to this perspective on the world are clear: the ghost of Salman Rushdie lurks behind a number of the statements, as, for example, in the reexpression of item nine; the existence of Israel and the renewed emphasis on the Jews and the theological disputes revivified from the Middle Ages with the Christians are clear in the extension of item three; the rejection of the modern conception of the notion of religion as an internal matter in the comments added to item four; the rejection of modern animosity to certain religious symbols provided as examples in item six. As an aside, it is hard not to observe the impact of translation in the move from an Arabic-reading audience to an English-reading one and the influence of the worldwide context of the Internet in producing the softening of some of the aspects of Ibn Baz's statement (which remains recognizably strident even in its more polite English version).

I would not claim that I can draw any profound conclusions from this examination of these theological debates. These observations do not come anywhere near approaching a general answer to the relationship between religion and violence in Islam. But a few comments may be put forth in the hopes that they might provide a firm basis for further reflection on the complexities of the situation. Times of crisis in Islamic history have been marked by tensions among Muslims regarding membership in their community. A threat to the unity and stability of the community, widely felt and deeply perceived, tends to provoke a spirit of Islamic renewal that has been, in some of its manifestations, oriented toward a strict delimitation of the boundaries of Islamic identity. The Wahhabi movement is one such tendency, and that continues today in the Salafi movement in Saudi Arabia. The pressures are there—the threat of people leaving Islam, especially, due to the attractions of the world around—and the desire to be able to tell friend from foe becomes more critical. There are definite authoritarian aspects to these proclamations, and those who support them are firm in their belief that they are correct. That violence may erupt in such a situation is, unfortunately, a reality.

## Notes

1. W. Montgomery Watt, *Muhammad, Prophet and Statesman* (London: Oxford University Press, 1961).
2. The document is found in Ibn Ishaq, *Sirat rasul Allah*, trans. Alfred Guillaume, *The Life of Muhammad: A Translation of [Ibn] Ishaq's* Sirat Rasul Allah (Oxford: Oxford University Press, 1955), pp. 231–233.
3. The following summary of the positions of the early theological schools is based on material in my *Muslims: Their Religious Beliefs and Practices*, 2nd ed. (London: Routledge, 2001), chap. 5.
4. Cited in Kenneth Cragg and Marston Speight, *Islam from Within: Anthology of a Religion* (Belmont, Calif.: Wadsworth, 1980), p. 119.
5. It is worth noting that the term Kharijite is used in modern intra-Muslim polemic with a derogatory connotation and some religious extremists have taken pains to avoid being labeled in this way. See the discussion in Jeffrey T. Kennedy, "Jews, Kharijites, and the Debate Over Religious Extremism in Egypt," in Ronald L. Nettler and Suha Taji-Farouki, eds., *Muslim-Jewish Encounters: Intellectual Traditions and Modern Politics* (Amsterdam: Harwood Academic Publishers, 1998), pp. 65–86.
6. The nature of the Kharijite movement in the earliest period of Islam (as compared to the later legal/theological schools which emerged) is a much-discussed topic in scholarly writing. See, for example, Wilfred Madelung, *The Succession to Muhammad* (Cambridge: Cambridge University Press, 1997), and G. R. Hawting, "The Significance of the Slogan *la hukma illa li'llah* and References to the *hudud* in the Traditions about the Fitna and the Murder of Uthman," *Bulletin of the School of Oriental and African Studies* 41 (1978): 453–463.
7. The question of the duty that Muslims have to try to stop other people from doing wrong, especially when it comes to dealing with political power, is extensively and compellingly treated in Michael Cook, *Commanding Right and Forbidding Wrong in Islamic Thought* (Cambridge: Cambridge University Press, 2000).
8. Frank Griffel, "Toleration and Exclusion: al-Shafi'i and al-Ghazali on the Treatment of Apostates," *Bulletin of the School of Oriental and African Studies* 64 (2001): 339–354, provides an excellent treatment of some of the ramifications of this topic as they changed between the eighth and the eleventh century. Al-Ghazali (d. 1111) held that Islamic law "must not shy away from the threat posed to the Islamic community by the activities of secret apostates" (p. 353), whereas earlier "it had, in theory at least, been impossible to pass the death penalty on a supposed Muslim apostate who was not willing to die for his convictions."

9. On the Wahhabis, see Esther Peskes, "Wahhabiyya," *Encyclopaedia of Islam,* new ed (Leiden: E. J. Brill, 1960—in progress).

10. I previously drew attention to this document in my article "What has Osama bin Laden done to Islam and where does it go from here?" in Karim-Aly Kassam, George Melnyk, and Lynne Perras, eds., *Canada & September 11: Impact and Responses* (Calgary: Detselig, 2002), pp. 195–203, an article that has also been published in a slightly different form in the booklet *Responses to Terrorism* (Victoria, B.C.: Division of Continuing Studies, University of Victoria, 2002).

11. I would like to thank Rosalind Gwynne of the University of Tennessee for providing me with a copy of this text. It was Dr. Gwynne's on-line article "Al-Qacida and al-Qur'an: The 'Tafsir' of the 'Tafsir' of Usamah bin Ladin," available at http://web.utk.edu/~warda/ bin_ladin_and_quran.htm, that first piqued my interest in this document.

12. See R. Strothmann and Moktar Djebli, "Takiyya," *Encyclopaedia of Islam*, new ed. (Leiden: E. J. Brill, 1960—in progress).

# CHAPTER EIGHT

# Disarming Phineas

## Rabbinic Confrontations with Biblical Militancy

ELIEZER SEGAL

Traditional Jewish piety is expressed largely through commitment to a comprehensive system of religious commandments. Beyond the rituals and acts of devotion that Western liberalism recognizes as the legitimate domains of religious activity, the Torah establishes a judiciary structure to administer civil, criminal, and cultic offenses. It regulates the appointment of judges (Dt 16:18–20), as well as the rules of testimony (e.g., Dt 17:6–7) and punishment (e.g., Dt 25:6–7). No person, including royalty or the priesthood, is above the law; and violations of the law are to be adjudicated according to due process (see Dt 17:5–13). To be sure, the Torah tells of individuals who took the law into their own hands and acted with violent impetuosity against wrongdoers, such as when Simeon and Levi massacred the Shechemites for dishonoring their sister Dinah (Gn 34). Their actions were not portrayed in a favorable light, and the incident belongs, after all, to the era prior to the Torah's revelation. So, too, when the young Moses slew the Egyptian taskmaster (Ex 2:12) he was not yet subject to the Torah's standards. In his later years, after the receiving of the divine law, Moses' leadership was typified by his reluctance to issue decisions without explicit direction from the Almighty. We discern this trait, for example, when an individual was arrested for gathering sticks on the Sabbath (Nm 15:32–36); or when adjudicating the inheritance claims of Zelophehad's daughters (Nm 27:1–11).

A blatant exception to the Torah's insistence on judicial processes is the episode related in Nm 25, where Phineas spontaneously executes an

Israelite leader and his Midianite consort who were openly participating in
the idolatrous and licentious cult of Baalpeor:

> And, behold, one of the children of Israel came and brought unto
> his brethren a Midianitish woman in the sight of Moses, and in the
> sight of all the congregation of the children of Israel, who were
> weeping before the door of the tabernacle of the congregation.
> And when Phineas, the son of Eleazar, the son of Aaron the priest,
> saw it, he rose up from among the congregation, and took a
> javelin in his hand. And he went after the man of Israel into the
> tent, and thrust both of them through, the man of Israel, and the
> woman through her belly. So the plague was stayed from the chil-
> dren of Israel.[1]

Many issues arise from this story, but we will focus here on the one that
drew the most attention from the rabbinic interpreters and homilists: What
normative lessons are we expected to derive from Phineas' act of zealous
assassination?[2] Phineas' role was sometimes contrasted with that of Moses,
who appears conspicuous in his inactivity in the face of an extreme provo-
cation of idolatry, promiscuity, and insubordination.[3]

The rabbinic references to the Phineas episode have been explored
extensively by scholars dealing with ideological foundations of the Zealot
movement during the Second Temple era. The most significant study of that
sort is Martin Hengel's monumental investigation of the Zealots.[4] The present, narrower treatment of the question will differ from Hengel's in several
respects. Most importantly, my principal concern is not to scour the rabbinic corpus for evidence of the pre-rabbinic Zealot philosophy, but rather
to study the talmudic and midrashic materials for their own sake and on
their own terms, paying attention to how the rabbis interpreted Phineas'
action, and how their rhetorical and hermeneutic approaches allowed them
to take a critical view of this biblical hero without calling into question the
authority of the Torah.

A second difference between this study and Hengel's has to do with the
narrower definition given here to the phenomenon of "rabbinic literature."
Hengel[5] made generous use of medieval compendia such as *Numbers
Rabbah*,[6] *Exodus Rabbah*,[7] and assorted minor works from the medieval
era.[8] Although he is cognizant of some of the methodological problems
associated with this approach, and makes strong arguments for the antiquity of some of the exegetical traditions that show up in late sources,[9] I am
nonetheless convinced that it is more valid to base conclusions on texts that
can be reliably classified as "rabbinic." In the present context, this meant
restricting my analysis almost exclusively to the *Sifré on Numbers* and the

two Talmuds, while using other works mostly as textual witnesses for the earlier collections.

## Phineas in the Second Commonwealth

In diverse ways, the rabbinic texts indicate that they associated Phineas' violent impetuosity with the events and attitudes of the Second Temple era, between the Hasmonean revolt and the destruction of the Jerusalem Temple in 70 C.E. Such an association is implied in the way that the rabbinic expositions of Nm 25 connect it to an anonymous teaching of the Mishnah (*Sanhedrin* 9:6) that "One who has sexual relations with an Aramean woman,[10] zealots [*qanna'in*] attack him."[11] The descriptive style and invocation of extralegal sanctions set this passage apart from the customary discourse of rabbinic legal literature, which is normally addressed to the sages and courts that are charged with the administration of ritual or judicial cases, and is couched in conventional categories of innocence, guilt, penalties, and compensation. The treatment of this mishnah in subsequent talmudic and midrashic discussions reflects the rabbis' assumption that it derived from a particularly ancient oral tradition. On the whole, it would appear that the rabbis were correct in identifying the mishnah passage as belonging to a pre-rabbinic stratum, a dating that is borne out by, among other factors, its juxtaposition with other motifs that belong to the Second Temple era.[12]

The early midrashic tradition, however, takes this premise a giant step further by assuming that the mishnah about Zealots avenging dalliances with foreign women originated at Mount Sinai itself and was part of a body of halakhic teachings that was revealed orally to Moses simultaneously with the written text of the Torah.[13]

In the expanded midrashic narrative,[14] this assumption functions as a justification for Phineas' apparent violation of judicial protocol in acting without authorization from Moses, his master. The midrash resolved this difficulty by asserting that Phineas was acting on the basis of an explicit ruling of the oral Torah, one that had been momentarily forgotten by Moses himself.[15]

Indeed, the Babylonian Talmud (*Sanhedrin* 82a) explicitly ascribes the mishnah to the Maccabean revolt when it relates that:

When Rav Dimi came[16] he stated that the court of the Hasmoneans decreed that one who has relations with a gentile woman incurs guilt on the counts of: menstrual impurity, having relations with a slave and with a married woman. When Rabin came, he said: he incurs guilt with respect to menstrual impurity, having relations with a slave, with a gentile, and a harlot.[17]

An additional indication of how the rabbis associated Phineas' exploits with the radicalism of the Second Commonwealth may be discerned in an ostensibly trivial detail that they injected into their retelling of the biblical narrative: "'And took a javelin in his hand'—He removed the metal point and placed it inside his bosom; and leaned himself on the wooden rod, out of fear of [Zimri's] tribe who were surrounding him."[18]

In its midrashic context, the story of Phineas' concealing the spear blade under his cloak does not appear to be a response to any textual stimulus; at most it serves to explain how he was able to gain close access to Zimri and Cozbi by disguising the javelin as a walking-staff.[19] However, the image evokes the vivid image of the Sicarii, the Zealot faction of the Great Revolt who derived their name precisely from their attachment to this practice, as recorded by Josephus (*Wars* 2:13:3 [255]; cf. *Antiquities* 20:8:12 [186]):[20] "Sicarii, who slew men in the day time, and in the midst of the city; this they did chiefly at the festivals, when they mingled themselves among the multitude, and concealed daggers [*sica*] under their garments, with which they stabbed those that were their enemies."[21]

On the whole, the rabbis were accurate in their perception that the impetuous zealotry that animated Phineas' violent response to Zimri's abomination was representative of the temperament of the late Second Temple era, a time when devotion to the Israelite covenant often took the form of armed resistance to Hellenistic or Roman authority or to a Jewish leadership that was believed to have deviated from the true path.[22] The author of 1 Maccabees (2:26) invoked the precedent of Phineas in describing how Mattathias the Priest incited the revolt against the Hellenistic persecutions by slaying a Jew who was offering up heathen sacrifices.[23] In 4 Maccabees (18:12), the mother of the seven martyred children mentions Phineas as an inspirational model for heroic resistance. Even the conservative priest Ben Sira (45:23) is full of praises for Phineas' zeal in warding off evil from his people.[24]

### Phineas in the Midrash

The earliest rabbinic midrash on the Phineas episode is contained in the *Sifré on Numbers*, a tannaitic compilation ascribed to the school of Rabbi Ishmael.[25] The *Sifré* introduces twelve miracles[26] that were performed for Phineas in the course of his impaling the iniquitous Zimri and Cozbi. The rabbinic preachers had a proclivity for magnifying the supernatural dimensions of biblical narratives, as a way of glorifying God and underscoring his influence over events,[27] particularly in instances when the divine participation is not obvious from the surface reading.[28] In the present passage, most of the miracles supplied by the midrash seem to promote the specific objective of making the offense clearly visible to all observers.[29] To this pattern belong the following:

[1] The culprits were forced to remain coupled together *in flagrante delicto*.

[3] The javelin impaled them both in their genitals "and everyone could see his maleness and inside her vagina; this was on account of the fault-finders[30] who might otherwise have argued that he had only gone in there for personal reasons."

[4] They did not slide off the javelin, but remained impaled on it.

[5] An angel raised the doorway so that people could see above his shoulder.

[7] The javelin was elongated to allow it to impale both bodies.

[8] Phineas was given the strength to carry them out.

[9] The javelin was strong enough not to snap under the burden.

[12] "Normally, the upper body drops to the bottom on a javelin. In this case, however, a miracle was performed and Zimri was flipped on top of Cozbi as they had been at the time of their deed; and all Israel saw them and declared them deserving of capital punishment."

By linking the Torah's approval of Phineas' violence with a sequence of uniquely miraculous circumstances, the *Sifré* has implicitly challenged its status as a precedent for emulation even under otherwise identical conditions. This is an inference that will have an impact on the subsequent discussions in the Talmuds.[31]

The Jerusalem Talmud (*Sanhedrin* 9:6; 27b), after a brief exposition of the Phineas episode in connection with the allusion to Zealots in the mishnah, cites a tannaitic tradition to the effect that he had acted "contrary to the will of the sages."[32] There follows the following pericope:

Could Phineas have acted contrary to the will of the Sages?!
Says Rabbi Judah ben Pazi:[33] They wanted to place him under the ban, but for the fact that the holy spirit leaped upon him and declared: "And he shall have it, and his seed after him, even the covenant of an everlasting priesthood, etc." (Nm 25:13).

The audacity of this discussion is astonishing in the way that it pits the authority of mortal judges against the dictates of the Almighty.[34] What might have been implicit in the *Sifré* is stated explicitly by Rabbi Judah: if the Jewish courts had been allowed to deliberate without divine interference, then Phineas' impetuous violence would never have been condoned. It was a violation of proper judicial process, as well as an infringement of the protocol that forbids a disciple to issue a ruling in the presence of his master (in this case, Moses).[35]

The Babylonian Talmud (*Sanhedrin* 82b) contains the following passages[36] attached to the mishnah about Zealots attacking sinners:[37]

> Rav Kahana inquired of Rav: If the zealots did not attack him, what is the law?
> Rav could not recall his received tradition.
> They[38] recited to Rav Kahana in his dream: "Judah hath dealt treacherously, and an abomination is committed in Israel and in Jerusalem; for Judah hath profaned the holiness of the Lord which he loved, and hath married the daughter of a strange god" (Mal 2:11).
> He [Rav Kahana] went and said to him [Rav]: Thus have they recited to me. . . .

In the meantime, Rav recalled his received tradition. The Talmud now goes on to expound each of the transgressions enumerated in the Malachi verse and concludes as follows:

> "Judah hath dealt treacherously"—This refers to idolatry.
> "And hath married the daughter of a strange god"—This refers to one who marries a gentile woman.

And immediately following this it states (verse 12):

> "The Lord will cut off the man that doeth this, the alert ones and the responders, out of the tabernacles of Jacob, and him that offereth an offering unto the Lord of hosts."
> —If he is a scholar, he shall have no "alert ones" among the sages, and none "responding" among the disciples.
> —If he is a priest, then he shall have no son who will offer up a meal offering unto the Lord of hosts.

This exchange between two third-century Babylonian scholars goes a long way toward diminishing the severity of the crime and its punishment.[39] The same transgression that would provoke assassination at the hands of the Zealots would, under different circumstances, be left to divine retribution. God's penalties appear relatively benign by comparison: depriving a teacher of students and colleagues and a priest of offspring who would inherit his sacred vocation. Although these examples were obviously influenced by the wording of the biblical verse, they also reflect a homiletical setting in which the chastisements were being addressed to a law-abiding community of scholars. The authors seem to have resigned themselves to the fact that the meting out of penalties for offenses of this sort requires knowledge of motives that are inaccessible to mortals and is therefore best left to the omniscient deity.[40]

The pericope continues with the following more explicit discussion of the normative status of Phineas' deed:

> Says Rav Ḥisda:[41] If someone were to consult about how to proceed, they should not be instructed to act in that manner
> So too was it stated: Rabbah bar bar Ḥana[42] says in the name of Rabbi Joḥanan:[43] If someone were to consult about how to proceed, they should not be instructed to act in that manner
> Even more so: If the culprit had succeeded in disengaging himself, and Phineas had then killed him, then he [Phineas] would have been judged guilty of homicide; whereas if Zimri had managed to turn around and kill Phineas, he would not be subject to the death penalty because it would have been deemed an act of self-defense.

The implications of these talmudic discussions were not lost on the traditional Jewish exegetes of the medieval and modern eras. Notwithstanding the diversity of their interpretations, most of them operated within a consistent set of parameters, assuming that Phineas' zealous attack had been justified by a special constellation of circumstances, personality traits, and motivations that were virtually irreproducible.[44]

Ultimately, the normative status of Phineas' action for Jewish practice was determined by the interpretations of the medieval codifiers.[45] The foremost of these, Maimonides (*Issurei Bi'ah* 12:4), summarizes the talmudic discussion as a normative regulation, which he classifies as an ancient oral "halakhah to Moses from Sinai." Zealots may attack individuals involved in sexual acts with heathen women only if the conditions that existed in Phineas' case are all satisfied:[46] the offenders must be caught in the act, and in public. Nevertheless, no court must ever instruct an individual to emulate Phineas' zealotry. The divinely ordained penalties that were designated for these sinners in lieu of judicial sentences were equated by Maimonides with the biblical punishment *karet* ("cutting off"; usually understood as a supernaturally inflicted premature demise).

## Conclusions

The course of events that we have traced demonstrates an unmistakable shift by the rabbis vis-à-vis the dominant values of the Bible and Second Temple documents, all of which extolled Phineas' zeal as a model to be emulated and as a hero whose decisively violent response to sacrilege and immorality merited divine commendation. While nominally accepting that Phineas' assault had been justified in its distinctive circumstances, the upshot of the expositions in the midrashic and talmudic sources was to relegate the episode to the past, if only as recent as the Second Commonwealth.

As we attempt to account for the shift in attitude, it is tempting to ascribe it to the changed historical circumstances, as the rabbis accommodated themselves to a new situation in which zealous violence was no longer a realistic option. An instructive parallel may be discerned in Josephus Flavius' marginalizing of the Zealots in his accounts of the Jewish Wars. Josephus' policy was likely motivated by his intention to persuade his Roman patrons and gentile readership that the recent revolt had been instigated by a small group of fanatics and did not enjoy the support of the wider Jewish populace, who were nothing more than unfortunate victims of the political dynamics. By exonerating the mainstream movements, particularly the Pharisees, from the taint of Zealot sympathies, these parties could still be proposed as acceptable candidates for leadership in the post-70 reality.[47]

On further reflection, it does not seem plausible to ascribe such an agenda to the rabbinical sages who assumed the mantle of Jewish leadership in the wake of the Temple's destruction.[48] Rabbinic literature is no less uncompromising than the Zealots in its hatred and demonization of the evil Roman Empire, an attitude that can be discerned in countless homilies in Palestinian aggadic midrash, is not lacking from the Babylonian Talmud, and was given normative status in the mandatory prayers. Like the Zealots, the rabbis were outspoken in their conviction that acceptance of "the yoke of the kingship of Heaven" implied a rejection of heathen rule, even if the religious ideology could not be applied in the present circumstances.[49] A popular insurrection against Rome did arise in 132–135 C.E., with the support of some of the same rabbis whose views were incorporated into the Mishnah and kindred works.[50]

Nevertheless, the talmudic sages may well have been reacting to the violent excesses that had led to tragic consequences in the previous era, excesses that they ascribed to the "baseless hatreds" of religious fanaticism and factionalism.[51]

It seems preferable to regard the talmudic attitude not so much as a response to historical circumstances, but as a fundamental philosophical mind-set, perhaps even a psychological one, that strove to impose moral and legal order on the world through the instrument of the halakhah. Religious and communal leaders who are responsible for the orderly administration of their societies will inevitably be wary of all ideologies that encourage passion, subjectivity, or charisma as grounds for policy. At the core of rabbinic discourse, whether in the courtroom or the academy, is an emphasis on free and rational discussion, wherein every opinion must be defended against opposing arguments or proof texts, and even the most senior judges and scholars are not immune from challenge.[52] Appeals to emotion or supernatural revelation were antithetical to that process and were not considered acceptable justifications in a halakhic debate.[53] Needless to say, the potential for disaster is far more daunting when human lives are placed on the scales. Seen this way, what requires an explanation is not the rabbis' neutralization of the Torah's endorsement of Phineas, but the attitude of the Torah itself.

The case of Phineas' zealotry is but one example of the rabbis' efforts to diminish the impact of a biblical validation of uncontrolled violence. The same combination of reverence for scriptural authority, hermeneutic daring, and sensible humanism is discernible in their treatment of other Torah institutions that chafed at the sages' orderly and moderate sensibilities. Some conspicuous instances that come readily to mind are: the *lex talons* (Ex 21:24, etc.), the city seduced to idolatry (Dt 13:12–18), the rebellious son (Dt 21:18–23), and the institution of capital punishment.[54] Each case requires a thorough analysis that would take us far beyond the scope of the present study.

## Notes

1. The older source-critical theories ascribe Nm 25:1–9 to the Priestly source incorporating narrative elements that had been merged into JE; see George Buchanan Gray, *A Critical and Exegetical Commentary of Numbers*, International Critical Commentary on the Holy Scriptures of the Old and New Testaments (New York: Scribner, 1906), pp. 380–387; Martin Noth, *Numbers, a Commentary*, Old Testament Library (Philadelphia: Westminster, 1968), pp. 196–199; Norman Henry Snaith, *Leviticus and Numbers*, Century Bible (London: Oliphants, 1969), pp. 302–304. A more nuanced hypothesis is offered by Israel Knohl, *Miqdash Ha-demamah: 'Iyun Be-rovde Ha-yetsirah Ha-Kohanit Sheba-Torah [The Sanctuary of Silence: A Study of the Priestly Strata in the Pentateuch]*, Publications of the Perry Foundation for Biblical Research in the Hebrew University of Jerusalem (Jerusalem: Magnes, 1992), pp. 92, 96. Knohl notes that the Phineas

episode differs from the normal style of P, but exhibits typical signs of the Holiness Code (H). See also Ps 106:30–31.

2. An instructive summary of the exegetical puzzles may be found in the 'Aqedat Yiṣḥaq by the fifteenth-century Spanish commentator R' Isaac Aramah [Sefer 'Akedat Yitshak 'al Ḥamishah Ḥumshe Torah ve-'al Ḥamesh Megillot . . . R' Yiṣḥaq 'Aramah . . ., ed. Hayim Yosef Pollak (Pressburg: Verlag von Victor Kittseer, 1849)] [Hebrew], 4:126b–127a, #83: "What was it that Phineas saw which was not evident to Moses? And why did he act without being commanded to do so? And if it was proper to act in that manner, then why was it not commanded?"

   Virtually every study of the Zealot ideologies during the latter part of the Second Commonwealth focuses on the archetype of Phineas. See Martin Hengel, The Zealots: Investigations into the Jewish Freedom Movement in the Period from Herod I until 70 A.D, trans. David Smith (Edinburgh: T. & T. Clark, 1989); A. Stumpff, "ζῆλος, ζηλόω, ζηλωτής, παραζηλω," in Theological Dictionary of the New Testament, ed. Gerhard Kittel, Gerhard Friedrich, and Geoffrey William Bromiley (Grand Rapids: Eerdmans, 1985), pp. 877–888; William Klassen, "Jesus and Phineas: A Rejected Role Model," Society of Biblical Literature Seminar Papers 25 (1986): 490–500; David Rhoads, "Zealots," in The Anchor Bible dictionary, ed. David Noel Freedman (New York and Toronto: Doubleday, 1992), pp. 1043–1054.

3. See Louis Ginzberg, The Legends of the Jews, trans. H. Szold, 7 vols. (Philadelphia: Jewish Publication Society of America, 1909–1939), 3:384 ; 6:136–137, n.792, for a survey of midrashic passages that offer favorable or critical assessments of Moses' passivity.

4. Martin Hengel, Die Zeloten: Untersuchungen zur jüdische Freiheitsbewegung in der Zeit von Herodes I. bis 70 n. Chr, 2. verb. und erw. Aufl. n ed., Arbeiten zur Geschichte des antiken Judentums und des Urchristentums (Leiden: Brill, 1976). I will be citing the work according to the English translation: Hengel, The Zealots. The most crucial section for our purposes is IV B (pp. 149–177).

5. He acknowledges the help provided by Paul Billerbeck and Hermann Leberecht Strack, Kommentar zum Neuen Testament aus Talmud und Midrasch (München: Beck, 1922).

6. See Günter Stemberger and Hermann Leberecht Strack, Introduction to the Talmud and Midrash, trans. Markus N. A. Bockmuehl, 2nd ed. (Minneapolis: Fortress Press, 1996), pp. 309–311.

7. Stemberger and Strack, Introduction to the Talmud and Midrash, pp. 308–309.

8. A definitive argument for the classification of "late midrashim" as medieval, rather than as rabbinic documents, was made by Joseph

Dan, *The Hebrew Story in the Middle Ages*, Sifriyyat Keter (Jerusalem: Keter, 1974), especially pp. 15–23 [Hebrew]. Of relevance to our topic is the typology of medieval Jewish eschatological scenarios, as described there, pp. 33–46.

9. Note particularly the "Phineas is Elijah" tradition, which Hengel, *The Zealots* (see pp. 162–177), dates to Second Temple Zealot traditions, though it does not appear explicitly in Hebrew sources prior to the Middle Ages. Some of his arguments (though assuredly not all of them) are supported by references to medieval "midrashim" and Targums [and cf. Avigdor Shinan, *The Embroidered Targum: The Aggadah in Targum Pseudo-Jonathan of the Pentateuch*, Publications of the Perry Foundation for Biblical Research in the Hebrew University of Jerusalem (Jerusalem: Magnes Press, 1992), pp. 193–198 (and n. 13) [Hebrew] on the dating of Targum Ps. Jonathan]. On the other hand, some current research by J. Yahalom, D. Boyarin, and others might ultimately strengthen Hengel's hypothesis that ideas that were suppressed in "official" rabbinic works (including distinctive Priestly values) survived in the popular Targums, *piyyuṭ* and other genres of the same era.

10. "Aramean" is the conventional equivalent of "gentile" or "heathen" in Jewish Aramaic dialects, including the biblical Targums. On this usage see: Saul Lieberman, *Greek in Jewish Palestine* (New York: The Jewish Theological Seminary of America, 1942), p. 86, n. 130; Geza Vermes, "Leviticus 18:21 in Ancient Jewish Bible Exegesis," in *Studies in Aggadah, Targum, and Jewish Liturgy in Memory of Joseph Heinemann*, ed. Jakob J. Petuchowski and Ezra Fleischer (Jerusalem: Magnes Press and Hebrew Union College Press, 1981), pp. 108–124; M. Sokoloff, *A Dictionary of Jewish Palestinian Aramaic*, Dictionaries of Talmud, Midrash, and Targum (Ramat-Gan: Bar-Ilan University Press, 1990), p. 76.

11. See Hengel, *The Zealots*, p. 158. Rabbinic Hebrew routinely employs the present participle in a jussive sense, indicating what must, should, or may be done; see Moses Hirsch Segal, *A Grammar of Mishnaic Hebrew*, reprint ed. (Oxford: Clarendon Press, 1986), p. 159, #331. Thus, it is not clear whether our passage should be read as normative—"the zealots ought to strike him"—or as descriptive. The assigning of the punishment to the Zealots serves to inject a measure of contingency into the matter, as if to say: "if there are zealots present, then they will attack him."

12. Benzion Lurie, *Megillat Ta'anith with Introduction and Notes* (Jerusalem: Bialik Insitute, 1964), pp. 20–26 [Hebrew]; Hengel, *The Zealots*, pp. 67, 215. The Mishnah juxtaposes three offenses that are

avenged by Zealots: (1) stealing a sacred bowl from the Temple; (2) cursing through sorcery; and (3) intimacy with gentile women. Luria suggests that the background for (1) can be explained in terms of issues and events from the Hellenistic reforms prior to the Hasmonean uprising.

13. See Stemberger and Strack, *Introduction to the Talmud and Midrash*, pp. 31–44, for a summary and bibliography of rabbinic beliefs about the antiquity of the oral Torah. In relatively few instances do the talmudic sources insist on a belief in a literal received tradition dictated to Moses, as distinct from Sinaitic authorization of the interpretations and enactments of the sages through history.

14. Ginzberg, *The Legends of the Jews*, 3:383–388, 6:135–138.

15. Sifré on Numbers #131 [H. S. Horovitz, ed., *Siphre D'Be Rab: Siphre ad Numeros adjecto Siphre zutta*, 2nd ed. (Jerusalem: Wahrmann, 1966), pp. 172–173 (Hebrew)]; *Tanḥuma Balaq* 21; Solomon Buber, ed., *Midrash Tanḥuma*, 2 vols. (Vilna,1885); *Balaq* 30 (p. 2:148) [Hebrew]; *TP Sanhedrin*; *TB Sanhedrin*.

16. Rav Dimi and Rabin belonged to the class of *naḥote* who brought traditions from the Land of Israel to Babylonia.

17. There is some confusion regarding the respective mnemonics in the text. This seems to be the best reading.

18. Sources are listed in Ginzberg, *The Legends of the Jews* , 6:137, n. 796. The texts employ different terms to designate the javelin's blade.

19. Cf. Mishnah *Sheqalim* 3:2.

20. Ralph Marcus, ed., *Josephus with an English Translation*, The Loeb Classical Library (London and Cambridge, Mass.: William Heineman and Harvard University Press, 1966), 2:422–423, 9:488–491, and notes. *Sicarii* are mentioned occasionally in rabbinic literature; see, e.g., Mishnah *Makhshirin* 1:6, *Avot de-Rabbi Natan* B 7 [Solomon Schechter, ed., *Aboth de Rabi Nathan*, newly corrected ed. (New York: Feldheim, 1967), p. 20 (cf. A 7)] [Hebrew]; *TB Giṭṭin* 56a; Hengel, *The Zealots*, pp. 50–56.

21. Menahem Stern, "Zealots," *Encyclopedia Judaica Year Book*, vol. 1 (1973). The same midrashic tradition has Zimri's bodyguards comment sardonically as he enters the tent: "Let him go in! The Pharisees have permitted it" [i.e., Zimri's idolatrous deeds]. This rare rabbinic usage of the term Pharisee (following the usual pattern, the word is being used by their opponents) further demonstrates how the rabbis linked the episode to the Second Commonwealth setting, when the Pharisees existed as a distinct movement. Notwithstanding Josephus' attempts to distance the Pharisees from the Zealots, even he cannot avoid acknowledging the fundamental closeness of the two "philosophies"; see *Antiquities* 18:23; Hengel, *The Zealots*, pp. 77, 80.

22. Virtually all scholarly accounts on Second Temple Zealotry make reference to the impact of Phineas in the consciousness of the Zealots, whether in the Hasmonean revolt or the struggle against Rome. See Morton Smith, "Zealots and Sicarii: Their Origins and Relations," *Harvard Theological Review* 64 (1971): 1–19; H. P. Kingdon, "The Origins of the Zealots," *New Testament Studies* 19 (1972–1973): 74–81; Valentin Nikiprowetzky, "Josephus and the Revolutionary Parties," in *Josephus, the Bible, and History*, ed. Louis H. Feldman and Gohei Hata (Detroit: Wayne State University Press, 1988), pp. 216–236.

23. The Septuagint renders the Hebrew *romaḥ*, conventionally translated as a spear or javelin, as *seiromasten*, a kind of dagger.

24. The Qumran scrolls, to the best of my knowledge, do not focus especially on Phineas.

25. Stemberger and Strack, *Introduction to the Talmud and Midrash*, pp. 247–251, 266–268. Cf. Hengel, *The Zealots*, p. 156.

26. The enumeration is divided into two lists of six. I have been unable to identify any qualitative, logical, or narrative difference between the two lists. Evidently, they were taken by the redactor from separate sources. See Ginzberg, *The Legends of the Jews*, 6:137, n. 798.

27. Conveniently ascribed to the activity of angels.

28. See Isaac Heinemann, *Darkhei ha'aggadah* (Jerusalem and Tel-Aviv: Magnes and Masadah, 1970), pp. 80–82 [Hebrew]; Eliezer Segal, *The Babylonian Esther Midrash: A Critical Commentary*, Brown Judaic Studies (Atlanta: Scholars Press, 1994), 3:254–256.

29. This interpretation forms the basis of Rashi's commentary to the parallel passage in *TB Sanhedrin* 82a, where six of the miracles are enumerated with some variations. Items #10 and #11 were designed to prevent the priestly Phineas from contracting impurity through his contact with a corpse. The midrashic expansion of the passage cannot be seen as a response to any textual stimulus or difficulty.

30. The Hebrew expression appears in many forms in the various manuscripts and parallel versions, though the sense is clear from the context.

31. Hengel, *The Zealots*, p. 160, who assumes a more extreme contrast between the attitudes of the *Sifré* and the Talmuds.

32. Cf. Hengel, *The Zealots*, p. 159 and n. 75. This kind of anachronistic projection of rabbinic institutions ("sages") onto the Bible is, of course, a familiar trope of midrash. A different understanding of the discussion may be found in the traditional commentary *P'nei Mosheh* by Rabbi Moses Margalit.

33. R' Judah, the son of R' Simeon ben Pazi, was a prominent Palestinian teacher known chiefly for his homilies. See Stemberger and Strack, *Introduction to the Talmud and Midrash*, p. 94.

34. A general discussion of this tension may be found in Eliezer Berkovits, *Not in Heaven: The Nature and Function of Halakha* (New York: Ktav, 1983).

35. The question of why God endorsed Phineas' action in this case is one that occupied the post-talmudic exegetes; see below.

36. The passages does not present any major textual difficulties. For purposes of my translation and discussion I have consulted R. N. N. Rabbinowicz, *Diqduqé Soferim, Variæ Lectiones in Mishnam et in Talmud Babylonicum*, reprint ed., 2 vols. (New York: M. P. Press, 1976) *ad loc.* [Hebrew]; Samuel K. Mirsky, ed., *Sheeltot de Rab Ahai Gaon* (Jerusalem: Sura Research and Publication Foundation, 1963–1977) 5:75–77 [Hebrew]; and the fine Yemenite tradition of Z. M. Rabinowitz, ed., *Midrash Haggadol on the Pentateuch: Numbers* (Jerusalem: Mossad Harav Kook, 1973), pp. 440–443. [Hebrew].

37. It is not obvious which genre of rabbinic sources this passage belongs to, since it combines the elements of academic discussion with those of an aggadic narrative (apparently, one that took place outside the academic setting). See Eliezer Segal, *Case Citation in the Babylonian Talmud: The Evidence of Tractate Neziqin*, ed. E. S. Frierichs, Brown Judaic Studies (Atlanta: Scholars Press, 1990), vol. 1, pp. 63–64.

38. I.e., unspecified supernatural informants.

39. For biographical information see Stemberger and Strack, *Introduction to the Talmud and Midrash*, pp. 93–95. It is interesting to note that the same Rav Kahana would later commit an act of zealous violence by slaying an informer. See Isaiah Gafni, "The Babylonian *Yeshiva* as Reflected in Bava Qamma 117a," *Tarbiz* 49, no. 3–4 (1980), 292–301; Daniel Sperber, "On the Unfortunate Adventures of Rav Kahana," *Irano-Judaica* 1 (1982), 83–100.

40. As Arama explains it, this was the reason why Moses did not prosecute the case, since he represented the finite authority of the judicial system. Arama adds that this attitude should be read into the sequence of 1 Kgs 18–19, where Elijah (a figure who was regarded by Jewish tradition as a parallel to Phineas) massacred the prophets of Baal and was subsequently forced to flee into the wilderness under unbearable conditions, until he was told to go to Horeb and experience the presence of God in the same way that Moses had. Arama reads this whole episode as a punishment for Elijah's zealotry, and as a divine recommendation to follow Moses' ways, not Phineas'. To be sure, Arama is aware of rabbinic texts that prefer Phineas' activism to Moses' indecisiveness. However, he insists that Phineas' case was a unique one and was not intended to serve as a precedent for similar situations that might arise in the future.

41. Died in 309. See Stemberger and Strack, *Introduction to the Talmud and Midrash*, p. 101.

42. Stemberger and Strack, *Introduction to the Talmud and Midrash*, p. 101.

43. Stemberger and Strack, *Introduction to the Talmud and Midrash*, p. 94.

44. See S. Federbush, *Ha-Musar Veha-mishpaṭ Be-yisra'el* (Jerusalem: Mosad Harav Kook, 1979), pp. 135–136 [Hebrew]. A fine survey of the principal commentators to the passage may be found in Yehudah Nachshoni, *Studies In the Weekly Parashah*, trans. Shmuel Himelstein, 5 vols., Mesorah, vol. 2: Sh'mos (New York: ArtScroll, 1988), 4:1111–1121. See also Nehama Leibowitz, *Studies in Devarim (Deuteronomy)*, 3rd ed. (Jerusalem: World Zionist Organization, Dept. for Torah Education and Culture in the Diaspora, 1980), pp. 328–333.

45. See Mirsky, ed., *Sheeltot de Rab Ahai Gaon*, 5:75–77; Zwi Taubes, ed., *Otsar ha-Ge'onim Le-masekhet Sanhedrin* (Jerusalem: Mossad Harav Kook, 1966), pp. 444–446 [Hebrew]; Abraham Sofer, ed., *Beit Habbeḥirah 'al Massekhet Sanhedrin asher ḥibber Rabbeinu Menaḥem . . . Hamme'iri*, 2nd rev. ed. (Jerusalem: Kedem, 1974), 298–300 [Hebrew]; S. J. Zevin, ed., *Talmudic Encyclopedia*, 2nd rev. ed., vol. 1 (Jerusalem: Talmudic Encyclopedia Institute, 1969-), 3:14–16 [Hebrew].

46. See Gerald J. Blidstein, *Political Concepts in Maimondean Halakha* (Ramat-Gan: Bar-Ilan University, 1983), p. 224, n. 43 [Hebrew]. Blidstein argues that Maimonides limits the scope of the law to where the woman herself is an idolater.

47. Hengel, *The Zealots*, pp. 11, 14–16, 65–66, etc. Cf. Louis H. Feldman, *Studies in Josephus' Rewritten Bible*, Supplements to the Journal for the Study of Judaism (Leiden, Boston, and Köln: Brill, 1998), pp. 302–303.

48. On the diverse Pharisaic and rabbinic attitudes towards the Zealots and the post-Destruction Roman authorities, see E. Urbach, *The Sages: Their Concepts and Beliefs*, trans. I. Abrahams (Cambridge, Mass., and London: Harvard University Press, 1987), pp. 595–601.

49. One should not lose sight of the simple fact that the rule sanctioning attack by Zealots is, after all, preserved in that quintessential testimony to rabbinic legalism, the Mishnah.

50. As far as I can tell, there is insufficient evidence to determine whether the anti-Zealot views described here represent a consensus among the rabbis or were restricted to particular schools. It would not be surprising, for example, if the school of Rabbi Akiva, who supported the Bar Kokhba insurrection, were more sympathetic to biblical militants like Phineas and Elijah.

51. See Urbach, *The Sages*, pp. 540, 929 n. 53.

52. See, e.g., Mishnah *Sanhedrin* 4:1–4, 624–625.

53. See E. E. Urbach, "Halakha and Prophecy," *Tarbiz* 18 (1947), 1–27; Berkovits, *Not in Heaven*.

54. With respect to each of these instances, we know that there were rabbis, especially in the earlier stages of the talmudic era, who upheld the literal sense of the biblical commandments.

# CHAPTER NINE

# Hindutva and the Rhetoric of Violence

## Interpreting the Past, Designing the Future

RONALD NEUFELDT

The coming to power of the Bharatiya Janata Party (BJP) in India has brought to the fore, in the political landscape of India, a rhetoric concerning Hindu religion and culture that is quite different from the descriptions and analyses of Hindu religion and culture one normally gets in academic circles. The rhetoric of the BJP and its fraternal organizations is not a new rhetoric, but has its roots in the period leading up to the independence of India. It is a rhetoric that was born in the debates over independence and the debates over the direction that India was to take as a nation. Furthermore, it is a rhetoric aimed at the recovery of a lost part of the Hindu past, its allegedly martial character, and the revival of this character as an integral part of India's or Hindusthan's future. As such it is a rhetoric aimed at providing an alternative interpretation of Hindu history and culture in order to counter the allegedly misguided understandings based on Gandhian influence.

This chapter revisits one aspect, perhaps the most important, of this rhetoric: the language of Hindutva. The language of Hindutva was articulated publicly in 1923 by V. D. Savarkar in his monograph entitled *Hindutva: Who Is a Hindu?* The text of *Hindutva* not only set out the ideology of the Hindu Mahasabha but also the program of the Hindutva forces of today.[1] Much of the recent literature on Hindutva tends to focus on the revival of Hindutva rhetoric in the language and programs of the VHP and related organizations, and in the language of the Bharatiya Janata Party, particularly since its success at the polls in the 1990s. As important as it is to recognize the revival of the rhetoric of Hindutva in more recent developments, it is equally important

157

to recognize the persistence of the rhetoric in political and legal discourse even after the Hindu Mahasabha and the Rashtriya Swayam Sevak Sangh fell out of public favor.

In his prime V. D. Savarkar was, of course, a formidable opponent of M. K. Gandhi, taking issue with what he referred to as the Gandhist forces in the Congress movement, and in particular Gandhi's approach to independence and the business of nation-building. Indeed, Savarkar's biographer, Keer, suggests that *Hindutva* was, at least in part, an intense reaction to Gandhism, particularly with respect to the treatment of the antinational demands of the Muslims.[2] Savarkar's was a voice that Gandhi and the leaders of the Congress movement had to take seriously. They did so not only because Savarkar was a charismatic orator, but because he articulated a compelling interpretation of India's past and a program for the future.

While Savarkar's vision did not win the day, the language of Hindutva continued to be a critical factor: in the Constituent Assembly Debates, in Reports on Missionary Activities, in Freedom of Religion Bills (some of which became state statutes), in High Court and Supreme Court cases dealing with religious freedom, and more recently, in the language of the BJP and its supporting groups. In short, the language of Hindutva stayed alive only to emerge in the full light of day with the political victories of the BJP in the 1990s. In this chapter I wish, in the first instance, to return to V. D. Savarkar, to provide a brief analysis of salient features of Hindutva, focusing on his interpretation of the past and vision for the future; and second, to provide a brief examination of the influence of the language of Hindutva in the Constituent Assembly Debates, Reports on Missionary Activities, and Freedom of Religion Bills. My focus will be particularly on the influence of this language in attitudes to and prescriptions for non-Hindus, for it is here that one sees the potential for religiously and culturally motivated violence.

## Hindutva

*Hindutva: Who Is a Hindu*, although written by Savarkar in 1923, was destined to become the point of reference for much of what has been called Hindutva since then. As the title of this work indicates, Savarkar was interested in addressing what Hinduness means. In the process of defining Hinduness, he offered a reinterpretation, indeed, a rewriting, of India's past and a vision for the future of India. Hindutva, Savarkar claimed, is broader than the spiritual or religious history of India. It signifies the whole history of India, embracing "all departments of thought and activity of the whole Being of our Hindu race."[3] It is intrinsically tied to the idea of Hindu consciousness, a consciousness that is as old as the civilization that was fashioned in India by the ancient Aryans, and is therefore at least as old as the *Rig Veda*.[4]

Savarkar's rendition of the spread of this civilization reads like an expression of manifest destiny: "Tribe after tribe of the Hindus issued from the land of their nursery and led by the consciousness of a great mission and their Sacrificial Fire that was the symbol thereof, they soon reclaimed the vast, waste and but very thinly populated lands."[5] The point of this account was, of course, to counter two claims made about the origin and meaning of the term "Hindu." The first is that the term refers primarily to a religious tradition or family of traditions based on the Vedas. The second is that the term is of relatively recent origin. Savarkar's claim is fundamental to his argument for a Hindu Rashtra, something he developed in his presidential addresses to the Hindu Mahasabha. He seemed to feel that the claim of antiquity gave to the idea of a Hindu Rashtra a sense of truth and inevitability.

His account, however, begs an important question: Why was the term not in common use in the ancient texts? His response was clear: the name was forgotten as new colonies and a variety of peoples were incorporated into the Aryan or Hindu culture. As this happened, he argued, the term "Hindu" was replaced by regional terms. This changed, however, with the coming of Rama, whose advent signaled the real birth of the Hindu people. Here, too, we see the expression of a manifest destiny, but now a destiny fulfilled:

> At last the great mission which the Sindhus had undertaken of founding a nation or a country, found and reached its geographical limit when the valorous Prince of Ayodhya made the triumphant entry in Ceylon and actually brought the whole land from the Himalayas to the seas under one sovereign sway. The day when the Horse of Victory returned to Ayodhya unchallenged and unchallengeable, the great white Umbrella of Sovereignty was unfurled over the Imperial throne of Ramachandra, the brave, Ramachandra the good, and a loving allegiance was sworn, not only by the Princes of Aryan blood but Hanuman, Sugriva, Bibhishana from the South—that day was the real birth of our Hindu People.[6]

We see in this account an appeal to an idealized past, an appeal that Anderson and Damle have noted in their account of Hindu revivalism in general.[7]

The experiment in nation-building, Savarkar claimed, was almost undone by the rise of Buddhism. Savarkar's attitude was highly ambiguous on this point. On the one hand, Buddhism, along with the movement of

Hindus outside the borders of India, served to make India a pilgrimage destination of the then-known world.[8] On the other hand, the experiment with Buddhism proved to be a disaster for the national life of India. The problem with Buddhism was its teaching of *ahimsa*. In his view *ahimsa* was entirely unsuited for the rough-and-tumble world of political ambition and national and racial distinctions that drive people to do battle with each other. *Ahimsa* may do for a future universal human state based on universal righteousness[9] but not for the realities of the present time. The "mealy-mouthed formulas of ahimsa," he argued, simply invited invasion from hordes who could not appreciate the finer points of Hindu civilization.[10]

Thankfully, the resources for the revival of the nation were at hand. These could be found in the Vedas, the system of *varnas*, the *Laws of Manu*, and the ancient records of the Indian people kept alive in the Epics and the Puranas. Savarkar's language is graphic: "So the leaders of thought and action of our race had to rekindle their Sacrificial Fire to oppose the sacrilegious one and to reopen the mines of Vedic fields for steel, to get it sharpened on the altar of Kali, 'the Terrible so that Mahakal—the Spirit of Time' be appeased."[11] The appeal to Kali is an instructive one. It is an appeal to a terrific deity, a terrible warrior if you will. This, in effect, is an appeal to the martial heritage of Hindus, a heritage that had allegedly been lost and must now be recovered if the dream of *Hindurashtra* was to be realized.

The recovery of national pride resulted in one hundred years of peace and plenty, broken finally by the invasion of the Muslims. Savarkar argued that the invasions served as never before to unite Hindus into a nation. The seers, statesmen, and martial heroes who rallied the people did so by appealing to Hindutva and Hindusthan. Significantly, among the heroes listed, pride of place belongs to warriors, and they are the ones credited not only with the protection of the Hindu civilization but also of Hindu religion. "For it was the one great issue to defend the honor and independence of Hindusthan and maintain the cultural unity and civic life of Hindutva and not Hinduism alone, but Hindutva,—i.e. Hindudharma that was being fought out on hundreds of fields of battle as well as on the floor of the chambers of diplomacy."[12] It is here that one sees with some clarity Savarkar's vision for India and the meaning he gave to terms such as "Hindu" and "Hinduism." Hinduism is a religious term meaning the ideological systems based in some sense on the Vedas. He, by contrast, made the point that a person can be a Hindu *without* believing in the Vedas.[13] The term "Hindu" is a broader category referring to those who are not only residents of India or Hindusthan, but also to those who defend the honor and independence of Hindusthan and Hindutva, the Hindu civilization based on Hindu dharma (law, virtue, truth). He recognized, in effect, three requisites for being recognized as a

Hindu: being a person of the soil of India, recognizing India as Fatherland or Motherland, and recognizing India as Holyland.[14]

Savarkar went to great lengths to point out that love for India as Fatherland is not enough. If it were, Christians and Muslims could be called Hindus, and this he did not want to allow. Muslims and Christians may love India as a Fatherland, they may even observe caste rules, but India is not a Holyland for them in the sense that Hindu dharma has ceased to be a salvific dharma for them. By adopting a new religion they have cast their lot with a different cultural unit and have ceased to have a loving attachment to Hindu civilization and dharma.[15] Savarkar's language on this issue is instructive. It is the language of adulteration. Indian Christians and Muslims have become infected by an alien adulteration.[16]

This raises two significant issues. One is the business of dual loyalties, something which Savarkar saw as destructive of any attempt at nation-building. His view was that any minorities who love India as Fatherland only cannot be completely loyal to India.

The second issue is the business of conversions. Savarkar supported the program of *Buddhi*, but for him this meant more than simply a religious conversion. He accepted the possibility of conversion to Hinduism (the religion as opposed to the civilization), but this is not enough. To his mind, a mere conversion to Hinduism does not qualify one as a Hindu. For that to happen the alien adulteration must be removed, but this can only happen if one accepts India as Fatherland and Holyland.

In his study of Hindu nationalism in modern India Hansen has pointed out that there are two important coordinates in Savarkar's Hindutva, territoriality and culture.[17] It should be added that this is culture with a special meaning. Indeed, for Savarkar, to be a nation or a people meant to have a common culture, a common language, a common history, a common religion, and to claim "this Bharatbhoomi from the Indus to the Seas as his Fatherland and Holyland."[18] This is the meaning of the term "Hindusthan," a term that supposedly had its roots in the Vedas and was allegedly appealed to over and over in the defense of Hindu dharma throughout India's history. The independence of India was, for Savarkar, synonymous with the establishment of Hindusthan.

In principle, Savarkar saw the idea of territorial unity alone as deeply flawed. It was, in the first instance, a product of the denationalization of India that had occurred through the introduction of Western education.[19] In the second place, Muslims of India had never bought into the idea of a territorial unity. They wanted a nation, but it must be a nation built on cultural, religious, and racial unity; in other words, a Muslim nation. Savarkar accused Congress of pushing a brand of pseudonationalism and of being anti-Hindu.[20] He argued that Congress nationalism is a communal nation-alism because it recognizes a majority and a minority.

At issue here is the business of dual loyalties. For him it was simply impossible to be loyal to the Indian State on the one hand and to have a loyalty to a non-indigenous religion on the other. As much as he tried to downplay the importance of religion in defining Hindu and Hindutva, here he chose not to ignore it. Rather, he emphasized it.

> Whatever may happen some centuries hence, we cannot ignore the solid fact of today that religion wields mighty influence on the minds of men in Hindusthan and, in the case of Mohammedans especially, their religious zeal more often than not borders on *fanaticism*! Their love toward India as their Motherland is but a handmaid to their love for their Holyland outside India. Their faces are ever turned toward Mecca and Medina. But to Hindus, Hindusthan being their Fatherland as well as their Holyland, the love they bear to Hindusthan is undivided and absolute.[21]

Muslims, in Savarkar's view, could not even buy into territorial alle-giance; their theology, theoretical politics, and stage of development prevent it. They were still at the stage of intense religiosity (read fanaticism) and a concept of the state that divides the world into Muslims and non-Muslims. A faithful Muslim could not swear loyalty to any state that is ruled by non-Muslims, but "is called upon to do everything in his power by policy or force or fraud to convert the non-Muslim there to the Muslim faith, to bring about its political conquest by a Muslim power."[22] Muslims, Savarkar claimed, have a "secret urge goading (them) to transform India into a Moslem state."[23]

The appropriate response to the proselytizing activities of Christians and Muslims was to engage in an aggressive policy of *Buddhi* (conversion), rather than the Gandhian program of appeasement and its misplaced opti-mism about Hindu–Muslim unity. Given Savarkar's definition of Hinduism, and his call to reestablish the organic Hindu nation, the call for aggressive *Buddhi* could only mean a call to increase the number of Hindu voters to counteract the perceived growth of the Muslim population and conversions to Islam. If there were indeed two nations, a Hindu nation and a Muslim nation, then as far as Savarkar was concerned the only way to assure the reestablishment of the Hindu nation on its proper footing was an aggressive campaign of reconversion. In this campaign Savarkar worked hand in glove with the Arya Samaj, the original proponents of *Buddhi*.

While the vision of Savarkar and the Hindu Mahasabha did not win the day—indeed, while the Hindu Mahasabha fell out of favor after the assassination of Gandhi—the language of Hindutva continued to be a significant factor in the political arena, both at the Centre and in the States. Hindutva rhetoric was very much a part of the Constituent Assembly Debates, Reports on Christian Missionary Activities, and, more recently, Freedom of Religion Bills at the state level. It is to these that I now turn.

## The Constituent Assembly Debates

There is no question that the Hindutva language as it was spelled out by Savarkar played a role in the Constituent Assembly Debates. This was so whether in the Resolution on Aims and Objectives, or the debates over fundamental rights, religious rights, or minority rights. A few examples taken from the debates over religious freedom and minority rights will suffice. Debates over the fundamental rights to be included in the Constitution began in March 1947 with the discussion of draft articles to be included in the interim report of the Subcommittee on Fundamental Rights. Involved were proposals for religious freedom. Despite arguments that propagation of religion or preaching was divisive and destructive of attempts to build national unity, the Advisory Committee on Minorities and Fundamental Rights had seen fit to recommend the inclusion of the right to propagate religion. Not to do so, it was argued, would be to place an undue restriction on the exercise of religious freedom. Both the Subcommittee and the Advisory Committee saw a clear connection between the right to propagate religion and the probability of conversion from one religious community to another. Such shifts in communal loyalties were not, however, seen as detrimental to the business of nation-building, despite arguments suggesting that extraterritorial allegiances of Christians and Muslims were problematic. Accordingly, the Interim Report issued in April 1947 included the right to practice, profess, and propagate religion. It also included the prohibition of conversion brought about by coercion and undue influence.[24]

The issue of conversion triggered considerable debate, some of which was informed by concerns over a perceived dwindling Hindu population, the eventual loss of an overall Hindu majority, and the problematic nature of dual loyalties. Algu Rai Shastri (Representative for the United Provinces) raised these issues forcefully in his criticism of the proselytization efforts of Christian missionaries.

> The consequence, as Algu Rai Shastri argued, is that grown-up people in such castes as the *bhangies* and *chamars* are converted, and with them their children also go into the fold of the new religion. They should be affectionately asked to live as brothers, he said. This is what has been taught by prophets, angels, and leaders. But this is not being practiced today. Instead, he explained, we are

in search of opportunities to indulge in underhand dealings. We go to people and tell them "you are in darkness; this is not the way to your salvation." Thus, everyone can realize how all possible unfair means have been adopted to trample the majority community underfoot. It is in this way, he insisted, that the foreign bureaucracy has been working here and has been creating vested interests in order to maintain its political stranglehold over the people.[25]

The debates over the Supplementary Report on Fundamental Rights elicited the expression of similar concerns, particularly in the discussion of the clause prohibiting conversion by coercion and undue influence. The clause had been sent back to the Advisory Committee for further consideration but was brought back to the Assembly unchanged. In expressing his concerns over the erosion of the Hindu community, R. V. Dhulekar (Representative for the United Provinces) raised directly the issue of the loyalty of the Muslim community, arguing that to be Muslim meant to be disloyal and subversive: "In the present environment, all sorts of efforts are being made to increase the population of a particular section of this country. There is ample proof both within this House and outside that many who live in this country are not prepared to be citizens of this country. Those who have caused the division of our land desire that India may be further divided."[26] He went on to imply that all conversions to Islam had been conversions by force or fraud.

While such comments express concerns similar to those raised by Savarkar in his articulation of Hindutva ideology, it was left to Lokanath Misra (Representative for Orissa: General) to explicitly raise the concern over the erosion of Hindu culture; this was the so-called culture card, as it has been labeled in present-day expressions of Hindutva. In February 1948 the draft Constitution was submitted to the Assembly for debate. Included in the Fundamental Rights was the right to propagate religion. This elicited considerable discussion in the context of which Lokanath Misra raised quite explicitly concerns over Hindutva or the health of Hindu culture in an environment of religious competition:

> Gradually it seems to me that our "secular State" is a slippery phrase, a device to by-pass the ancient culture of the land. . . . Do we really believe that religion can be divorced from life, or is it our belief that in the midst of many religions we cannot decide which one to accept? If religion is beyond the ken of our State, let us clearly say so and delete all references to rights relating to religion. If we find it necessary, let us be brave enough to say what it should be. . . . Justice demands that the ancient faith and culture of the

land should be given a fair deal, if not restored to its legitimate place after thousands of years of depression.[27]

Ancient Indian culture, he claimed, excluded nothing, and as "an integrated vision and philosophy of life and manners"[28] would have resulted in a "perfectly secular and a homogeneous state"[29] had it not been disturbed by Islam. In present-day Hindutva rhetoric this has become a call for the development of a truly Indian secularism, based on ancient Indian texts and culture, and the rejection of the pseudosecularism adopted from the West.

Like Savarkar, Misra called for the recognition of Hindu culture as the majority culture. Like Savarkar, he saw foreign religions as a threat to that culture because propagation would inevitably lead to the swelling of the non-Hindu ranks in India. Like Savarkar, he argued that Hinduism both as a way of life and as a religion should be restored to its rightful place of supremacy on the political, social, and religious landscape of India. This religion and way of life, he insisted, must be protected from the undermining that will inevitably occur through propagation by Christians and Muslims, if this is freely allowed.

The same concerns over the threat to the Hindu majority, if too many rights were to be accorded to the minorities, were expressed in the debates over the Report of the Advisory Committee on Minority Rights (August 1947). Here it was cast in terms of tyranny by the minorities. This case was made explicit by P. S. Deshmukh (Representative for the Central Provinces and Berar), who argued that Muslims enjoy privileges everywhere far in excess of what was fair.[30] As it had been with Savarkar, the tendency was to equate nationalism with things Hindu and with things regarded to be indigenous. To be Hindu was to be truly nationalist. To belong to non-indigenous religious communities was to be less than loyal, indeed to be tainted by foreignness and suspected of subversion. To convert was to cast one's lot with something foreign and in an obviously significant way to turn one's back on India. This was, in fact, expressed and rejected passionately by Frank Anthony (Representative for C.P. and Berar: General), who took direct aim at what he saw as attempts at Hindu revivalism that threatened minority communities:

> We see, Sir,—I say it without offence—we see members of this great party who technically are members of the Congress, but spiritually are members of the R.S.S. and the Hindu Mahasabha. Unfortunately I read speeches day in and day out by influential and respected leaders of the Congress Party, who say that Indian Independence can only mean Hindu Raj, that Indian culture can only mean Hindu culture.[31]

## Reports on Missionary Activities

Let us now consider state-level events, specifically reports on Christian missionary activities and Freedom of Religion Bills. Although the discussions of fundamental rights in the Constituent Assembly Debates elicited the expression of concern over the presence of the Muslim community in the context of nation-building, we now focus on the Christian community. When it comes to Christian missionary activity, the most often cited report is *The Report of the Christian Missionary Activity Enquiry Committee*, Madhya Pradesh (commonly referred to as the *Niyogi Report*). This was published in 1956. A lesser-known report, but equally as important, is *The Christian Missionary Enquiry Committee's Report*, Madhya Bharat, published in the same year. It is important to note that these reports, particularly the *Niyogi Report*, continue to find a prominent place in Hindutva inspired rhetoric, particularly in books and pamphlets dealing with the topic of conversion.[32] The concerns giving rise to both enquiries were similar: mass conversions, fraudulent conversions, conversions brought about by illegitimate means, the use of schools and medical and social services to gain converts, and criticism of Hindu beliefs and practices. The *Niyogi Report* is of particular importance.

The Christian Missionary Activities Enquiry Committee, Madhya Pradesh, chaired by M. B. Niyogi, was appointed on April 14, 1954, to look into allegations of widespread conversions of illiterate and backward peoples through force, fraud, or promises of monetary gain. Ostensibly, the committee was concerned with examining objections to methods used to convert, not the business of preaching or conversions itself. The general issues were summarized clearly in the *Report*: "There was a general tendency to suspect some ulterior political or extrareligious motive, in the influx of foreign money for evangelistic work in its varied forms. The concentration of missionary enterprise on the hill tribes in remote and inaccessible parts of the forest areas, and their mass conversion with the aid of foreign money, were interpreted as intended to prepare the ground for a separate independent State on the lines of Pakistan."[33]

This quotation points to the central concerns: conversions were being conducted on a mass scale, the methods used for conversion were illegitimate, the motives for seeking conversions were political, and these political motives were supported by foreign money. Thus, from this perspective, the attempt to seek conversions amounted to a foreign conspiracy to subvert the national aspirations of the great majority of Indians. While the *Report* stated that the purpose of the committee was to investigate these expressed concerns, there is every reason to believe from the *Report* itself that the committee (if Niyogi speaks for the whole of the committee) felt from the start that these concerns did, in fact, express the reality of the situation on the ground. This is certainly evident in both the accounts of missionary activities as well as the recommendations of the committee.

It was argued, for example, that the missionary organizations seem to constitute a state within a state.[34] While the *Report* placed the origin of the idea that conversion means a change in nationality at the feet of the missionaries themselves, the *Report* itself seemed to accept this idea and to operate on the basis of such an understanding.[35] If it did indeed operate on the assumption that indigenous religion is an essential ingredient of nationalism, then it was operating on an assumption voiced by Savarkar in his explanation of Hindutva. Evidence for this can be found in the *Report*'s extensive critical comment on the conversion of aboriginals to Christianity. The work of social uplift and educational and medical work undertaken by missionaries, it was claimed, had the effect of turning these simpleminded tribals against Hindus and therefore against loyalty to the nation.[36] More important, it was assumed that the tribals were Hindu, that the tribals had become Hindu by way of an unconscious evolution within the context of the caste system. "Where a tribe has insensibly been converted into a caste, it preserved its original name and customs, but modified its animistic practices more and more in the direction of orthodox Hinduism."[37]

Such comments would appear to be based on arguments made by Savarkar in support of Hindutva. India has from ancient times been recognized as a Hindu nation. The glue that has held this nation—or the idea of this nation—together was Hindu culture.

The way of Hindu India has always been to assimilate foreign invaders or migrants under the umbrella of Hindu culture. Attempts to convert are not only antinational but also unnecessary since Hindu culture has, from the beginning, excluded nothing. Nonetheless, despite the obvious religious and ethnic pluralism of India, there is such a thing as Hindu culture, which is to create a national bond among the Indian people. Therefore, attempts by missionaries to convert ignorant and easily duped tribals from Hinduism are both deemed reprehensible and antinational.

Furthermore, inasmuch as much of the Christian propaganda comes out of America, proselytization has to be seen as an American plot to gain a foothold in Indian society and turn the underprivileged against their own country. That proselytization is seen as a program to undermine national unity, and ultimately to make it possible to establish a Christian party that will lay claim to a separate state as did the Muslim League, is made abundantly clear by the aims of proselytization outlined in the *Report*.[38]

Given what has been said so far it is clear that the *Report* rejected the possibility of dual allegiances. To proclaim allegiance to god over allegiance to the state is in effect an act of denationalization. Ironically, the *Niyogi*

*Report* admitted that Christians do profess loyalty to India but insisted nonetheless that such professions should be viewed with suspicion, given foreign influence over Indian Christians. One is tempted to suggest that there is here an echo of Savarkar's idea that loyalty to the state means nothing unless one sees India as Holyland as well as Fatherland.

## Freedom of Religion Bills

The Constituent Assembly Debates registered considerable concern over the conversion of minors, tribals, and women. Clauses for the protection of the so-called weaker elements of society were put forward, as were clauses that would make it mandatory to register conversions. Such clauses, however, did not make it into the final draft of the Constitution. This did not, however, mean that these concerns died out. They reappeared, not only in reports such as the *Niyogi Report*, but also in the form of Freedom of Religion Bills at the state level. From 1967 to 1978, Freedom of Religion Acts were brought into force in three states—Orissa (1967), Madhya Pradesh (1968), and Arunachal Pradesh (1978).[39] While these Acts were labeled Freedom of Religion Acts their intent was to curtail the incidence of conversion of the weaker sections of society, particularly to an alien religion. In general, the Acts were aimed at eliminating conversion on the ground that conversion undermines faith. This could only be directed at perceived attempts to undermine indigenous faith, for at issue was conversion away from Hinduism, not conversion to Hinduism. The Orissa Act states:

> Conversion in its very process involves an act of undermining another's faith. The process becomes all the more objectionable when this is brought about by recourse to methods like force, fraud or material inducements and exploitation of one's poverty, simplicity and ignorance. Conversion or attempt at conversion in the above manner, besides creating various maladjustments in social life, also give rise to problems of law and order. It is therefore important to provide measures to check such activities which also directly impinge on the freedom of religion.[40]

The concern over conversion in general as an undermining act was surely based on a belief in the kind of rhetoric that we have seen in Savarkar's understanding of Hindutva. If there is to be a Hindu Raj, then conversion cannot be contemplated except conversion in the other direction, that is, back to Hinduism.

Indeed, the Arunachal Pradesh Act—in its original name, the Arunachal Pradesh Freedom of Indigenous Faith Bill—brings us back to the language of Hindutva that had been enunciated by Savarkar. While it is in some respects similar to the Orissa and Madhya Pradesh Acts, it goes considerably beyond those Acts in its explicit mention of the protection of indigenous faiths. Indigenous faith, not surprisingly, is defined as:

> Such religions, beliefs and practices including rites, rituals, festivals, observances, performances, abstinence, customs as have been sanctioned, approved, performed by the indigenous communities of Arunachal Pradesh from the time these communities have been known and includes Buddhism as prevalent among the Monpas, Menbas, Sherdukpens, Khambas, Khamtis and Singphoos, Vashnavism as preached by Noctes, Akas and Nature worships including worships of Dogi-Polo, as prevalent among other indigenous communities of Arunachal Pradesh.[41]

The implications of the language are obvious. Non-indigenous faiths are seen as alien and endangering the national interests. Indeed, indigenous faith and nationalism are viewed as synonymous in some respects. Conversions from indigenous faiths are seen as unwelcome, but no such displeasure is expressed in the other direction—that is, conversions to indigenous faiths.

Similar in intent to the State Acts were a number of bills put forward at the Centre—the Indian Converts Regulation and Registration Bill of 1954, the Backward Communities Religious Protection Bill of 1960, the 1978 Freedom of Religion Bill, and the Compulsory Registration of Religious Conversions Bill of 1981. Of these, the most interesting for my purposes is the 1967 Bill. The object of this bill was "to protect members of Scheduled Castes, Scheduled Tribes and Backward Classes from proselytizing activities of foreign Christian missionaries."[42] In the statement of objects and reasons a direct connection was made to the *Niyogi Commission Report*. It was asserted that the findings of the commission have been agitating the mind of the public and have caused considerable tension.[43] Of greater import is the definition given to religion of Indian origin. This includes Hindu religion in any of its forms, Buddhism, Jainism, Sikhism, or any religion whose founder was born in India.[44] Any change to a religion not of Indian origin is to be accepted only after filing of written statements, enquiry by the District Magistrate, and registration. These same restrictions are not to apply to a change of religion back to one's ancestral religion or to a religion of Indian origin.[45] What was at issue here, as was the case with the *Niyogi Report* and the Freedom of Religion Bills, was the shape of the nation and the understanding of nationalism. The assumptions, even if they were not stated, have to be that the nation is to be defined in terms of Hindu culture, that indigenous religion is an integral part of this culture, and that belonging to a religious tradition that is not seen as indigenous undermines in a fundamental way one's loyalty to the state. There is a true Indian or Hindu culture. To be part of this culture means to revere in some sense the ancient heroes of the Epics. Anyone who cannot do this is guilty of disloyalty to the nation.

### Conclusion

In a recent study I dealt with Savarkar's critique of Gandhi.[46] Given that both were in the business of interpreting India's past and proposing a vision for the future, some of the conclusions arrived at in that study are pertinent here. What Savarkar proposed against Gandhi was a vision for a state in which the number of Hindus was of paramount importance in both the religious and the political sense. In the language of Hindutva, India was to be a Hindu State in which all citizens viewed India as Fatherland and Holyland. In such a vision there could be no room for dual loyalties, loyalty to India on the one hand and loyalty to an "alien" religion on the other. Such language was quite foreign to Gandhi, who chose rather to speak in terms of Indian nationalism, citizens of India, or an India that took seriously the concerns and even demands of its minorities. He believed in the possibility of a pan-Indian (not a pan-Hindu) civilization that would recognize the multiple diversities and identities, and in which these diversities would somehow be united in a larger cause. Sumit Sarkar, in his analysis of Hindu nationalism, has argued compellingly that Gandhi worked on the basis of the assumption that human communication was possible even across the sharpest of divides.[47] The Hindutva ideology seems to run in the other direction; that is, it serves to set up barriers.

Furthermore, it is a kind of language that is used, and has been used, to support violence of one religious group against another, of one cultural group (to use Hindutva language) against another. It has long been suspected that recent upsurges of violence against Christians in Gujarat, Madhya Pradesh, and Orissa have been fueled, at least in part, by Hindutva rhetoric. Without question, that rhetoric has played a role in the recent Hindu–Muslim riots over attempts to construct a temple on the ruins of the destroyed mosque in Ayodhya. That this is the case should not be surprising. For if one defines the nation as Hindu and regards certain faith traditions as alien, then converts to such faith traditions can be seen as guilty of treason, to be dealt with in the way that treason frequently is—with violence.

## Notes

1. See Lise McKean, *Divine Enterprise: Gurus and the Hindu Nationalist Movement* (Chicago: University of Chicago Press, 1996), pp. 71–96. See also Walter K. Anderson and Shridar Damle, *The Brotherhood in Saffron: The Rashtriya Swayam Sevak Sangh and Hindu Revivalism* (New Delhi: Vistar Publications, 1987), pp. 26–30.
2. Dhananjay Keer, *Veer Savarkar* (Bombay: Popular Prakashan, 1988), p. 162.
3. V. D. Savarkar, *Hindutva: Who Is a Hindu* (New Delhi: Bharti Sahitya Sadan, 1989), p. 4.
4. Savarkar, *Hindutva*, p. 8.
5. Savarkar, *Hindutva*, p. 10.
6. Savarkar, *Hindutva*, pp. 11–12.
7. Anderson and Damle, *The Brotherhood in Saffron*, p. 11.
8. Savarkar, *Hindutva*, p. 17.
9. Savarkar, *Hindutva*, p. 38.
10. Savarkar, *Hindutva*, p. 19.
11. Savarkar, *Hindutva*, p. 21.
12. Savarkar, *Hindutva*, pp. 45–46.
13. Savarkar, *Hindutva*, p. 81.
14. While the term "Fatherland" seems to play a dominant role for Savarkar in his references to India, it is also the case that he uses the term interchangeably with "Motherland."
15. Savarkar, *Hindutva*, pp. 100–101.
16. See Savarkar's discussion in *Hindutva*, pp. 91–92.
17. Thomas Blom Hansen, *The Saffron Wave: Democracy and Hindu Nationalism in Modern India* (Princeton: Princeton University Press, 1999), p. 77.
18. V. D. Savarkar, *Hindu Rashtra Darshan*, 3rd ed. (Bombay: Veer Savarkar Prakashan, 1992), pp. 8–10.
19. See Savarkar, *Hindu Rashtra Darshan*, pp. 37–39.
20. Savarkar, *Hindu Rashtra Darshan*, p. 73.
21. Savarkar, *Hindu Rashtra Darshan,* pp. 14–15. (Italicization taken from the text).
22. Savarkar, *Hindu Rashtra Darshan*, p. 49.
23. Savarkar, *Hindu Rashtra Darshan*, p. 89.
24. *CAD*, Vol. 2, p. 298.
25. *CAD*, Vol. 3, p. 498.
26. *CAD*, Vol. 5, p. 364.
27. *CAD*, Vol. 7, p. 823.
28. *CAD*, Vol. 7, p. 824.

29. *CAD*. Vol. 7, p. 822.
30. *CAD*, Vol. 5, p. 201.
31. *CAD*, Vol. 8, p. 328.
32. See, for example, Arun Shourie, *Missionaries in India, Continuities, Changes, Dilemmas* (New Delhi: ASA Publications, 1994). See also *Religious Conversions, Frequently Asked Questions* (Mumbai: Hindu Vivek Kendra, 1999).
33. *Report of the Christian Missionary Activities Enquiry Committee* (Nagpur: Government Printing, 1956), p. 3 [hereafter referred to as *Niyogi Report*].
34. *Niyogi Report*, p. 27.
35. *Niyogi Report*, pp. 52–53.
36. See the discussion in the *Niyogi Report*, pp. 24–31.
37. *Niyogi Report*, p. 27.
38. *Niyogi Report*, p. 62.
39. It is important to note that there were precedents for such laws. Donald Eugene Smith has pointed out that at the time of independence seventeen princely states had anticonversion provisions in effect. Some of these provisions were similar to those found in the Orissa, Madhya Pradesh, and Arunachal Pradesh Acts. See Donald Eugene Smith, *India as a Secular State* (Princeton: Princeton University Press, 1963), pp. 177–179.
40. Lalit Mohan Suri, ed., *The Current Indian Statutes* (Chandigarh, 1968), p. 5.
41. Bojendra Nath Banerjee, *Religious Conversions in India* (New Delhi: Harnam Publications, 1982), p. 262.
42. Bill No. 134 of 1967, as introduced in Lok Sabha on 1 December 1967, p. 4.
43. Bill No. 134, p. 4.
44. Bill No. 134, p. 2.
45. Bill No. 134, p. 3.
46. The study is forthcoming in a volume on Indian Critiques of Gandhi, to be published by State University of New York Press.
47. See Sumit Sarkar, "Indian Nationalism and the Politics of Hindutva," in *Making India Hindu*, ed. David Ludden (New Delhi: Oxford University Press, 1966), p. 274.

# CHAPTER TEN

# Buddhism and Violence in Modernity

## ROBERT E. FLORIDA

Buddhism, generally speaking, has the image of a faith dedicated to peace and peacemaking, perhaps even as a way of pacifism. In picturing exemplars of the faith today, one thinks of the typical Theravada monk, clad in saffron robes, walking calmly and carefully with downcast eyes, so dedicated to the welfare of all beings that he treads carefully so as not to harm crawling insects. Or one remembers the current Dalai Lama, head of the Gelugpa sect and figurehead of the Tibetan Government in Exile, accepting the Nobel Peace Prize for his work in tring to solve the Tibetan-Chinese confrontation by peaceful means. However, in actuality, the relationship between Buddhism and violence, particularly state-sponsored violence, is complicated and not nearly so pure as might be expected. This chapter will present some basic Buddhist teachings about war and militarism found in the early period and then will look at some surprising later developments.

For the sake of brevity, Thailand will be the primary focus for the Theravada tradition and Tibet for the Mahayana. Japan[1] and Sri Lanka[2] also provide striking examples of how the Buddhist tradition, in confronting the realities of modern nationalism and technological advances, actually provided some major support to militarism and state brutality. Thai and Tibetan examples were chosen as being somewhat less well known and thus perhaps more graphic. Both examples may seem to present contemporary Buddhists in a bad light, which is not the intent, and counterexamples will be briefly noted.

## Basic Principles

On the whole, the Buddha taught little that directly concerned political issues and seemed to go out of his way not to advocate anything that would lead to radical social change.[3] Accordingly, Buddhist scriptures record only a very few incidents where Buddha dealt with soldiering and warfare. The *Vinaya*, the portion of the Buddhist canon that contains the rules and traditions of the monks and nuns, has two accounts of soldiers converting to Buddhism. In the case of the General Siha,[4] who became a lay disciple, Lord Buddha enjoined him to follow Buddhist moral precepts, to purify himself from all evil inclinations of the heart, and to be generous in almsgiving.[5] Although the first precept of Buddhist morality is to take no life (especially human life) and the overall message of the Buddha was one of nonharm and benevolence, General Siha's line of work was never raised, either by him or by his teacher. This seems to be the general position for Buddhist laymen: it is not necessary to give up being a soldier, and the term "warrior" does not appear on the lists of professions considered to be the wrong livelihood.

However, there is evidence from the earliest times that some Buddhist soldiers found the conflict between the teachings against violence and the nature of their job to be hard to bear. The second *Vinaya* story about soldiers converting was set in the context of a border conflict in the powerful Magadha nation ruled by King Bimbisara, who was one of Lord Buddha's most powerful patrons.[6] At that time, some of the finest soldiers thought: "We, who go (to war) and find our delight in fighting, do evil and produce great demerit. Now what shall we do that we may desist from evil doing and may do good?"[7] They resolved to become ordained as Buddhist monks, whose strict vows of nonharm were respected and protected by the king. When the officers found that a number of their crack troops had defected to the Buddhist monastic life, they complained to the king, who asked his judicial officers what should be done. Their answer was that the monk who led the ordination service deserved to be beheaded, the monk who recited the verses should have his tongue torn out, and all the others present should have half their ribs broken.

The king quickly had a word with Lord Buddha, reminding him that his order was under royal protection and that an upset king could make life very unpleasant for the monks. He concluded with the request that no more persons in royal service be ordained, and so the Buddha introduced such a rule, which continues to the present time. This story shows a certain moral queasiness in Buddhism about the legitimacy of war. But it also shows the recognition that a mutual relationship between the secular powers and the order of monks had to be maintained. Another clear indication that early Buddhists wanted monastics to keep a very healthy distance from the military is a series of three minor offences detailed in the section of the *Vinaya* recited twice monthly by the monks and nuns to test their adherence to the discipline. It was improper for a world renouncer to go to see an army fight, to stay more than two or three nights with an army if such a visit were necessary, or to seek out military displays or fighting during one's stay with the army.[8]

Without the power of the state, which in the Indian traditional view necessarily involves the use of force, the conditions necessary to maintain the order of Buddhist mendicants cannot be sustained. Thus, Buddhists never denied that it was legitimate for the ruler to use force both internally and externally, and certain rules to exclude soldiers, thieves, slaves, debtors, and others from ordination were enacted in order to maintain social order.[9] Those soldiers wanting ordination in order to practice the principle of non-harm and improve their karma would first have to get a discharge from the military.

One of the fundamental notions in Buddhism is compassion, the deep intuitive reaction to the suffering of one's fellow human beings, and indeed of all sentient beings. This is both one of the fruits of attaining great insight through meditation practices and a quality to be cultivated by all persons who are on the path of enlightenment. In the biographical accounts of Lord Buddha, and of other Buddhist saints and sinners, incidents motivated by compassion play a major role. There is at least one scriptural example in which Lord Buddha himself intervened for compassionate reasons to prevent a war.

It involved a quarrel between his countrymen, the Sakhyas, and their neighbors over water rights in a time of drought.[10] Lord Buddha intervened by using his supernormal powers and shamed the kings from battle by getting them to acknowledge that it was not sensible to set flowing rivers of human blood for the sake of a little water. The story ends with three verses of praise, extolling lives lived in freedom from hatred, sickness, and desires—even in a world that is afire with all three. These scriptural passages pretty well illustrate the basic Buddhist scriptural responses to war and the military. First, the orders of monks and nuns, who are set apart from the world to perfect themselves, should have nothing to do with the business of shedding blood. War involves clear violations of the first precept against killing, and war feeds on the three fundamental moral poisons of hatred, selfish grasping, and delusion. However, with the ordinary world such as it is, a strong state and even an army are necessary evils; therefore, it is permissible for a lay Buddhist to serve as a ruler or a soldier, and the monastics undertake not to recruit soldiers. In the story of the war that nearly broke out over water, the first problem was a selfish refusal to share a scarce resource. This rapidly led to hatred and escalating violence. But it was all steeped in delusion—none of the officers had the slightest idea what had started the war. When Lord Buddha, acting from wisdom and compassion, made all this clear to the combatants, the quarrel naturally evaporated. However, there was no suggestion that the armies should have been disbanded.

## The Ideal Monarch and Emperor Asoka

The *Digha Nikaya* is the canonical collection of early teachings preserved in the Theravada branch of Buddhism that contains a concentration of material about civil as opposed to monastic governance. "The Sermon on the Knowledge of Beginnings" (*Agganna Sutta*)[11] teaches that government came about when the people elected a man who embodied morality and virtue to impose order after the first humans, who had evolved at the beginning of this cosmic era, had fallen into a violent and chaotic situation. This first king had the duty "to show anger where anger was due, [to] censure those who deserved it, and [to] banish those who deserved banishment."[12] In return for this unsavory but necessary task, the people promised to support the king by giving him a share of their rice crop.

The ideal Buddhist king, described as the wheel-turning king, is described in some detail in the twenty-sixth book of the *Digha Nikaya*, the *Cakkavatti-Sihanada Sutta*, or the "Lion's Roar on the Turning of the Wheel." Again the context is a cosmic one: wheel-turning kings like Buddhas occur at certain times during the great cycles of evolution and decay. Just as worlds and the cosmos as a whole are subject to the process of evolution and dissolution, so, too, individual sentient beings are caught up in the wheel of birth, death, and rebirth. He is called the wheel-turning king because one of his seven sacred treasures is an actual wheel, a mark of his virtuous rule.[13] Wherever he rolls this wheel, the people of that realm submit to him.[14] No violence occurs at all; the people are conquered by the righteousness alone and happily join in the empire of righteousness.

In the words of the Turning of the Wheel chapter, the king is enjoined as follows to exemplify Buddhist virtues:

> Yourself depending on the Dharma, honouring it, revering it, cherishing it, doing homage to it and venerating it, having the Dharma as your badge and banner, acknowledging the Dharma as your master, you should establish guard, ward and protection according to Dharma for your own household, your troops, your nobles, and vassals, for Brahmins and householders, town and country folk, ascetics and Brahmins, for beasts and birds. Let no crime prevail in your kingdom, and to those who are in need, give property.[15]

There is no attempt in this to eliminate social distinctions: the king is greater than his nobles, who in turn are greater than the vassals. The king rules absolutely, and there is no hint of democratic procedures or egalitarianism. Activities counter to dharma—crime, for example—cannot be tolerated, which implies that the use of state force is acceptable.

One of the greatest figures in Indian history is Asoka, the Mauryan Emperor, who reigned from around 269–232 B.C.E. and expanded the boundaries of the empire to include most of the subcontinent. He had a number of inscriptions engraved on pillars and natural stone faces, leaving the most detailed historical record of any ancient Indian monarch. His last great campaign was against the Kalinga nation, whose army he destroyed. One of the rock inscriptions noted that the war cost the Kalingas 100,000 killed on the battlefield, 150,000 taken captive, and many others dead from what we would now call collateral damage. He said, "All suffer from the injury, slaughter, and deportation inflicted on their loved ones . . . all men share in the misfortune, and this weighs on [the King's] mind."[16] The inscription continued to say that now the emperor would regret to kill even a thousandth as many as he did in Kalinga. Since becoming a Buddhist, he had practiced the following: "Even a person who wrongs him must be forgiven for wrongs that can be forgiven." Although he attempted to reform the troublesome hill tribes, he reminded them that he continued to exercise "the power to punish, despite his repentance, in order to induce them to desist from their crimes and escape execution."[17]

Asoka never eliminated capital punishment, but he did very much temper the violence of traditional rule. He initiated public health projects and public works and strongly encouraged vegetarianism. He was a patron of Buddhist and other religious sects and undertook to regulate the activities of all the religious orders in the empire. After the final battle against Kalinga, he gave up warfare, except in self-defense, and established a policy of "conquest through righteousness" (dharma), sending missionaries to his neighbors and as far away as Europe. Although the record is not altogether clear, he claimed that many kingdoms joined the empire because they saw the advantage of living under the rule of dharma. In any case, Buddhists take Asoka as an ideal monarch, one who approached the status of a wheel-turning king. Yet, his chilling warning to the hill tribes, quoted earlier, shows that he did not renounce violence altogether and was willing to use the standing army he maintained.

## Thailand

Thailand, where more than ninety percent of the people are Theravada Buddhists,[18] is the country where the traditional pattern of Buddhist monarchical rule is most intact today, even though the monarchy has been limited in its powers since the revolution of 1932. All of the other states that used to run this way, Laos, Cambodia, Burma, and Sri Lanka, for example, have been changed fundamentally by years of Western colonial rule or by communist regimes. In Thailand, generally speaking, the monks have minded their religious business and stayed out of direct politics. A rare exception occurred in the period of chaos after the Burmese (also a Theravadan people) destroyed the Ayutthyan kingdom in 1767, when some monks organized an army and temporarily seized power in the northern city of Pistsanulok.[19] Taksin, the mercurial general who rallied the Siamese people to expel the Burmese, became king in 1770, establishing his new capital in Thonburi across the river from where Bangkok was later built. In the same year Taksin turned his attention to the north and easily beat the army led by the rebellious monks. As we have seen, one of the primary duties of a good Buddhist monarch is to purify the *sangha* when the monks have lost their discipline, violating the *Vinaya*, neglecting learning, or going astray in doctrine. Taksin, who had earlier been a dedicated monk himself for some three years, immediately set out to cleanse the northern *sangha*.[20] Although the ringleader monk had escaped, his major monastic lieutenants and a large number of monks who had taken up arms were captured. Those who admitted to having broken the rules against killing, theft, or sexual misconduct were immediately disrobed and given jobs in the new administration. Those who protested their innocence were tried by water ordeal, and those who failed were executed. Many were proven innocent, and they were allowed to continue as monks under the supervision of fifty learned clerics sent up from Thonburi. The king generously donated to some of the northern monasteries and gave honors to leaned monks throughout the country. The people of Siam approved of his firm treatment of the monks who had violated their vows by entering military service and appreciated his patronage of the *sangha* in general.

King Wachirawut (Rama VI), who ruled Thailand from 1910 to 1925, like his better-known immediate predecessors, was very much aware of the danger to Thai sovereignty posed by European colonial powers and worked hard to instill a sense of patriotism and national unity. He formulated an ideology of where the nation (people), the Buddhist religion, and the monarchy worked together to sustain the independence of the Siamese. He very clearly formulated a Just War doctrine, arguing that the Buddha taught that "it was the duty of able men to fight against enemies who invade with the intention to take our land, to jeopardize Buddhism, and to destroy our sovereignty . . . let us make it known to the world that we, the Thai, are determined to protect our nation, religion, and monarchy."[21] He saw Siam as the last line of defense for Theravada Buddhism, since Ceylon and Burma were under foreign control.[22]

Subsequent to the 1932 democracy revolution in Thailand, there have been several periods of military rule where the government relied highly on the people, religion, and monarchy ideology for legitimacy. Their particular slant tended to identify the army as the people and pictured the military as the protectors of the king and of the religion. When there were democratically elected regimes, the same threefold ideology was used, but it was argued that the message of the Buddha actually favored social justice, democratic values, and human rights. For its part, the Thai Buddhist hierarchy helped by legitimating the monarchy and especially after the 1960s by providing monks to work in missions to the non-Buddhist, non-Thai hill tribes and in development work with the peasants as part of government plans to strengthen the nation.[23] While individual monks and religious laypeople and organized Buddhist groups have supported both conservative and progressive forces,[24] the clerical hierarchy has more often than not allied itself with the conservative and military interests of the country, actively cooperating with the Communist Suppression Operations Command in the 1960s and later. In this context, Sulak Sivaraksa, a well-known Buddhist lay leader, who has worked very bravely as the leader of democratic and peace-oriented people for more than thirty years, must be acknowledged.

Perhaps the most striking case of a Thai monk speaking out politically was that of Bhikku Kitthiwuttho, who was a strong supporter of right-wing causes in the 1970s.[25] At that time there was a communist insurrection in the country, and in the aftermath of the Vietnam War, Pol Pot's regime was ruthlessly wiping out Buddhism in Cambodia while the communist regime in Laos was more humanely attempting to eliminate Buddhist influences. There was a well-founded fear in Thailand that the country might suffer a similar fate. In any case, Kitthiwuttho delivered a notorious speech in 1976 entitled "Killing Communists Is Not Demeritorious." He argued that soldiers who protected the nation, Buddhism, and the king by killing communists gained more merit than they lost by taking human life. He went so far as to argue that some people were so worthless that killing them was like ridding the body of impurities. The crimes against religion and the death of millions that were taking place in the communist regimes in China, Laos, and Cambodia justified killing to defend the Thai nation. If the intent was self-defense, then there was no fault incurred by killing. Progressive Buddhists in Thailand vigorously opposed these arguments, but Bhikku Kitthiwuttho has remained a powerful figure, and the relationship between the Buddhist hierarchy and the Thai state remains problematical.

## Tibet

Geoffrey Samuel, Chair of the Religious Studies Department at Lancaster University, subtitled his groundbreaking study of Tibetan Buddhism "Buddhism in Tibetan Societies,"[26] which underlines the differences that marked the various divisions of the Tibetan world. What they held in common was their Tibetan culture and language, especially their unique form of Vajrayana Buddhism. However, their religion, too, was quite complex, as there were four major Tibetan Buddhist schools, each with distinctive practices and doctrine, each led by incarnate lamas, and each in competition for political, economic, and spiritual power. From 1642 to 1959, when removed by the Chinese, the Dalai Lama, who was the leader of the Gelugpa sect and was understood to be an incarnation of the Bodhisattva Avalokitesvara, headed the Lhasa government.[27] The Gelugpas attained their position with the aid of Mongol military power; and before them, from the thirteenth century, the Sakhya school was in ascendance, also originally with Mongol support. The political power of the Dalai Lama derived in large part from his status as an incarnation of the highest order; but, in practice, the Dalai Lama's managers handled most of the day-to-day secular governance. Because of the considerable time lag between the recognition of the new incarnation as a young child and his taking power around the age of twenty-one, regents ruled the country during most of the Gelugpa hegemony. Also, many of the Dalai Lamas died very young, perhaps under "encouragement," which ensured that power would remain with regents and officials. From the death of the Great Fifth Dalai Lama in 1682 to the Great Thirteenth, who reigned from 1895 to 1933, none actually governed for more than a few years.

The focus of this study will be on some aspects of institutionalized violence centered in the major Tibetan monasteries in the Lhasa region in the last years of the traditional government, that is, in the first half of the twentieth century. The Tibetan system of governance, with direct rule by Buddhist monastics, was unique in the Buddhist world, and some of the ways that their monasteries functioned were found only in Tibet. A very high proportion of the population of Tibet lived as monks.[28] In 1951, there were around twenty-five hundred monasteries in Tibet, with some 115,000 monks, or between ten to fifteen percent of the male population. The custom in Tibet was for families to place their sons as novices at the age of seven or eight, and the boys were expected to stay until they died. In contrast, most Thai monks enter the order for only a few months or years as young men, and there is no disgrace if one chooses to return to the secular world. The proportion of men who are monks in Thailand has been put in the range of one to two percent.

Some Tibetan monasteries had thousands of residents, supported by endowments of money, land, and bound labor, and run to generate enough profit to support the religious activities of the monks and their supporters. Others were very modest indeed. Monasteries had considerable autonomy and the central government rarely intervened in internal issues, with the larger monasteries having the authority to discipline their members for all crimes save treason and murder.[29] The three largest Gelugpa monasteries, known as the Three Seats, all near Lhasa, were enormously powerful.[30] These mass institutions were by no means quiet retreats for scholars and meditators, although they did produce and maintain a relatively small number of excellent scholars and practitioners. Most of the monks were engaged in practical pursuits to support themselves and their monasteries. Many worked on building and maintenance projects; some poor monks were servants to the higher monks; some served as administrators of the vast monastic holdings. Nonscholar monks, in addition to the moneymaking work they did, also participated in rituals as musicians, dancers, chanters, and the like. Goldstein reports that the Three Seats comprised around 10,000, 7,000, and 5,000 monks respectively in 1951.[31] Those engaged in higher studies constituted some thirty percent of the total, with most of those never advancing far in their learning.[32] The *dobdos*, or warrior-monks, made up from ten to fifteen percent of the population of the Three Seats.[33]

A rare eyewitness account of the details of monastic life in the Three Seats comes from a Japanese Buddhist priest and scholar, Ekai Kawaguchi, who spent three years in Tibet at the turn of the twentieth century. Tibet was closed to foreign travelers, but Kawaguchi was able to pass as a Tibetan, due to his mastery of the language and his appearance. Kawaguchi enrolled as a student in the Sera Monastery, one of the Three Seats and the one with a reputation for having the fiercest *dobdos*. From his point of view, there were three classes of monk at Sera, all of which were engaged in moneymaking activities: "[M]ost of them are engaged in trade. Agriculture comes next to trade, and then cattle-breeding. Manufacturers of Buddhist articles, painters of Buddhist pictures, tailors, carpenters, masons, shoemakers and stone-layers are found among the priests."[34] He reported that the highest class of monks lived extremely well, with private quarters and up to sixty or eighty servants, while the serious students were the poorest, as the course of study was so difficult that they were unable to earn extra money and often went hungry. On the other hand, the *dobdos*, though very poor, were able to get by as they worked as guards or laborers.[35]

Kawaguchi had some medical knowledge and became friends with the *dobdo* whose wounds he treated after duels. "They scarcely ever fight over a pecuniary matter, but the beauty of young boys presents an exciting cause, and the theft of a boy will often lead to a duel."[36] They fought with swords, generally until one or both were wounded, and then retired to the inns of Lhasa to reconcile over drinks. While the Japanese priest was put off by their rude manners and uncouth appearance, Kawaguchi, on the whole, admired the fighting monks for their good-natured honesty and valor.[37] In commenting on the very small Tibetan army, Kawaguchi said: "The warrior-priests are far more soldier-like than the regular soldiers; they have no wives nor children to take care of, and have therefore nothing to fear. They are indeed far more estimable than the professional soldiers."[38] Indeed, at the time Kawaguchi was in Lhasa, the *dobdo* forces of the Three Seats outnumbered the soldiers of the central government, which gave the great monasteries an effective veto on decision-making. The clerical powers did not hesitate to call out their troops from time to time, with profound effects on the future of Tibet.

## Monastic Opposition to Reform in Tibet (1900–1950)

From 1913 to 1933, the thirteenth Dalai Lama attempted several modernizations in Tibet, in large part because he had become convinced in his period of exile[39] that the future independence of the country could only be maintained through building a modern army and improving other state facilities.[40] He fled to Mongolia and China after the British military excursion into Tibet in 1903–1904, then to India when the Chinese occupied Lhasa in 1909. All in all he was gone from 1904 to 1912, returning when China was in turmoil from the Republican revolution. The young army officers, who had fought the British and the Chinese and who knew firsthand that their traditional fighters, no matter how courageous, could not withstand a sustained invasion by modern armies, were the strongest supporters of modernization. The side that most strongly opposed change was the Three Seats, supported by their squadrons of *dobdos*.

At first the thirteenth Dalai Lama was inclined to follow the advice of the soldier faction and proceeded slowly to build up a strong, modern army to protect the borders and sovereignty of the country and provide a countervailing force to the monastic troops. In 1921, he used the small but effective army against the Loseling College of the Drepung Monastery, one of the Three Seats.[41] In the 1911–1912 war with Chinese forces, the Loseling College supported the Chinese side, refusing to send warrior-monks to help rid Lhasa of Chinese forces and then protecting the Chinese political officer when he fled. In the context of a conflict over property, the central government punished two high College officials who had helped the Chinese, and then a crowd of monks from Loseling besieged the Dalai Lama, who was in retreat in the Norbulinga, his summer palace. "While the senior monks shouted and prostrated, the younger monks urinated and defecated all over the Dalai Lama's gardens, pulled up and trampled the Dalai Lama's flowers, broke the statues, and sang as loudly as possible in order to disturb him."[42] At that moment, there were not enough troops to control the situation, but within a few days, some three thousand soldiers were brought together to confront the College, which backed down without a single shot being fired. About sixty ringleader monks were seized and punished by light flogging, being shackled and put into cangues (heavy wooden yokes), and then being put under house arrest under the care of various nobles.[43] There was no general punishment and no confiscation of property. This incident changed forever the relationship between the forces of the central government and the forces of the Three Seats and showed the value of an effective army to the interests of the Dalai Lama. It also reinforced the conservative forces in their opposition to a modern army and other progressive changes.

Buddhist institutions in traditional Tibet loaned out their enormous endowments at twenty to thirty percent rates of interest to support their annual cycle of rituals and other activities. In 1944, a group of monks primarily from the Sera Che College were sent to Lhundrup Dzong, a district north of Lhasa, to collect the interest on such a loan. This ordinary act precipitated an incident that had dangerously destabilizing effects on the country. It illustrated the political power of the ecclesiastical institutions, showed how tenaciously they defended their economic interests, and also showed how ordinary citizens were protected to some degree by the central government from the demands of their overlords.[44] It began when the debtor peasants complained to the district commissioner that they could not afford to pay what they owed. The central government had a new policy to relieve some of the financial burdens of the peasantry, and the commissioner instructed the monks not to force payment until the government had investigated the situation, much to the anger of the loan collector monks. The abbot of the College instructed them to do whatever they had to do to get the money.

Around November 1944, the party of collectors presented themselves to the district commissioner, bringing with them traditional gifts, including a dried leg of mutton. Each side stubbornly held its position. "In the series of increasingly insulting exchanges that followed, one monk, in a frenzy, started hitting the district commissioner on the head with the dried meat."[45] The others joined in, stabbing and pummeling the hapless official with tea utensils and whatever else came to hand. He was very severely injured and died a few days later after the number and nature of his wounds were carefully catalogued. The central government appointed a very high-level committee of inquiry into this violent act and ordered that the College hand over the monks who were involved for questioning. The College refused, saying that the monks were not acting for themselves and never meant to show disrespect to the government. They offered instead to pay a fine on behalf of the institution. Neither side would compromise. The government quietly waited while reinforcing its troops around Lhasa and acted in June 1945 to remove the abbots of Sera Che and the other college that supported them. At first the abbot wanted to offer armed resistance—they had some two thousand rifles and the usual cadre of fighting monks—but the largest subunit of the College would not agree. The abbot fled to the Chinese-controlled section of Tibet, with his bodyguards fighting the pursuing troops. He later returned to Lhasa with the Chinese Peoples Army.

With the abbot out of the way, the government seized all of the monks that were directly involved in the Lhundrup Dzong killing. Two of them, the most defiant, were whipped severely in the course of the hearings, and fourteen were convicted and punished. Two years later, things came to a head again when the monks of Sera Che revolted against the central government.[46] It began on April 16, 1947, when the unpopular new government-appointed abbot publicly supported the regent in a move against his rival. Spontaneously a group of his monks armed themselves with swords, knives, and an axe. They pursued the abbot across the roof of Sera Che, eventually cornered him, and then stabbed and hacked him to death.[47] The rebellion lasted with sporadic fighting until the twenty-ninth of April when it was put down in a decisive battle by the government forces. One of the most violent episodes occurred on the twenty-third and twenty-fourth, when a force of armed monks surrounded and slaughtered a small group of soldiers who were guarding a confiscated property.[48]

In the days of fighting, it was estimated that perhaps two or three hundred monks were killed, with only some fifteen soldiers having died. Twenty-two monks who led the rebellion were flogged severely, with one hundred to two hundred lashes, and then placed in irons and in cangues. Five received life in prison, and the others were kept under house arrest in various aristocratic estates.[49] While the rebellious monks were completely crushed, the country was left "hopelessly fragmented . . . [with no] chance that Tibet would be able to present a unified front to the inevitable Chinese threat to its de facto autonomy."[50] At the time of all this turmoil, it should be remembered that the fourteenth Dalai Lama, who remains the incumbent today, was only thirteen years old and that officers of his regency made all of the political decisions. It was reported that he was most distressed by the harsh treatment of the leading rebels.[51]

## Conclusion

While individual Buddhists are encouraged to cleanse their own hearts from violent impulses and avoid violent acts, Buddhists generally have not advocated pacifism as a policy for the state to follow. Buddha's social and political thought had rather a hard-nosed realism to it, recognizing that men and women in society were caught up in webs of delusion and desire, which inevitably led to injustice and violence. A strong ruler, who combined a concern for the practical welfare and spiritual progress of his people, was the solution offered. Such a ruler, by the very nature of social reality, would have to use force to restrain and punish the most greedy, violent, and lustful of his subjects when they oppressed their weaker neighbors. The ruler also had the positive duty to take steps to see that the nation prospered and then to see that the wealth was used to support spiritual groups, particularly, the Buddhist orders.

Individual monks and nuns, who renounced the world to live in the Buddhist orders, were expected to live according to much higher moral standards than the laity. Their lives were regulated by strict rules conducive to nonviolence, chastity, and nonacquisitiveness. In large part, the monastics were supported or not depending on how well kept their many precepts. This, of course, was not easy to do in traditional times and even less in modernity. In Thailand, this interrelation between the worldly and the world-renouncers has been maintained as an ideal, but has been put under considerable strain by the threats to the country from both Western imperialism and communist expansionism.

Tibet's Buddhism evolved very differently, with the governance of the state overlapping considerably with the monastic establishments. Monks held key political offices, participated fully in the economy, and even served in military positions. While this system provided relative stability and reasonably good government for some centuries, in the modern era it would seem that the political and economic interests of clerical forces fatally undermined the independent survival of the country as a whole. This sort of outcome may well partially explain why the Buddha taught in the *Vinaya* that monastics should keep themselves at arm's length from political, economic, and military power. Of course, in the case of Tibet, where the monasteries were mass institutions rather than elitist, effectively autonomous as economic, political, and even military structures, it was not possible to follow the rules that separated monks from worldly spheres of activity. One hundred years ago, Kawaguchi noted approvingly the words of his Tibetan teacher:

> I do not know whether to rejoice at or to regret the presence of so many priests in Tibet. Some seem to take this as a sign of the flourishing condition of the national religion and on that ground seem to be satisfied with it. I cannot quite agree with this argument; on the contrary I rather hold that it is better to have even two or three precious diamonds than a heap of stones and broken tiles.[52]

In exile today the Dalai Lama and his followers have renounced most direct political power and have reformed many of the economic and other practices of the monasteries.[53] In Tibet, the monasteries, which have begun to rebuild after the worst excesses of Chinese repression were relaxed, are limited in size and restricted from political and economic activities and are monitored to see that they support the current regime.[54]

## Notes

1. Brian (Daizen) Victoria, *Zen at War* (New York: Weatherhill, 1997).
2. H. L. Seneviratne, *The Work of Kings: The New Buddhism in Sri Lanka* (Chicago: University of Chicago Press, 1999).
3. Richard Gombrich, *Theravada Buddhism: A Social History from Ancient Benares to Modern Colombo* (London: Routledge and Kegan Paul, 1988), chap. 2.
4. T. W. Rhys Davids and Hermann Oldenberg, *Vinaya Texts,* (Oxford: Oxford University Press, Sacred Books of the East, three volumes, 1881 ff, reprinted, Delhi: Motilal Banarsidass, 1966), Mahavagga, VI. 31, SBE, vol. XVII, pp. 108–117.
5. Davids, *Vinaya,* Verses 8 and 13.
6. Davids, *Vinaya,* Mahavagga, I. 40, SBE, vol. 13, pp. 194–196.
7. Davids, *Vinaya,* Mahavagga, I. 40, Verse 2, p. 194.
8. Davids, *Vinaya,* SBE, vol. 13, p. 43; Charles S. Prebish, *Buddhist Monastic Discipline: The Sanskrit Pratimoksa Sutras of the Mahasamghikas and Mulasarvastivadins* (University Park: Pennsylvania University Press, 1975), pp. 81–82 and 86.
9. Davids, *Vinaya,* Mahavagga, I. 39-I. 52.
10. Watson Burlingame, trans., *Buddhist Legends Translated from the Original Pali Text of the Dhammapada Commentary,* vol. 3 (London: Pali Text Society, 1969), pp. 70–72. For a commentary, see John A. McConnell, "The Rohini Conflict and the Buddha's Intervention," in Sulak Sivaraksha et al., eds., *Radical Conservatism: Buddhism in the Contemporary World* (Bangkok: Thai Inter-Religious Commission for Development, 1990), pp. 200–208.
11. Maurice Walshe, trans., *Thus Have I Heard: The Long Discourses of the Buddha: The Digha Nikaya* (London: Wisdom, 1987), the twenty-seventh chapter, pp. 407–415.
12. *Digha Nikaya,* Sutta 27, v. 20.
13. *Digha Nikaya,* Sutta 26, v. 2.
14. *Digha Nikaya,* Sutta 26, v. 6.
15. *Digha Nikaya,* Sutta 26, v. 5.
16. N. A. Nikam and Richard McKeon, *The Edicts of Asoka* (Chicago: University of Chicago Press, Phoenix Books, 1966), p. 29.
17. Nikam and McKeon, *Edicts,* p. 30.
18. The Theravada form of Buddhism has been dominant in Thailand for hundreds of years. For details, see Gombrich, *Theravada Buddhism.*
19. B. J. Terwiel, *A History of Modern Thailand 1762–1942* (St. Lucia: University of Queensland Press, 1983), pp. 43–49; Somboon Suksam-

ran, *Buddhism and Politics in Thailand* (Singapore: Institute of Southeast Asian Studies, 1982), p. 118.

20. Terwiel, *History*, pp. 36–37.
21. Somboon, *Buddhism*, pp. 124–125.
22. Somboon, *Buddhism*, p. 125.
23. Somboon, *Buddhism*, pp. 128ff.
24. Swearer, *The Buddhist World of Southeast Asia* (Albany: State University of New York Press, 1995), pp. 110ff.
25. Swearer, *Buddhist World*, pp. 113–114.
26. Geoffrey Samuel, *Civilized Shamans: Buddhism in Tibetan Societies* (Washington, D.C.: Smithsonian Institution Press), 1993.
27. Melvyn C. Goldstein, *A History of Modern Tibet, 1913–1951: The Demise of the Lamaist State* (Berkeley: University of California Press, 1989), pp. 41–42.
28. Goldstein, *History*, p. 21; and Melvyn C. Goldstein, "The Revival of Monastic Life in Drepung Monastery," in Melvyn C. Goldstein and Matthew T. Kapstein, *Buddhism in Contemporary Tibet: Religious Revival and Cultural Identity* (Berkeley: University of California Press, 1998), pp. 15–22.
29. Goldstein, "Revival," p. 19.
30. Goldstein, *History*, pp. 24–36.
31. Goldstein, *History*, p. 25.
32. Figures from the Mey College of the Sera Monastery (Goldstein, *History*, p. 24).
33. For the *dobdo*, or *dobdob* (*ldab ldob*, in standard transliteration from Tibetan) see Melvyn C. Goldstein, "A Study of the Ldab Ldob," *Central Asiatic Journal*, vol. 9, no. 2 (1964): 125–141; Goldstein, "Revival," p. 19; David Snellgrove and Hugh Richardson, *A Cultural History of Tibet* (Boulder, Colo.: Prajna Press, 1980), pp. 240–241; R. A. Stein, *Tibetan Civilization* (London: Faber and Faber, 1972), pp. 140–141.
34. Ekai Kawaguchi, *Three Years in Tibet* (Madras: Theosophical Publishing Society, 1909), p. 325.
35. Kawaguchi, *Three Years*, pp. 326–328.
36. Kawaguchi, *Three Years*, p. 292.
37. Kawaguchi, *Three Years*, pp. 291–294 and 301.
38. Kawaguchi, *Three Years*, p. 551.
39. Goldstein, *History*, chap. 1.
40. Goldstein, *History*, pp. 89–93.
41. Goldstein, *History*, pp. 104–110.
42. Goldstein, *History*, p. 106.

43. For an account of Tibetan judicial punishments, see Kawaguchi, *Three Years*, pp. 374–387.
44. Goldstein (*History*, pp. 427–445) reviews the disputed events of this complex incident. The present study presents a bare outline of what happened. An important underlying factor was the rivalry between the regent (Taktra), who was currently governing on behalf of the young Dalai Lama, and the former regent (Reting), who was eager to regain the position. Most of the monks and the abbot of Sera Che college strongly supported Reting.
45. Goldstein, *History*, p. 429.
46. Again, events were very complicated and centered in large part on the struggle between the two main contenders for the regency. See Goldstein, *History*, chap. 14.
47. Goldstein, *History*, pp. 486–491.
48. Goldstein, *History*, pp. 516–520.
49. Goldstein, *History*, p. 505.
50. Goldstein, *History*, p. 521.
51. Goldstein, *History*, p. 521n.
52. Kawaguchi, *Three Years*, p. 430.
53. http://www.tibet.net.
54. Goldstein, "Revival."

# Conclusion

## The Ascension of Mars
## and the Salvation of the Modern World

### MICHAEL L. HADLEY

*Now entertain conjecture of a time/*
*When creeping murmur and the poring dark/*
*Fills the wide vessel of the universe.*
　　　　　　　—Shakespeare, *Henry V*

Images of combat abound in the media—in fiction, fantasy, and fact. Whether in reports of the Gulf War, Rwanda, Bosnia, or Afghanistan, or in the daily outpourings of Hollywood-style infotainment and "breaking news," the message is clear: violent responses to critical situations can effectively resolve conflicts. Indeed, so the tacit argument runs, violence can redress wrongs, create justice, destroy evil; it can even redeem. Humankind has, of course, indulged in this approach at various times throughout recorded history, but modern technology, global economics, and the rise of Western wealth and power have given it new life. Mars, the ancient god of war, has ascended with a messianic force previously unknown.

This "redemptive violence," as Walter Wink has persuasively argued, "is the ideology of conquest" in which "the god favours those who conquer."[1] Redemptive violence is carried out by individuals against each other and against established authorities; by factions against the demonized "enemy other." As an instrument of power projection, it is carried out by armies on behalf of states. Its core convictions argue for "peace through war; security through strength." It stands for winning at whatever moral cost. It draws on the language and emotional energy of religious convictions

189

in order to legitimize oppressive power. It has one self-serving purpose: to establish order over a seemingly threatening chaos. Wink's analysis found redemptive violence to be a pervasive phenomenon in contemporary Western society: in television, sports, nationalism, militarism, televangelism, foreign policy, religious-right movements, and self-styled militia groups. It is no less pervasive in cultures that feel threatened by Western hegemony. In short, wide-ranging cultural evidence suggests that adherents of redemptive violence subscribe today to an uncompromising view: "We need a messiah, an armed redeemer, someone who has the strength of character and conviction to transcend the legal restraints of democratic institutions and save us from our enemies." Redemptive violence, Wink concludes, "is the most dominant religion in our society today."[2]

In its declarations of war on everything from drugs to terrorism, Western culture, more than any other time in its history, promotes the Domination Theory of social progress. No longer content with the vocabulary of "competition," "challenge," "debate," or even mere differences of opinion, exponents of this theory resort to the language of battle to promote their causes and dominate their field. They do so in commerce ("trade wars," "fashion wars"), in education ("war on illiteracy"), social welfare ("war on poverty"), criminal justice ("war on drugs"), and in a variety of combative enterprises from sports to medical research. Talk of war has become a very glib affair, masking, as it does, a range of conflict once differentiated with subtle precision. This widespread mind-set endorsing combat in all walks of life—with all the vocabulary of violence, subjection, and conquest—is at once both banal and pernicious. But the attitude highlights an understanding that is new to our era: war is no longer considered a defined event with a beginning and end, a tragic event marked by a legal declaration of war and a negotiated peace; it is now a protracted condition of crisis with ill-defined borders, a diffuse, extenuated flash point in a continuous spectrum of armed, or threatened, conflict. War, in short, is now a "way of being."

The thought is disturbing to those who know the history of the past hundred years. After all, the twentieth century is noted for its savage high-tech wars that devastated whole countries, killing or maiming millions of people, including innocent civilians. History of the period offers graphic evidence of the real nature of war: over a hundred years of arms races, worldwide armed conflict among nations, and weapons of mass destruction, thousand-bomber raids, atomic warfare. As a conservative estimate, World War I (1914–1918) alone accounted for some ten million killed and twenty million wounded. World War II (1939–1945) cost the lives of some fifteen million military personnel, two million of whom were Russian prisoners of war. Significantly, that war took the lives of thirty-five million noncombatant civilians. A litany of suffering punctuates the century: the

Korean War (1950–1953), the Vietnam War (1962–1975), the Iran-Iraq War (1980–1988), to mention but three. In the latter, 1.5 million lives were lost with neither side making any strategic gains whatever.

Yet on the eve of the twenty-first century, proponents of Domination Theory and redemptive violence still speak as though the violence and carnage of the past held little meaning for us except to endorse simplistic and violent solutions to complex current issues. Indeed, despite detailed and nuanced analyses that explore and explain the multilayered complexities of the twentieth century's conflicts, many popular accounts today still hold to the superficial understandings of propaganda and bias that inform the legacy of what one popular television series has called "The World at War." By contrast, spokespersons for the twenty-first century resort to convenient clichés about homeland defense, national interest, and power projection, all by way of justifying and promoting the mind-set of military force. In fact, one can characterize a whole range of persuasive rhetoric—ranging from official propaganda and disinformation to fanciful fiction and advertising—as "The Great War of Words."[3]

The communication of cultural myth is a natural, largely unreflective, and unconscious, projection of a given culture's self-understanding. Cultures project their "way of being" through all the distinctive symbols, stories, and psychosocial artifacts that form their character. Even liberal cultures engage in establishing boundaries, for liberalism, as Hauerwas has argued, "is not simply a theory of government but a theory of society that is imperial in its demands."[4] But cultural myths have also been manufactured as a vital tool of governments, especially of intelligence and information services, worldwide. Where intelligence serves to gain insights in support of one's own military operations, its handmaiden propaganda aims at destabilizing the enemy and motivating the home front. In fact, the creation of departments of military propaganda over a hundred years ago is arguably the forerunner of modern intelligence-gathering services. As professionals have observed when reflecting on the current post-9/11 war on terrorism, "the media and the military will continue to walk hand in hand in a blissful, bittersweet union."[5] This marriage of convenience has a lengthy history. A case in point is Grand Admiral Alfred von Tirpitz's creation of the Press and Information Branch during the British–German naval arms race of 1880–1914. It was designed to influence both parliament and the people and did so by serving up economic and military arguments directed at nonspecialists. Marshalling a broad spectrum of officers, writers, and well-known academics to his banner, von Tirpitz launched the modern era of military propaganda.[6] Von Tirpitz's "bandwagon provide[ed] a scaffold of cultural, economic, political, military and vulgar Darwinistic timber for the new structure."[7] Nor were things very different under British intelligence. As Peter Buitenhuis has shown, during the period 1914–1933 the British employed writers of every hue, who distorted the facts of combat in order to create new political realities for public consumption. Thus, in the Great War of 1914–1918 in which casualties amounted to between five thousand and fifty thousand per day, writers transformed lost battles into victories and desperate "backs-to-the-wall" reversals into uplifting advance. Significantly, these well-known writers— H. G. Wells, Arnold Bennett, John Galsworthy, John Masefield, John Buchan, Edith Wharton, and Henry James among them—created self-serving national myths. These myths failed to withstand subsequent scrutiny.

This type of mythmaking is what Paul Fussel's magisterial study of the interrelationship between the Great War and modern memory has termed "that contempt for life, individuality, and privacy, and that facile recourse to violence that have characterized experience in the twentieth century."[8] Small wonder, then, that the predominant mood after World War I was disillusionment. Small wonder, too, that the misuse and abuse of language continued despite the experience that in any kind of war the first casualty is always truth. Again, in World War II, nations mobilized their writers and thinkers in another "war of words" in support of the military enterprise.[9] The language of Nazi Germany is what Siegried Bork first explored as a "model case," offering an urgent "warning to the future" about the dehumanizing effects of attempting to manipulate language.[10] His graphic study serves as a warning to those cultures that embed their rhetoric in their axioms of values and myths of origin. On the linguistic level, Germany's successful attempt at bringing idiom into line with ideology is an early example of political correctness. Bork shows how the Nazis deployed words propagandistically as a weapon against truth and objectivity.[11] They used the language of technology and industry as a means of combating reflection and sensitivity. Thus, they spoke of their troops as "human material" now "welded together" in "iron resolve" to assert German supremacy. They resorted to the language of combat ("struggle for lost honor," "struggle against Jewry") in order to present their national interests as black-and-white issues of crass survival. They mobilized the language of sport not only to characterize the physical toughening of the body for the demands of the "struggle"; they also invoked sport as a metaphor for the training of both character and the intellect. The whole point of what Bork called the "sportification of language"—expressions like "knock-out punch," "kick-off," "beat"—was to make political realities seem close to the people; in effect, it amounted to a "dumbing-down" of complex issues. Anti-intellectualism permeated the political and military culture. Indeed, official documents themselves exemplify the jargon of action before thought.

Nazi Germany's "misuse and abuse" of language set the stage with classic examples of political euphemisms: "final solution" (*Endlösung*) for genocide, "special treatment" (*Sonderbehandlung*) and its abbreviation *S.B.* for political murder, and "cleansing" (*Säuberung*) for disposing of unwanted persons such as homosexuals, gypsies, Jews, and the mentally impaired. Even Germany's war of aggression was justified in response to the nation's perceived need for "living space" (*Lebensraum*), or room to breathe. Indeed, weapons themselves merged with humans as a new life force. Thus, the German submarine of World War II was regarded in its day as "a remarkable and miraculous synthesis of spirit and heart-blood of comrades, of steel body and cable nerves."[12] Yet, these "steel sharks," as they were dubbed, quickly became the "iron coffins" of a whole generation of seafarers who perished in the mythmakers' protracted war at sea. The language of modern warfare redefines its terms. From the euphemisms of Goebbels' Ministry of Propaganda it was but a small step to the language of "ethnic cleansing" in Bosnia in the 1990s. In his reflections at the time of the outbreak of the 1991 Gulf War, Rowan Williams reminds us of a classic instance from the more recent past, when in the name of "village pacification" U.S. soldiers murdered up to five hundred unarmed civilians, including women and children, during the infamous My Lai massacre of March 16, 1968. Like the justifications for Bosnia, the Vietnam reasons were striking: "In order to save the village, it became necessary to destroy it."[13] Such language, Williams cautioned, "makes us forget human truth."

Today, U.S. forces and their coalition partners mask aggression by speaking of "anticipatory retaliation" and "sanitizing" enemy-held territory. Reports of their using "smart weapons" and "brilliant weapons" to effect "surgical strikes" are meant to persuade us of intelligently applied clinical accuracy under sterile conditions. They speak of "regime change" when referring to their plans to overthrow foreign governments through unilateral military intervention and covert operations. Meanwhile, the Israelis speak of "point-point operations" and "routine patrols" to mask their savage reprisals against the Palestinians, and "the neighbor procedure" when using Palestinians as human shields.[14] As in the case of the assassination of Hamas leader Abdul Rahman Hamad by an Israeli government sniper on October 14, 2001, they speak of "permissive termination" and "calculated elimination." Elsewhere, to use a contortion of euphemistic language, opponents of oppressive regimes in Latin America have been "disappeared"—kidnapped and eventually killed—by members of the military and the police.[15] All this euphemism amounts to using the logic of violence in order to control violence. As has been argued in Wittengenstein's terms, "words somehow emerge out of the social collective" and it makes sense "for that collective to agree on expressions for brute reality that are simpler than the reality itself."[16]

War, as John Keegan has shown in his critique of Clausewitz, "is always an expression of culture, often a determinant of cultural forms, in some societies the culture itself."[17] This thesis has been widely affirmed, but nowhere more forcefully than in Germany in 1995. Triggered by national debate about the traveling exhibition "War of Annihilation: Crimes of the German Military 1941–1944," organized by the Hamburg Institute for Social Research, Germans have again attempted to come to grips with their past. This has required their confronting not only military history, but literature, moral theology, and, of course, linguistics. Successive official speakers at the various exhibition sites emphasized that point. In his introductory words at the opening of the exhibition, historian Jan Philipp Reemtsma explained: "War is a social condition that plays throughout all levels of the society that wages war: at the front, in the support bases, at home where letters arrive from the front, where the arms industry works, wherever images of war circulate."[18] Indeed, he argues, war as trauma and cultural identity insinuates itself into every nook and cranny of society long after the actual battle is over. That was as true for Germany after World War II as it was for the United States in the aftermath of Vietnam; it is as true for the genocidal civil war in Rwanda that savaged not only its own people but the ill-prepared U.N. peacekeepers and their traumatized Canadian commander as well.[19] Wars, in the words of Robert S. McNamara, former Secretary of Defense for Presidents Kennedy and Johnson, "generate their own momentum and follow the law of unanticipated consequences."[20]

One consequence, however, seems both inevitable and contradictory: while war may be a cultural condition, *effective* warfare is a product of the civilizing influences of Western philosophy, science, and civics. This, at least, is one of the many disturbing conclusions of Victor Davis Hanson's important study of landmark battles in the rise of Western power.[21] Central to his view is his notion of civic militarism: the rise of the citizen soldier who embodies the principles of freedom, consensual government, and dissent. These principles, he argues, gave in the past a greater "resiliency" to Western armies and allowed them greater "margins of error" in the conduct of war, thus enabling them to risk losing battles without sacrificing Western culture to the enterprise. In military and economic terms, this "Western" tradition prevails as the dominant global force, with the United States as its fiercest proponent and most dominant power. Hanson is not interested here in questions of morality, but in the principles of military power alone. Thus, he writes on the eve of the New Millenium—his book *Culture and Carnage* was published in 2001—that our besetting peril is not, in the first instance, the proliferation of atomic weapons. Rather, "the most obvious worry is the continual spread of Western notions of military discipline, technology, decisive battle, and capitalism *without* the accompanying womb of freedom, civic militarism, civilian audit, and dissent."[22] In other words, the greatest threat to the Western enterprise remains "the dissemination of knowledge, rationalism, the creation of free universities, perhaps even the growth of democracy, capitalism, and individualism themselves throughout the world."[23] For him, these principles do not necessarily contain the oft-touted seeds of eternal peace, tolerance, and security that they seem to have promised. In fact, they have created "the world's deadliest armies in the past." Paul Kennedy expresses this insight in less ideological terms when tracing the rise and fall of the Great Powers through four centuries of economic competition and military conflict: "In a long-drawn-out Great Power (and usually coalition) war, victory has repeatedly gone to the side with the more flourishing productive base—or, as the Spanish captains used to say, to him who has the last escudo."[24] Successful warfare and productive capacity are indisputably and causally linked. Westerners concerned for their own national or cultural security might take comfort in this militaristic social Darwinism: "History teaches us," Hanson insists, "that Westerners can still field in their hour of need grave, disciplined, and well-equipped soldiers who shall kill like none other on the planet."[25]

The horrifying destruction of the World Trade Center towers in New York on September 11, 2001, set a dramatic benchmark in international relations and American national resolve. This traumatic "first war of the Information Age," as Richard B. Myers, Chairman of the U.S. Joint Chiefs of Staff and former Commander-in-Chief of the North American Aerospace Command (NORAD) called it six months after the event, required a decisive response. To his mind, it "highlighted two imperatives facing the militaries of North America and Europe. First, we must win the global war on terrorism; and second we must prepare our forces for other future challenges."[26] Touted in the United States as "a second Pearl Harbor," comparable to the first in its suddenness, savagery, and devastation, it awakened us to the fact "that armed conflict can take forms we had not previously imagined, except in technothriller novels."[27] Despite the fact that some sectors of the American intelligence community had warned of such an assault, the actual attack took everyone by surprise. In the words of U.S. General Richard B. Myers, "You hate to admit it, but we hadn't thought about this."[28]

From the perspective of technology and logistics alone, the American military response was, and remains, impressive. Controlled from Central Command (CENTCOM) in Tampa, Florida, with a breathtaking array of advanced technology, it provides what is called "real-time connectivity" to a variety of armed forces—naval, air, ground, and Special Operations—operating over seven thousand miles away. Indeed, wherever forces are deployed—from some 267 bases, in some thirty locations in fifteen different countries, or while overflying forty-six independent nations in the course of operations—they are actually able to "see" the battlefield by means of sophisticated computerized data-linking and imaging as events unfold. As foreshadowed during the Persian Gulf War, never before have military forces enjoyed such all-encompassing, detailed, graphic, and immediate situational awareness. Never before, for that matter, have noncombatants in their own homes even thousands of miles from the action been so regaled by infotainment offering up-to-the-minute battle-action images and commentary as the conflict unfolds.

This, then, is "technothriller" combat: subsea, surface, and supersonic attack systems capable of massive destruction, unprecedented psychological and electronic warfare, unmanned aerial "spy" vehicles, satellite photography and navigation, precision-guided "smart" munitions, "stealth" bombers flying nonstop United States to Afghanistan and return, and, of course, a seemingly infinite supply of armament, supplies, and financial backing. We can expect exponential increase in the complexity, magnitude, and flexibility of military power projection.[29] Reliable witnesses such as *Jane's International Defence Review* and *Jane's Defence Weekly* offer striking evidence of increasing technological sophistication in global warmaking. The gains made by leading producers of weaponry spill over into other regions as well, for instance, in the Middle East.[30] Yet technological capability brings with it moral baggage that is only rarely addressed in military journals. By distancing combatants from their human "targets," by providing them tools such as "fire-and-forget" weapons that allow them to disengage emotionally and spiritually from the implications of combat, technology helps military personnel "overcome natural resistance, and makes killing easier."[31]

Yet, despite moral reservations, the sheer force and strategic opulence available to the United States seem to confirm Hanson's view about the capacity of Western culture to predominate in managing its carnage. Well before the Persian Gulf War, Paul Kennedy observed: "The United States now runs the risk, so familiar to the rise and fall of previous Great Powers, of what might roughly be called 'imperial overstretch.'"[32] In short, American interests are so widespread globally that the United States cannot intervene simultaneously in all the "hotspots" requiring its attention. It must choose where to apply its "redemptive violence"—Persian Gulf (because of oil), Afghanistan (because of the "terrorist" threat to Western "freedom")—or where to abstain—Rwanda and Zimbabwe (no oil, no threat to "freedom"). These choices are fraught with far-reaching moral dilemmas.

For example, the U.S. decision not to participate in U.N. peacekeeping, while condemned by some, is excused by arguing that such participation is unnecessary because of a vital quid pro quo: the United States's vastly superior infrastructure and the intelligence network on which the West depends. Unmentioned is the fact that whoever controls intelligence also controls propaganda. Truth becomes monolithic, and the Domination theory is proved correct. Both morally and ethically, this catches governments in a double bind. For as Robert S. McNamara asked rhetorically, "How, in times of war and crisis, can senior government officials be completely frank to their own people without giving aid and comfort to the enemy?"[33]

In a world dominated by a single superpower, even friendly voices express concern for what they perceive as American unilateralism and isolation. Canada's former foreign minister, for example, has spoken of American "disdain" of international treaties and multilateral cooperation.[34] Former South African president Nelson Mandela stated in press and radio that "the attitude of the United States of America is a threat to world peace."[35] America's will to "go it alone" seems to emerge from its deeply rooted and frequently articulated civil religion, that fervent patriotism that claims a divine purpose for the United States. Indeed, this messianic view has been reiterated by generations of U.S. presidents.[36] What other nations might see as unilateralism or intransigence, U.S. policy frames as a mission. As a Canadian scholar explained in the case of the American refusal to subscribe to the International Criminal Court: "The real reason for U.S. intransigence on the ICC is that the U.S. feels itself to be a sacred nation, the Holy Land of the new world, 'one nation under God.' For those who feel so," he explained, "it would not just be bad politics to permit U.S. service personnel to be tried by the ICC, if it ever came to that; it would also be sacrilege."[37] In terms of American civil religion it would also be sacrilege *not* to resort to power projection through the exercise of redemptive violence.

The terrifying attacks on the World Trade Center have also had an impact on language. After September 11, 2001, among other things, the ubiquitous jetliner was officially regarded as a potential "weapon of mass destruction." Under the banner of "Operation Infinite Justice" President George W. Bush's declaration of "war on terrorism" countenanced military intervention and reprisal that would respect no sovereign national boundaries and would target any country even suspected of harboring people sympathetic to alleged terrorists. The rhetoric of "sacred duty," of "bringing the evildoers to justice," of invoking "American justice" while mobilizing the military, the FBI, and the CIA was clearly retributive in intent. Journalists blamed "Muslims" and "Islamic fundamentalists" and "Holy War" (jihad); they saw the new world order framed by a clash of civilizations. Not since the Middle Ages, voices claimed, had Islam offered such a threat to the Christian world. Underpinned by Huntington's persuasive theory about a clash of cultures so powerful as to "remake the world order," many feared the worst.[38] Yet the flawed either/or ideology of this approach soon gave way to more nuanced views.[39] Rapidly, international pressure and the intervention of lobby groups from various faith traditions forced a change of operational name. Recognizing that the title "Operation Infinite Justice" was likely to offend Muslims, U.S. Defense Secretary Donald Rumsfeld saw to it that—in a journalist's words—"the operation to get Osama bin Laden was christened Operation Eternal Freedom."[40] The fact of "christening," rather than merely "renaming," the military initiative is striking, for it contributed to the "clash-of-civilizations" paradigm that saw the twenty-first century emerging into a new tribalism. Indeed, the destruction of the World Trade Center seemed to confirm a special version of that view: U.S.-style democracy on the one hand and "rogue states" like North Korea, Iran, and Iraq on the other. A Korean cartoonist responded by depicting George Bush as a devil with horns.

In announcing his "War on Terror" at a joint session of Congress on September 20, 2001, President George W. Bush evoked worldwide images of national flags, candlelight vigils, mourners at prayer, and global solidarity with America. Throughout the coming year, the media would project stirring images of commemoration ceremonies, memorials, grieving, and military buildup, culminating on the occasion of the first anniversary in daylong programs on television and radio. In the vocabulary of the media, "ground zero" became a focus of "pilgrimage" to a sacred site. The fault lines between good and evil, so Bush stated to Congress, ran through "a world where freedom itself is under attack."[41] The president polarized "civilization" on the one hand and "enemies of freedom" on the other. Indeed, "This is the world's fight. This is civilization's fight. It is the fight of all who believe in progress and pluralism, tolerance and freedom." In singling out al-Queda, which his speech writers termed "a fringe form of Islamic extremism that has been rejected by Muslim scholars [and which] perverts the peaceful teachings of Islam," the president focused on a terrorist organization intent on "remaking the world—and imposing its radical beliefs on people everywhere." Given the enormity of the threat, he issued an uncompromising challenge: "Every nation, in every region, now has a decision to make. Either you are with us, or you are against us." This biblical injunction would be evoked repeatedly in the coming months. By way of encouragement, he reported that "the civilized world is rallying to America's side." Only the barbarous hesitated or abstained. "The advance of human freedom—the great achievement of our time, and the great hope of every time—now depends on us. Our Nation." Thus, his address set the stage for an essentially theological understanding of the issues involved in this "war" between "freedom and fear, justice and cruelty." Significantly, he concluded, "We know that God is not neutral between them." In all, the address reflected the ideas of St. Paul: our fundamental conflict is not with human ambitions and territorial claims, but with principalities and powers of a higher order.

For Prime Minister Tony Blair as well, the Millenium's "turning point in history" was triggered by "an act of evil."[42] His speech to the Labour Party's conference, an address decried by some for its religiosity and messianic tones, proclaimed solidarity with the United States: "We will assemble a humanitarian coalition alongside the military coalition," Blair affirmed. "The world community must show as much its capacity for compassion as for force." But like President Bush a couple of weeks earlier, Blair would countenance no compromise in responding to al-Queda and bin Laden: "Let there be no moral ambiguity about this." Where the president had railed against al-Queda for their attempt at "remaking the world," Prime Minister Blair now promised to join forces with the United States in order "to reorder this world." Indeed, he noted, "this is a battle with only one outcome: our victory, not theirs."[43] For Blair, however, the goal was a cosmopolitan, compassionate, and tolerant global community—though one forged, if necessary, through military force. Seen in this light, the new concept of warfare could even expand "just war" theory to include "international humanitarian coercive action."[44]

By all accounts, the most compelling aspect of the State of the Union address in January 2002 was President George W. Bush's ultimatum that the American "war on terrorism" would not only target groups such as al-Queda, but any country even sympathetic to terrorists. "States like these and their terrorist allies," he was widely quoted, "constitute an axis of evil."[45] Again widely covered in the press, the destruction of the World Trade Center was depicted as the action of "evildoers," of "terrorists," of people with no moral conscience. As many observers in the media explained, this kind of warfare is new because it is "a struggle of ideas rather than a territorial conflict."[46] Equally troubling, the attacks had demonstrated that "not even the world's largest defense budget can buy insulation from the world's demons any more."[47] Understandably, many commentators saw the Bush administration as taking the moral high road. It could do so because of its reliance on a Power even greater than a national budget. As one of many apologists explained: "While people of good will can disagree about America's war on terrorism, we must surely agree that America was attacked by evildoers, as Mr. Bush calls them. Its response—to seek to eradicate international terrorism and its state sponsors—is virtuous in intent. To that extent, at least, God is on America's side."[48] In this light, the terrorists—while also claiming to fight in God's cause—were labeled the "Zealots" and ideologues. In a statement widely reported in the press, U.S. Brigadier-General Frank Hagenbeck said of the al-Quaeda and Taliban forces: "Local fundamentalists have called a jihad against the Americans and their coalition partners." This was technically correct, for al-Qaeda had reportedly issued a formal declaration in 1996, urging expulsion of Americans from the Arabian peninsula.[49] Repeated in the media, comments on jihad conveniently overlooked the spectrum of meanings attached to the term; rarely did commentators explain that, from a Muslim perspective, "even if war is morally tolerable, it must be prosecuted legitimately."[50] The Hagenbeck response brooked few nuances: "We'd like them to surrender, but if they want to come into the combat area, we're more than willing to kill them."[51] As articulated in newspapers and popular magazines, such "strike back" attitudes support the application of force to expunge evil. Supporters of the "war against terrorism" claimed that al-Qaeda were motivated solely by their "zealotry," by their purely ideological commitment to "holy war," and their thoroughgoing evil. Implied, though not directly quoted, were the Judaic and Christian biblical traditions assuring that "the Lord loves those who hate evil" (Ps 97:10), and thus tacitly enjoining the righteous to take action. Of course, the rhetoric of the Religious Right is the rhetoric of the Hebrew Bible, the Christians' Old Testament: "The fear of the Lord is hatred of evil" (Prv 8:13); "Do they not err who plan evil?" (Prv 14:22); "The evil have no future" (Prv 24:20); and "The evil do not understand justice" (Prv 28:55). Scripture itself would seem to offer redemptive value in validating retaliation by violent means: "Blows that wound clean away evil" (Prv 20:30). However, nowhere was it suggested that the United States and its coalition partners were themselves on a "crusade"—a term the U.S. president first used, but later retracted.

In what televangelist Pat Robertson, speaking on CNN, called a "brilliant" White House statement, President George W. Bush "touched all the bases" (in Robertson's phrase) in assessing the situation on June 24, 2002. Again, the statement was embedded in biblical subtext: "If all parties will break with the past, and set out on a new path," the president said, "we can overcome the darkness with the light of hope."[52] Like the address to the Joint Session of Congress before it, this well-crafted address also established the theological context for what amounted to a shift from politically motivated battle to a cosmic war of ultimate principles.[53] Indeed, this is the very religious zeal of which the United States was born.[54] In the president's richly biblical allusion to the many passages that exhort to changing one's life— repentance, putting on "the new man," putting on "the whole armor of God"—what was clearly meant was that *others* should break with the past and give up their "evil" ways. He made no allowances for ambiguity, doubt, or nuances of interpretation: "I've said in the past that nations are either with us or against us in the war on terror." Here, Bush drew on the striking words of Jesus: "Whoever is not with me is against me, and whoever does not gather with me scatters" (Mt 12:30; Lk 11:23). These words are taken from a passage in which Jesus is casting out devils and is himself accused of being in league with the very devil he was attempting to cast out. The devil in question in the biblical text was Beelzebub, the Baal of the Syrians. From the Hebrew perspective in scripture, this Baal was a "lesser god" than Jehovah. Thus, in offering the world an either/or proposition, Bush has cast himself in the role of upholding the interests of the greater god. This is a case of demonization as a means of self-identity.[55]

Exhorting to action, the president called on "every leader actually committed to peace [to] end incitement to violence in official media and publicly denounce homicide bombings." Of course, American bombings would continue in Afghanistan in order to end the "homicide bombings" that the president intended to eradicate. He then called upon every nation committed to peace to cut all aid "to terrorist groups seeking the destruction of Israel, including Hamas, Islamic Jihad and Hezbollah." Of course, generations of vicious PLO terrorist attacks against Israeli targets are a matter of public record.[56] The names of these organizations alone—Hezbollah ("Party of God"), Fedayeen ("those who sacrifice themselves"), Islamic Jihad, and al-Aqsa Martyrs' Brigade in Yasser Arafat's Fatah ("conquest") organization—underscore their sense of holy mission. At the same time, Bush's bias toward Israel, a country that receives more U.S. military aid than any other nation in the world, is unequivocal. Indeed, a congressional resolution in May 2002 had supported Israel 352 to 21 with 29 abstentions.

Concluding his statement, the president again asserted the old dichotomy of good versus evil. Again, he couched the dichotomy in Christian scriptural terms: "The choice here is stark and simple, the Bible says: 'I have set before you life and death, therefore choose life.' The time has arrived for everyone in this conflict to choose peace and hope and life." Here he drew upon the book of the prophet Jeremiah: "And death shall be chosen rather than life by all the residence of them that remain in this evil family" (Jer 8:3); or again: "Thus saith the Lord, I have set before you the way of life and the way of death"(Jer 21:8). Choosing life, both in the Hebrew Bible and in the Christians' New Testament, means choosing the side of God against evil. Significantly, this moral tone was missing when Rwanda was being savaged, and when both the United States and Britain refused the U.N. permission to send the necessary military aid to the U.N. contingent under General Romeo Dallaire. As we have seen, U.S. morality in the "war on terror"—which now includes U.S. policy on the Palestinians—is highly selective.

The rhetoric of the "war on terror"—on all sides of the conflict—has polarized international conflict by casting its ideologies in apocalyptic terms. In doing so, it encourages the view of a final cosmic battle between good and evil as prefigured in the Book of Revelations.[57] Significantly, as traces of bin Laden were gradually lost during military assaults on Afghanistan, U.S. attention turned to another "evil," Iraq's Saddam Hussein.[58] This shift allowed for a seamless continuation of the rhetoric of war against terror and what Hall has called the "exemplary dualism" of the either/or proposition. By this means, complex human relationships are reduced to crass distinctions between good and evil; and evil is repeatedly found in anything outside the moral sensibilities of the "good."[59]

The battle cries of the new millenium ring with urgent messages of "reordering" or "remaking" the world, recalling the title of Huntington's book. Whether through terrorism or counterterrorism, a first step in changing the balance of power has been to evoke the myth of redemptive violence: the oft-repeated story of the victory of order over chaos by means of violence, the use of force in the name of morality. It asserts the moral rights of the stronger to engage in unilateral preemptive strikes against the weaker: Russia against Chechnya, Israel against the Palestinian Authority, the United States against Iraq. Yet, however motivated, as former Canadian ambassador Kimon Valaskakis explained, such "unilateral pre-emptive war in the name of national interest opens up a Pandora's box much more dangerous than the problem it addresses."[60] Indeed, it threatens to upset a very fragile global balance of power. But the new war is rarely waged army against army. In the case of the "war on terror" the al-Qaeda model suggests a horizontal structure comprising some twenty-four constituent covert terrorist organizations with a global span, what Bush's National Security Strategy regards as "shadowy networks of individuals."[61] This al-Queda model lends new meaning to the concept of the futuristic "network-centric battlefield."[62] Significantly, the "new war" is asymmetric in three major areas: in weaponry (low-tech against high-tech), in organization (al-Qaeda versus the United States), and in morality.[63] The latter, as Michael Ignatieff has explained, is crucial, for what distinguishes the warrior, or professional soldier, from the terrorist is moral discrimination: the capacity to distinguish combatants from civilians and to keep violence proportional to objectives. Here Ignatieff seems in striking accord with the claims of Hanson's *Carnage and Culture* regarding the supremacy of the Western ways of warfare and "the singularity of Western military culture."[64] In a telling image, Ignatieff suggests that we have accustomed ourselves to believing that our discovery of a web means there must be a spider at the center. The new reality may be, however, that the real directing force is the net itself. All the more reason, as many have argued, to engage multilateral and multinational solutions to deep-layered problems.[65] Others call for deep spiritual changes in ourselves and our institutions.[66]

Meanwhile, the "war of words" continues: President George W. Bush's "moral" and "theological" arguments for preemptive retaliation, U.S. Defense Secretary Rumsfeld's apocalyptic pronouncements on threats to the United States, Israeli Prime Minister Ariel Sharon's biblical manifest destiny, Tony Blair's passionate urgings to strike against Iraq, and Vladimir Putin's hardline responses to Chechnya. If accepted as a universal principle, unilateral preemptive war could legitimately be used by any one country to bring about "regime change" in another. Labeled by critics as an evangelical tract, the National Security Strategy that President Bush sent to Congress on September 20, 2002, reflects imperial demands: it pledges to maintain global military dominance, to destroy terrorist threats even when they are not imminent, and to promote American values.[67] Some voices, that of the Saudi press among them, see in this the rise of a new Christian extremism. The language of this new kind of warfare, and the national symbols that underpin it, are about salvation, ultimacy, and power. Ironically, such rhetoric was once the preserve of the Church. For example, a tradition in the Anglican and Episcopalian liturgy holds that a preacher end a sermon with a rhetorical turn in which he ascribes to the Holy Trinity all "Might, Majesty, Dominion and Power, now and forever." Having proclaimed salvation through the Gospel, the priest now acknowledges a power beyond which there is no further ultimacy. In the words of St. Paul's letter to the Ephesians (1:21), "Far above all principality, and power, and might, and dominion" God reigns. Or in the Book of Zechariah (4:6): "Not by might [army], nor by power, but by my spirit, saith the Lord of hosts." Current military and political discourse seems to have appropriated the higher power unto itself. It suggests that ultimacy and its moral justification really rests with the one with the greatest military capability, and that Wink's theory of redemptive violence got it right.

### Notes

1. Walter Wink, *The Powers that Be: Theology for a New Millennium* (New York, London, Toronto: Doubleday, 1998), pp. 42–62.
2. Wink, *The Powers that Be*, pp. 50–51.
3. Peter Buitenhuis, *The Great War of Words: British, American, and Canadian Propaganda and Fiction, 1914–1933* (Vancouver: University of British Columbia Press, 1987).
4. Stanley Hauerwas, *Against the Nations: War and Survival in a Liberal Society* (South Bend, Ind.: University of Notre Dame Press, 1992), p.

18. See also the review by D. Stephen Long in *Journal of Law and Religion* 16, no. 2 (2001): 971–973.

5. "The Military and the Media: For Better or for Worse," *Military Review: The Professional Journal of the U.S. Army*, January–February 2002, pp. 48–71.

6. Michael L. Hadley and Roger Sarty, *Tin-Pots and Pirate Ships: Canadian Naval Forces and German Sea Raiders, 1880–1918* (Montreal and Kingston: McGill-Queen's University Press, 1991), p. 34. The German term for the Press and Information Office was *Abteilung für Nachrichtenwesen und allgemeine Parlamentsangenheiten*.

7. Holger H. Herwig and D. F. Trask, "Naval Operations Plans between Germany and the USA, 1898–1913: A Study of Strategic Planning in the Age of Imperialism," in *The War Plans of the Great Powers, 1880–1914*, ed. Paul M. Kennedy (London: George Allen & Unwin, 1979), pp. 39–74.

8. Paul Fussel, *The Great War and Modern Memory* (London, Oxford, New York: Oxford University Press, 1975), p. 322.

9. See, for example, Christopher Andrew, *Secret Service: The Making of the British Intelligence Community* (London: Heinemann, 1985).

10. Siegfried Bork, *Missbrauch der Sprache: Tendenzen nationalsozialistischer Sprachregelung* (Bern: A. Francke Verlag, 1970).

11. Bork, *Missbrauch der Sprache*, p. 5.

12. Michael L. Hadley, *Count Not the Dead: The Popular Image of the German Submarine* (Montreal and Kingston: McGill-Queen's University Press, 1995), p. 176.

13. Rowan Williams, "What Is Truth? A University Sermon on the Outbreak of the Gulf War (1991)," in Rowan Williams, *A Ray of Darkness: Sermons and Reflections* (Boston: Cowley Publications, 1996, p. 111.

14. John R. Hall, *Apocalypse Observed: Religious Movements and Violence in North America, Europe, and Japan* (London and New York: Routledge, 2000).

15. Priscilla B. Hayner, *Unspeakable Truths: Confronting State Terror and Atrocity* (New York and London: Routledge, 2001), p. 2.

16. John L. Casti, *The Cambridge Quintet: A Work of Scientific Speculation* (Reading, Mass.: Addison-Wesley, 1998), p. 72. See also James Dawes, *The Language of War: Language and Culture in the U.S. from the Civil War through World War II* (Cambridge, Mass., and London: Harvard University Press, 2002).

17. John Keegan, *A History of Warfare* (Toronto: Vintage Books, 1994; 1st ed. 1993), p. 12

18. Jan Philipp Reemstsma, "Begrüssungsworte," in *Krieg ist ein Gesellschaftszustand: Reden zur Eröffnung der Ausstellung,Vernich-*

*tungskrieg. Verbrechen der Wehrmacht 1941 bis 1944*, ed. Hamburger Institut für Sozialforschung (Hamburg: HIS-Verlagsgesellschaft, mbH, 1998), p. 13.

19. See, for example, Linda Melvern, *A People Betrayed: The Role of the West in Rwanda's Genocide* (London: Zed Books, 2000). Also Tana Dineen, "The Solitary, Tortured Nobility of Romeo Dallaire," *The Ottawa Citizen*, 13 July 2000.

20. Robert S. McNamara, *In Retrospect: The Tragedy and Lessons of Vietnam* (New York and Toronto: Random house, 1995), p. 174.

21. Victor Davis Hanson, *Carnage and Culture: Landmark Battles in the Rise of Western Power* (New York: Doubleday, 2001). By 'Western' Hanson refers to classical antiquity and its various inheritors up to and including today's predominant global culture.

22. Hanson, *Culture and Carnage*, p. 451.

23. Hanson, *Culture and Carnage*, p. 453.

24. Paul Kennedy, *The Rise and Fall of the Great Powers: Economic Change and Military Conflict from 1500 to 2000* (New York: Random House, 1987), p. xxiv.

25. Hanson, *Culture and Carnage*, p. 450.

26. Richard B. Myers, "Six Months After: The Imperatives of Operation Enduring Freedom," *RUSI Journal: Royal United Services Institute for Defence Studies* 47, no. 2 (April 2002): 11, 10–14.

27. Martin L. Cook, review of *Morality and Contemporary Warfare*, by James Turner Johnson (New Haven: Yale University Press, 1999), *Journal of Law and Religion* 16, no. 2 (2001): 1019.

28. General Richard B. Myers, cited in Joseph T. Jockel, "After the September Attacks: Four Questions about Norad's Future," *Canadian Military Journal* 3, no. 1 (Spring 2002): 11–16.

29. Kip P. Nygren, "Emerging Technologies and Exponential Change: Implications for Army Transformation," *Parameters: U.S. Army War College Quarterly* 32, no. 2 (Summer 2002): 86–99.

30. See, for example, Hirsh Goodman and W. Seth Carus, *The Future Battlefield and the Arab-Israeli Conflict* (New Brunswick and London: Transaction Publishers, 1990).

31. D. Keith Shurtleff, "The Effects of Technology on Our Humanity," *Parameters: U.S. Army War College Quarterly* 32, no. 2 (Summer 2002): 100–112 (105).

32. Paul Kennedy, *The Rise and Fall of the Great Powers*, p. 515.

33. McNamara, *In Retrospect*, p. 105.

34. Lloyd Axworthy, "Stop the U.S. Foul Play," *Globe and Mail*, 17 July 2002, sec. A13.

35. Cited, for example, in "U.S. Threat to World Peace, Mandela Says," *Globe and Mail*, 12 September 2002, sec. A13. See also Jeffrey

Simpson, "How the U.S. Fumbled the Post–Sept. 11 Ball," *Globe and Mail*, 10 September 2002, sec. A17; Simpson saw Bush as "acting in a neo-imperialist way."

36. Robert Booth Fowler, Allen D. Hertzke, and Laura R. Olson, *Religion and Politics in America: Faith, Culture, and Strategic Choices* (Boulder: Westview Press: 1999; 1st ed. 1995), pp. 258–260.

37. Donald Grayston, Letter, *Globe and Mail*, 4 July 2002, sec. A14. Grayston is Director, Institute for Humanities, Simon Fraser University, Vancouver, Canada.

38. Samuel P. Huntingdon, *Clash of Civilizations and the Remaking of World Order* (New York: Simon & Schuster, 1996).

39. For example, David Smock, "Clash of Civilizations or Opportunity for Dialogue?," U.S Institute of Peace, web posting, 11 September 2002. Web site http//www.usip.org.

40. See, for example, Margaret Carlson, "How Rumsfeld Rallies the Troops," *Time*, 26 September 2001.

41. Presidential Address to Joint Session of Congress, 20 September 2001, distributed by the Office of International Information Programs, U.S. Department of State. Web site

42. Tony Blair, "Speech at the Labour Party Conference," *The Guardian*, 2 October 2001. Unlimited Web site: www.guardian.co.uk.

43. For an example of widespread coverage of the speech see Michael White, "'Let Us Reorder This World'," *The Guardian*, 3 October 2001, online edition.

44. Lisa Sowle Cahill, review of *When War Is Unjust: Being Honest in Just War Thinking*, by John Howard Yoder (Maryknoll: Orbis Books, 1996), *Journal of Law and Religion* 16, no. 2 (2001): 1025–1029, 1027.

45. See, for example, John Ibbitson [Washington], "Bush Warns Rogue Nations," *Globe and Mail*, 30 January 2002, p. 1.

46. For example, "What September 11 Really Wrought," *The Economist*, 12–18 January 2002, p. 24.

47. "What September 11 Really Wrought," *The Economist*, 12–18 January 2002, p. 25.

48. John Ibbitson [Washington], "Trust Bush's Moral Compass," *Globe and Mail*, 18 February 2002, sec. A17.

49. Peter L. Bergen, *Holy War: Inside the Secret World of Osama bin Laden* (New York: Free Press, 2001), p. 79.

50. G. Scott Davis, book reviews of *The Holy War Idea in Western and Islamic Traditions*, by James Turner Johnson (1997), *Islam and War: A Study in Comparative Ethics*, by John Kelsay (1993), *Just War and Jihad: Historical and Theoretical Perspectives on War and Peace in*

*Western and Islamic Traditions,* ed. by John Kelsay and James Turner Johnson (1991), *Cross, Crescent and Sword: The Justification and Limitation of War in Western and Islamic Tradition,* ed. by James Turner Johnson and John Kelsay (1990), *Journal of Law and Religion* 16, no. 2 (2001): 999–1005.

51. Paul Koring, "Zealots Flock to Join Afghan Fight," *Globe and Mail,* 7 March 2002, sec. A1, A4.

52. Published in *Globe and Mail,* 25 June 2002, sec. A17.

53. For a discussion of the concept see Mark Juergensmeyer, "Sacrifice and Cosmic War," in *Violence and the Sacred in the Modern World,* ed. Mark Juergensmeyer (London: Frank Cass, 1991), pp. 101–117.

54. Robert Booth Fowler et al., *Religion and Politics in America,* p. 5.

55. Marc Gopin, *Between Eden and Armageddon: The Future of World Religions, Violence, and Peacemaking* (Oxford: Oxford University Press, 2000), p. 5.

56. For early examples see Chaim Herzog, *The Arab-Israeli Wars* (London: Arms and Armour Press, 1982).

57. Marc Gopin, *Between Eden and Armageddon,* p. 10.

58. See, for example, Andrew Koch, "Strategy to Oust Saddam," *Janes Defence Weekly* 37, no. 10 (6 March 2002): 21, and President George W. Bush's address to the nation on the first anniversary of the terrorist attacks, 11 September 2002.

59. Hall, *Apocalypse Observed,* p. 197.

60. Kimon Valaskakis, "Might Makes Right? Wrong," *Globe and Mail,* 17 September 2002, sec. A15; and "Vers le chaos?: La doctrine Bush risque de jeter par terre le fragile équilibre mondial," *La Presse,* 26 Septembre 2002, sec. A17. Valaskakis, Canada's former ambassador to the Organization for Economic Cooperation and Development, is currently president of the Club of Athens.

61. Paul J. Smith, "Transnational Terrorism and the al-Queda Model: Confronting New Realities," *Parameters: U.S. Army War College Quarterly* 32, no. 2 (Summer 2002): 33–46.

62. Paul Murdock, "Principles of War on the Network-Centric Battlefield: Mass and Economy of Force," *Parameters: U.S. War College Quarterly* 32, no. 1 (Spring 2001): 86–93.

63. For this and the following, see Michael Ignatieff, "Ethics and the New War," 2001 Young Memorial Lecture, 25 October 2001, *Canadian Military Journal* 2, no. 4 (Winter 2001–2002): 5–10.

64. Hanson, *Carnage and Culture,* p. 444.

65. Widely reported; see, however, "Iraq: Have We the Right to Attack?," *Globe and Mail,* 13 September 2002, sec. A15, that counterposes statements from George W. Bush and Kofi Annan.

66. For example, Michael N. Nagler, *Is There No Other Way?: The Search for a Nonviolent Future* (Berkeley: Berkeley Hills Books, 2001).

67. "Bush Sends New National Strategy to Congress," and text of "The National Security Strategy of the United States of America," 20 September 2002, U.S. Department of State, http://usinfo.state.gov/topical/pol/02092040.

# Contributors

CONRAD G. BRUNK is Professor of Philosophy and Director of the Centre for Studies in Religion and Society at the University of Victoria, Canada. From 1976 to 2002 he was Professor of Philosophy at Conrad Grebel University College, University of Waterloo, where he also served as Academic Dean. His areas of research and teaching include environmental and health risk management, environmental ethics, professional ethics, conflict resolution, and philosophy of law. He is co-author of *Value Assumptions in Risk Assessment* (Wilfrid Laurier University Press, 1991; 3rd ed. 1996), a book exploring how moral and political values influence scientific judgments about technological risks, and author of numerous articles in journals and books on ethical issues in technology, the environment, law, and professional practice. Dr. Brunk is a regular consultant to the Canadian government and international organizations on risk management and biotechnology. He is a member of the Canadian Biotechnology Advisory Committee, and he served as Co-Chair of the Royal Society of Canada Expert Panel on the Future of Food Biotechnology.

ROBERT E. FLORIDA is currently an Emeritus Fellow at the Centre for Studies in Religion and Society at the University of Victoria, Canada. He retired from Brandon University at the end of 1999 as Dean of Arts and Professor of Religion. He is currently working in the field of Buddhism and Human Rights and has published a number of book chapters and articles on Buddhist ethics, including "Buddhism and Abortion," in Damien Keown, ed., *Contemporary Buddhist Ethics* (Curzon, 2000).

TIMOTHY GORRINGE is St. Luke's Professor of Theological Studies at Exeter University, England. He is the author of several books, including *The Education of Desire* (SCM/Trinity Press, 2001), *A Theology of the Built*

*Environment* (Cambridge University Press, 2002), and *Karl Barth: Against Hegemony* (Clarendon Press, 1999).

MICHAEL L. HADLEY is Professor Emeritus, a Fellow of the Royal Society of Canada, Senior Member of Robinson College (Cambridge), and Associate Fellow in the Centre for Studies in Religion and Society, University of Victoria, Canada. Recognized internationally for his prize-winning works on naval history—particularly on German submarine warfare—he has in recent years been shifting his attention from the violence of war to the violence of crime in modern society. He is the editor of *The Spiritual Roots of Restorative Justice* (State University of New York Press, 2001).

DAVID J. HAWKIN is Professor of Religious Studies at Memorial University of Newfoundland, Canada, where he was Head of Department from 1992 to 2001. He is a former Executive Secretary of the Canadian Society of Biblical Studies and a former treasurer of the Canadian Corporation for Studies in Religion. His publications include *Christ and Modernity* (Wilfrid Laurier University Press, 1985), *The Word of Science* (Epworth Press, 1989), and *The Johannine World* (State University of New York Press, 1996).

DAVID R. LOY is Professor in the Faculty of International Studies at Bunkyo University, Chigasaki, Japan. His work is in comparative philosophy and religion, particularly comparing Buddhist with modern Western thought. His books include *Nonduality: A Study in Comparative Philosophy* (Yale University Press, 1988), *Lack and Transcendence: The Problem of Death and Life in Psychotherapy, Existentialism and Buddhism* (Yale University Press, 1996), *A Buddhist History of the West: Studies in Lack* (State University of New York Press, 2002), and *The Great Awakening: A Buddhist Social Theory* (Wisdom Publications, 2003). He has practiced Zen Buddhism for many years.

RONALD NEUFELDT is Professor of Religious Studies at the University of Calgary. The focus of his teaching and research has been India, particularly modern India. This interest has taken him to India a number of times, including a two-year period from 1993 to 1995, during which he served as Resident Director of the Delhi Office of the Shastri Indo-Canadian Institute. His publications include *Max Müller and the Rig Veda* (South Asia Books, 1979), *Readings in Eastern Religions*, co-edited with H. G. Coward and E. K. Dargyay (Wilfrid Laurier University Press, 1988), and *Karma and Rebirth: Post Classical Developments, Readings in Eastern Religions* (State University of New York Press, 1986).

JAY NEWMAN is Professor of Philosophy at the University of Guelph, where he has taught since 1971. He is a Fellow of the Royal Society of Canada and a past president of the Canadian Theological Society. He is the author of ten books, including *Religion and Technology* (Praeger, 1996) and *Inauthentic Culture and Its Philosophical Critics* (McGill-Queens University Press, 1997).

ROSEMARY E. OMMER is the Director, Special Projects, in the office of the Vice-President of Research at the University of Victoria, Canada, and Principal Investigator of the *Coasts Under Stress* project. She has formerly been the Director of the Calgary Institute for the Humanities and of the Institute for Social and Economic Research at Memorial University of Newfoundland. She was a member of the Social Sciences and Humanities Research Council of Canada and became the Principal Investigator on the Tri-Council Eco-Research project "Sustainability in a Cold-Ocean Coastal Environment," which was successfully completed in 1999. She is the author and/or editor of several books, including *Just Fish: Ethics and Canadian Marine Fisheries* (ISER Books, 2000); *Fishing Places, Fishing People: Issues in Canadian Small-Scale Fisheries* (University of Toronto Press, 1999), an interdisciplinary look at fisheries in Canada which she co-edited with Dianne Newell; and *The Resilient Outport* (ISER Books, 2002).

ANDREW RIPPIN is Professor of History and Dean of the Faculty of Humanities at the University of Victoria, Canada. His research interests include the formative period of Islamic civilization in the Arab world and the Qur'an and the history of its interpretation. His published articles and books include *Muslims, Their Religious Beliefs and Practices* (Routledge, 2001), *Textual Sources for the Study of Islam*, co-author (Manchester University Press, 1986), *The Qur'an: Formative Interpretation*, editor (Ashgate/Variorum, 2000), *The Qur'an: Style and Contents*, editor (Ashgate/Variorum, 2001).

ELIEZER SEGAL is Professor of Religious Studies and Head of Department at the University of Calgary. His scholarly publications include *Case Citation in the Babylonian Talmud* (Brown Judaic Studies, 1990) and *The Babylonian Esther Midrash: A Critical Commentary*, 3 vols. (Brown Judaic Studies, 1994), as well as many articles and book chapters. He has contributed to comparative studies on topics as diverse as afterlife beliefs, scriptures and traditions, religious practice, and criminal justice. He contributes the fortnightly "From the Sources" column to Calgary's *Jewish Free Press* and has a popular site on the World Wide Web: (http://www.acs. ucalgary.ca/~elsegal). Two collections of his nonspecialist articles have appeared under the titles *Why Didn't I Learn This in Hebrew School?* (Jason Aronson, 1999) and *Holidays, History and Halakhah* (Jason Aronson, 2000). His children's book, *Uncle Eli's Passover Haggadah* (No Starch Press, 1999), has been very successful, and will shortly be followed by a sequel.

# Index

213